T0319677

A Research Agenda for Arctic Tourism

Elgar Research Agendas outline the future of research in a given area. Leading scholars are given the space to explore their subject in provocative ways, and map out the potential directions of travel. They are relevant but also visionary.

Forward-looking and innovative, Elgar Research Agendas are an essential resource for PhD students, scholars and anybody who wants to be at the forefront of research.

For a full list of Edward Elgar published titles, including the titles in this series, visit our website at www.e-elgar.com.

A Research Agenda for Arctic Tourism

Edited by

OUTI RANTALA

Professor of Responsible Arctic Tourism, Multidimensional Tourism Institute, Faculty of Social Sciences, University of Lapland, Finland

DIETER K. MÜLLER

Professor of Human Geography, Department of Geography, Umeå University, Sweden

Elgar Research Agendas

Edward Elgar
PUBLISHING

Cheltenham, UK • Northampton, MA, USA

Published by
Edward Elgar Publishing Limited
The Lypiatts
15 Lansdown Road
Cheltenham
Glos GL50 2JA
UK

Edward Elgar Publishing, Inc.
William Pratt House
9 Dewey Court
Northampton
Massachusetts 01060
USA

A catalogue record for this book
is available from the British Library

Library of Congress Control Number: 2024938932

This book is available electronically in the **Elgar**online
Geography, Planning and Tourism subject collection
https://dx.doi.org/10.4337/9781035319992

ISBN 978 1 0353 1998 5 (cased)
ISBN 978 1 0353 1999 2 (eBook)

Printed and bound in Great Britain by
TJ Books Limited, Padstow, Cornwall

Contents

Figures

Contributors

June Anthonsen Røsbø is a lecturer in outdoor recreation/friluftsliv and Assistant Professor at the School of Sport Sciences at UiT – The Arctic University of Norway. She is currently doing a PhD, where her ethnographic research explores nature-based tourism, and how ski touring specifically, become part of place (re)making and destination development. Drawing on relational geography and materiality, as well as embodied perspectives, she seeks to shed light on how the offerings of peripheral northern places are activated in different spatial tourist and mobile networks. The study investigates constructions of place meanings and identities within nature-based tourism contexts, as well as changing power relations, changing landscape and human–nature relations. She has practical experience as a nature guide and educator in diverse nature environments and locations throughout the Northern Norway region. Additionally, she has contributed to the development of nature-based experiences for destinations and guide companies.

Suzanne de la Barre is an alumni faculty member of Vancouver Island University (VIU) and the World Leisure Centre of Excellence (VIU). She is involved in research and teaching through the UArctic Thematic Network on Tourism and the International Polar Tourism Research Network (IPTRN). Suzanne lives in Whitehorse, Yukon (Canada), and is engaged in research and practice in the areas of community economic development, tourism and the cultural sector.

O. Cenk Demiroglu is Associate Professor of Geography and an Affiliated Researcher of the Arctic Centre at Umeå University, Sweden. His main research interest is in climate crisis and tourism issues and, more recently, the application of geographical information systems (GIS) on the topic. Demiroglu is a Lead Expert of the Tourism Panel on Climate Change (TPCC), and the Co-chair of the Commission on Climate, Tourism and Recreation (CCTR) of the International Society of Biometeorology (ISB).

Brynhild Granås is Associate Professor in the Department of Social Sciences at UiT – The Arctic University of Norway. Her research on tourism's part in northern place development processes has a particular focus on nature practices, addressed through studies of human–non-human relational interactions. Recent and ongoing research projects include ethnographic studies of long-distance dog sledding, of the practising of allemannsretten (everyone's right/the right to roam) in contested periphery landscapes, and of human–seabird interactions in place processes. Her critical approach includes exploring power relations in tourism development as well as geographical, and historical interconnections that imprint on the remoulding of places through tourism practices within today's sustainability discourses.

Anne Hardy is Associate Professor in Tourism and Society at the University of Tasmania. Her research interests include tourist behaviour and sustainable tourism. Anne's most well-known research is the multiple award-winning project Tourism Tracer. This project was the first to track tourists, with their consent, for the duration of their holiday throughout entire destinations. It has been used in many other jurisdictions and has since been commercialized. Anne's Antarctic tourism research interests centre tourists' motivations, experiences and attitudes towards the continent. She also has a keen interest in the impact of citizen science activities upon tourists' perceptions of Antarctica.

Emily Höckert is a postdoctoral researcher in the Faculty of Social Sciences at the University of Lapland in Finland. Her research approaches the questions of hospitality and ethics of care at the crossroads of hermeneutic phenomenology, postcolonial philosophy, and feminist new materialism, asking how more-than-human actors welcome and take care of each other. Together with the "Intra-living in the Anthropocene" research group, and with support from the Research Council of Finland (PROFI 7, MESH, 2023-2028), she explores with the notion of "multispecies hospitality" in Arctic tourism settings.

Mats J. Hoel is pursuing a PhD in the Department of Social Science at UiT – The Arctic University of Norway, investigating the impact of nature-based tourism on society and the environment in Lofoten. Drawing on landscape and more-than-human theories, his research employs ethnographic methods to unravel the intricate relationship between tourism and society. With a decade-long tenure in tourism entrepreneurship, nature guiding, and destination management, he possesses a comprehensive understanding of the sector's practical challenges.

Edward H. Huijbens is an Icelandic geographer and graduate of Durham University, England. He chairs Wageningen University's research group in cultural geography. Edward works on spatial theory, issues of regional development, landscape perceptions, the role of transport in tourism and polar tourism. Edward has authored over 45 articles in several scholarly journals and edited volumes, published four monographs both in Iceland and internationally and co-edited four books.

Gunnar Thór Jóhannesson is Professor in the Department of Geography and Tourism at the University of Iceland. His recent research has been on destination dynamics, mobilities and placemaking with a focus on the entanglement of nature and culture. This has involved studies on entrepreneurship, innovation, tourism controversies and policymaking in the context of the Arctic and European High North. He is the vice lead of UArctic Thematic Network on Northern Tourism and a founding member of AIRTH – Alliance for Innovators and Researchers in Tourism.

Trine Kvidal-Røvik is Professor in Communication and Cultural Studies at UiT – The Arctic University of Norway in Alta. She does critical cultural research on place, identity, media and popular culture. In her research, she seeks to address issues of relevance to national minorities and Indigenous peoples in the North.

Patrick T. Maher is Professor in Physical and Health Education at Nipissing University. His research interests include nature-based tourism, outdoor/experiential learning, and sustainability with a particular focus on the Polar Regions. Pat's early work in Antarctica focused on the visitor experience as it leads to advocacy and ambassadorship. Pat is the lead of the University of the Arctic Thematic Network on Northern Tourism and the founder/former Chair of the International Polar Tourism Research Networks. He is a Fellow of the Royal Canadian Geographical Society, a 3M National Teaching Fellow, and Editor-in-Chief of the Journal of Adventure Education and Outdoor Learning.

Ulunnguaq Markussen is a PhD student in the Department of Culture, Language and History at Ilisimatusarfik (University of Greenland). In her project, Ulunnguaq investigates how to restore the resilience of small Arctic communities through business, cultural and democratic development, using Tasiilaq in East Greenland as a case study.

Stein R. Mathisen is Folklorist and Emeritus Professor of Culture Studies at UiT – The Arctic University of Norway. Major research interests include narratives and the constitution of identities, questions of heritage politics, and the history of cultural research in the northern areas. Publications in these fields relate to Kven, Sámi, Finn Forest, and Norwegian relations.

Dieter K. Müller is Professor of Human Geography at Umeå University, Sweden, where he also serves as Deputy Vice-Chancellor for research. His research focuses on economic dimensions of tourism in Arctic areas, on second-home tourism, and on the practice and development of tourism geographies. Müller is an elected member of the Royal Swedish Academy of Sciences and holds positions as co-editor of the Springer book series Geographies of Tourism and Global Change, as resource editor of the *Scandinavian Journal of Hospitality and Tourism*, and as an editorial board member of several leading tourism journals.

Kjell Olsen is Professor in Cultural Studies at UiT – The Arctic University of Norway. He has published extensively on identity processes, cultural heritage and tourism in Northern Norway.

Outi Rantala is Professor in Responsible Arctic Tourism at the University of Lapland, Finland and Adjunct Professor in Environmental Humanities at the University of Turku, Finland. She focuses in her research activities on creating critical, reflective and alternative narratives on northern tourism together with the members of Intra-living in the Anthropocene research group. Currently she leads a research profiling project on multispecies hospitality (Profi7 MESH, funded by the Research Council of Finland) and holds a position as Arctic Five Chair on Tourism and Climate Emergency. She also acts as a researcher in the ArcticHubs project funded by the European Union's Horizon 2020 research and innovation programme.

Carina Ren is Associate Professor in Tourism and Cultural Innovation at Aalborg University, Denmark and Head of AAU Arctic, Aalborg University's Arctic platform. Inspired by relational thinking, she researches how tourism interferes with other fields of the social, exploring the practices and events through which tourism takes and makes place. Geographically, her research is situated in the Nordic Arctic and Greenland. She has published widely on tourism and Arctic issues and co-edited books such as *Tourism Encounters and Controversies: Ontological Politics of Tourism Development* (2015), *Co-Creating Tourism Research: Collaborative Ways of Knowing* (2017) and *Collaborative Research Methods in the Arctic* (2020).

Seija Tuulentie is Research Professor of Arctic Sustainable Livelihoods at the Natural Resources Institute Finland (Luke) and Adjunct Professor in Environmental Sociology at the University of Lapland. Her research areas include nature-based tourism, rural development and land-use conflicts. She has particularly focused on the Arctic and northern issues in Finland and Scandinavia. Her PhD research dealt with the discussion of the legal claims of the Finnish Sámi from the perspective of national identity.

Alix Varnajot is a postdoctoral researcher at the University of Oulu, Finland, affiliated with the History, Culture and Communications Research Unit. He holds a PhD in Human Geography. His research interests include tourism geographies of the Arctic and Antarctica, dark tourism, last-chance tourism, and tourism adaptation to climate change in the Anthropocene. His most recent work also involves the study of collaborations between science and tourism in the context of polar expedition cruise tourism.

Preface

In Umeå (63°49'42" N) January 2024 started with some cold days and a temperature of -36°C. Two days later the thermometer showed +4°C and rainfall caused icy roads and a halt to public transportation in the region. While rapid changes of weather are not uncommon, certainly these quick shifts have become more frequent. They illustrate the changing climate in the Arctic and at the same time, they underline why it is worthwhile to study the Arctic as a region, where change is happening.

This volume focuses on tourism, which has become an important industry in the Arctic and a force that influences people, communities, business, and the environment, sometimes in very remarkable ways. Climate and geopolitical change as well as socio-economic development ambitions in northern communities and regions have paved the way for such development. Understanding these changes and their impacts has become a major research challenge, which has mobilized a community of researchers.

The University of the Arctic's Thematic Network on Northern Tourism was established in the early 2010s by a group of enthusiastic researchers under the lead of Arvid Viken, UiT – The Arctic University of Norway. It is a true satisfaction that this initiative results now in yet another scientific output with many of the founding members still onboard. The Arctic Five Chair collaboration under the lead of Outi Rantala, bringing researchers from the UiT – The Arctic University of Norway, Umeå University, Luleå University of Technology, University of Lapland, and Oulu University together contributed an important economic stimulus to the collaboration as did previous Nordic Council of Ministers' support, and the Nordplus mobility funding.

Particularly, the sessions of the research group at the Keropirtti lodge in Pyhä, Finland, in 2022 and 2023 contributed to turning the book from being an idea to a reality. Certainly, we would like to thank all the participants of these sessions, whether they attended physically or online, for their contributions and friendship during the years. We also would like to acknowledge Arvid Viken for his pivotal role in establishing this network.

Since the establishment of the network, it has brought not only the researchers but also students, PhD students and early career post-docs together, enabling collaborative learning across the Arctic. Indeed, during the Covid-19 pandemic it became very visible how close we are – despite the distances in the North – through our joint online courses, project meetings, and collective research processes.

Dieter would also like to thank his friends at the Department of Geography, Umeå University, and particularly Roger Marjavaara, Linda Lundmark, Cenk Demiroglu, Doris Carson, Marco Eimermann, Pamela Vargas-Bachmann, Håkan Appelblad, and Andreas Back for sharing an interest in tourism in the North and for making Umeå a great place of tourism geographies. Moreover, he would like to acknowledge the work of Keith Larsson and Peter Sköld, both Arctic Centre at Umeå University, Harri Malinen, University of Lapland, and Dag Avango, Luleå University of Technology, for their efforts for the Arctic Five collaboration. Moreover, inspiration and knowledge originate from the global tourism geographies community, and Dieter would like to thank C. Michael Hall, Jarkko Saarinen, Julie Wilson, Gijsbert Hoogendoorn, Carolin Funck, Hubert Job, Marius Mayer, Josep Cheer, Malin Zillinger, Jan-Henrik Nilsson, Robert Pettersson, Dimitri Ioannides, Albina Pashkevich and Manuela Gutberlet, to name just a few, for great discussions, inspiration, late night drinks and friendship.

Working together with Outi turned out to be a true pleasure and I enjoyed the extremely smooth and constructive collaboration very much. Since the next steps of our network collaboration are already under way, I know that there will be joint future undertakings and a lot of fun ahead as well. Certainly, I look forward to that.

Outi would like to thank also Ola Sletvold for the warm welcome to the planning of the network in 2008. Later, when she moved from the University of Lapland to UiT – The Arctic University of Norway for two years, it felt very cosy to have him and other Norwegian colleagues there, already familiar through the network's research activities. During these years, this feeling of cosiness has just increased. The latest three research projects – Envisioning proximity tourism (Research Council of Finland, University of Lapland), Mobility in Margins (Icelandic Research Fund, University of Iceland) and the contested nature of Allemannsretten (Research Council of Norway, UiT – The Arctic University of Norway) – have expanded our group and inspired our visions of Arctic tourism. Thank you all! Alongside the volume at the hand, the close collaboration on the forthcoming Annals of Tourism Research Curated Collection on Arctic tourism with Gunnar Thór Jóhannesson, Carina Ren and Kaarina Tervo-Kankare has motivated the reflections on the future of Arctic tourism. Special thanks go also to Minna Nousiainen, University of Lapland, for all the administrative work related to enabling the mobilities and networking of our students and researchers, for Trine Kvidal-Røvik, UiT – The Arctic University of Norway for our "almost" monthly walk and talk related to mundane academic life of tourism researchers in the North, and for Emily Höckert, University of Lapland, for always keeping up the hope for alternative futures of tourism in the North. Last but not least, I wish to thank Dieter for inviting me to co-edit this volume together with him. For me, you have always acted as a role model on what academic friendship can be – be it in the context of co-writing, project work, field travels, teaching or preparing a dinner for 24 people in a small cabin!

Finally, we would like to thank Katy Crossan and Stephanie Mills at Edward Elgar Publishing for their trust in the project and their great support throughout the production of the book.

January 31, 2024, Rovaniemi and Umeå
Outi and Dieter

1 Introduction: The need for a revised research agenda for Arctic tourism

Outi Rantala and Dieter K. Müller

Increased role of tourism in the Arctic

Ten years ago, Arbo et al. (2013) traced two main narratives related to the future of the Arctic. The first concentrated on the increasing economic activity in the Arctic and its environmental and societal impacts as an outcome of climate change and the receding sea ice cover. This narrative focused on population growth, increasing globalization, high demand for oil, gas, and other natural resources, technology development, regulatory frameworks, and the search for new shipping lanes. In contrast, the second narrative concentrated on issues relating to politics, governance, and security (Arbo et al., 2013, p. 176). Indeed, climate change, the potential emergence of new transportation routes, increasing access to natural resources and contested geopolitical orders all together have triggered lately a greater public awareness and interest in the Arctic region and its future.

On the future of the Arctic, what is interesting in the review by Arbo et al. is that although the prospects of new trans-arctic shipping routes attracted considerable attention together with the oil and gas development in the Barents Sea, at the same time, several other industries such as fisheries, mining, mineral industries and tourism, and the future development of these industries and their socio-economic consequences, were largely neglected in the studies they reviewed (Arbo et al., 2013, p. 176). Recently, industries such as aquaculture, forestry, mining and tourism have been named as the key industries in the European Arctic region, and – in line with Arbo et al.'s first narrative – the increased globalization and diverse related phenomenon such as global population growth, urbanization, digitalization and growing worldwide environmental concern are seen as major factors affecting these industries (Suopajärvi et al., 2022). What is more, even though it is recognized that the Arctic economy is increasingly shaped by globalization, with the future of the Arctic influenced by non-Arctic regional, social, political, and economic interests, it has also been recently pointed out that Arctic regions and communities are taking steps toward positioning themselves to tackle the challenges of economic development and embarking on fostering alternative, locally embedded economic activities – such as arts and crafts, tourism, small-scale manufacturing, and North-specific technological innovation (Larsen and Petrov, 2020; Müller et al., 2020).

Nowadays, it is evident that the Arctic areas have seen a boom in tourism during the last few decades. For instance, in 2017, tourism grew by 22% in Finnish Lapland (House of Lapland, 2019) and 24% in Iceland (Ferðamálastofa, 2019). Even though the COVID-19 pandemic had a major impact on the tourism industry, the growth has again been strong during winter 2023, and, for example, for Finnish Lapland new records are expected for 2024, while 2025 is forecasted to form a "super season" (Nieminen and Tolonen, 2023). Hence, tourism is of high importance for many local communities and regions in the sparsely populated North (Maher et al., 2022) and it is often seen as a sustainable alternative to the extractive industries in that it brings business opportunities, jobs and economic well-being to peripheral regions. Nevertheless, recent research has recognized that tourism in the region is variegated. Tourism in remote rural communities is accompanied by tourism in Arctic cities profiling themselves as global hubs for knowledge production and business (e.g. Müller et al., 2020). Despite these varieties, a clear seasonality underlined by (still) snowy and icy winters, the occurrence of northern lights and midsummer sun unites the region and contributes to a perceived exoticness. Being still a part of the cryosphere, iconic wildlife as well as specific landscape types are other ingredients of the mediated image of the Arctic region

Arctic areas are usually considered peripheries with limited access and remotely located at the lower end of a destination hierarchy (Lundgren, 1982) (Figure 1.1). In extreme cases, this requires specialized ad hoc transportation to backcountry settlements and destinations such as remote national parks. Hall (2005) relates this notion to gravity models, interaction, and distance decay ideas within geography. Accordingly, visitation to specific destinations is seen to decrease in relation to their relative distance from population centres, resembling the major demand markets for tourism. Consequently, peripheral locations are seen to have difficulties attracting larger volumes of tourists, simply because reaching them requires time and money. At the same time, a remote location may imply that environmental and cultural assets are less affected by land use competition and various kinds of global cultural influences, creating preconditions for nature-based and indigenous tourism (Hall and Boyd, 2005; Müller, 2015).

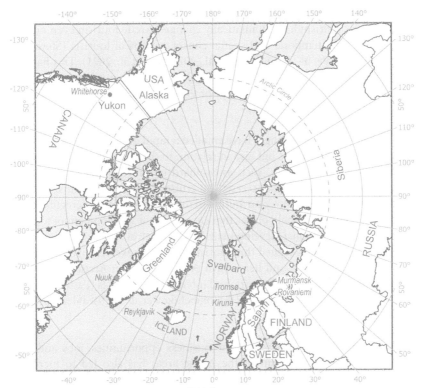

Source: Cartography: D. K. Müller (2024).

Figure 1.1   The Arctic and a selection of major destinations

Consequently, a location in the periphery at the lower end of a destination hierarchy affects the composition of the local businesses. Lundgren (1982) even argues that the peripheral location has led to a distinct business model, for example, the outfitters that equip tourists with specified services for a wilderness setting. While Lundgren's model is derived from a frontier context of the Canadian Arctic, Arctic areas in the European North are signified by a greater density of settlements and a history of resource extraction providing infrastructure for a secondary use through tourism (Lundgren, 1995; Müller, 2016). Hence, tourism businesses may have varying characteristics, also because Arctic tourism comprises increasingly urban places, entailing the inflow of non-specialized and less-prepared tourists (Müller et al., 2020). This implies improved accessibility including cheaper fares and greater volumes for tourism and consequently Arctic tourism businesses increasingly locate themselves close to gateways such as airports (Marjavaara et al., 2022). Furthermore, by packaging tourism in a Fordist manner, charter tourism as well as cruise tourism have dramatically changed Arctic tourism even outside Europe, creating temporal and spatial concentrations of tourists (Stewart et al., 2015; Rantala et al., 2019; James et al., 2020; Ren et al., 2021). This has also led to a softening of Arctic adventures making the high north accessible and enjoyable even for tourists lacking prior experiences, knowledge, or suitable equipment (Rantala et al., 2018).

The above-mentioned changes have entailed a rapid growth of Arctic tourism when it comes to volumes but also in relation to the geographical occurrence, where more remote places, such as Svalbard or the Canadian High Arctic are even in some instances accessed by cruise ships and air transportation (Lasserre and Têtu, 2015). Contributing to this is an increasing deregulation of tourism as well as national policies that encourage the development of tourism as a means for regional development (Dawson et al., 2017; Müller, 2011, 2021). It has also been argued that tourism is used to exercise national sovereignty (Timothy, 2010), and henceforth even the Russian Arctic has become increasingly accessible for domestic and international tourists (Pashkevich and Stjernström, 2014; Zelenskaya, 2018; Golubchikov et al., 2019), at least prior to the Russian invasion of Ukraine.

Aligned with the appreciation of the business opportunities, jobs and economic well-being, the boom in the Arctic areas has also led to increased recognition that the development of tourism in the North comes with unforeseen challenges to indigenous and local communities and non-human nature (Rantala et al., 2019; Olsen et al., 2019; Müller et al., 2020; Jóhannesson et al., 2022). It is clear that the dependency on pristine nature and local cultures makes the Arctic tourism industry fragile for critical approaches to sustainability. For example, even though the tourism industry contributes approximately 4% to observed human-induced global warming to date (Klöwer et al., 2021), the existing climate policies for aviation remain inadequate and technological advancements have limited capacity to compensate for those emissions caused by the rapid growth of tourism (Scott et al., 2016; Gössling and Humpe, 2020). Indeed, tourism in the North consists both of a fragile nature and infrastructure – including an increasing number of airports and related infrastructure that makes tourism initially possible (Ren et al., 2024).

Whilst the development of tourism in the Arctic has manifested itself in many parts as increasing international, economic activity steered primarily by non-local economic actors (Kulusjärvi, 2019), tourism researchers in the North have been concerned with how the current form of organizing tourism in the Arctic leaves limited possibilities to practice tourism in ways that would recognize local tourism relations and local economic agency as sources of social change (Kulusjärvi, 2019; Rantala and Höckert, 2024). Indeed, researchers have argued for marginal places to be recognized as "dynamic and mobile contact zones (Pratt, 1992; Clifford, 1997) that are characterised by how people travel in their dwelling and dwell in their travels (Clifford, 1997; Germann Molz, 2008)" (Jóhannesson et al., 2024, p. 4), and for a need to seek alternatives to the distancing, generalizing, and even apocalyptic future imaginaries of the Arctic (Rantala et al., 2024a). Therefore, this volume brings in-depth and innovative scholarship together with creative thinking across "tourism" disciplines in order to set a research agenda for future Arctic tourism that recognizes tourism as one future narrative for the Arctic – a narrative embedded in local human and non-human communities.

Research on Arctic tourism

The increased attention towards the Arctic is mirrored in plentiful publications and vibrant scientific exchange related to international organizations such as the International Arctic Science Committee (IASC), The International Arctic Social Science Association (IASSA) and the University of the Arctic (UARCTIC). While natural sciences have focused on the Arctic Oceans in a tradition established by the great explorers of the decades around 1900, social sciences have increasingly entered the arena addressing issues of indigeneity, community development, social and economic welfare, as well as business development in what has been called the "New Arctic" (Evengård et al., 2015). The New Arctic has shifted the focus to people in the Arctic and at the same time those borders of what is addressed under the Arctic label have been moved south.

In this context, even tourism has become a field of interest. The Arctic tourism research community is vibrant and active and is organized into two international organizations, the International Polar Tourism Research Network (IPTRN) and the University of the Arctic's Thematic Network on Northern Tourism. Both organizations regularly hold conferences and conduct joint research efforts. Altogether, the two networks gather between 80–100 researchers, mainly located in the Arctic states. However, there are numerous individual researchers with an interest in Arctic tourism beyond the circumpolar region. Furthermore, many universities offer programs on Arctic tourism or courses in Arctic/Northern studies programs (e.g. UiT The Arctic University of Norway, The University of Lapland, University of Oulu,

University of Iceland, Aalborg University, University of Alaska-Fairbanks, University of Paris-Versailles, Lakehead University) and many individual students specialize in Arctic tourism within their programs in tourism, geography, sociology, business or environmental studies.

With regard to Arctic tourism, numerous scientific articles and several collections of papers, often but not exclusively derived from the activities of the two networks, have significantly advanced the knowledge of tourism to the polar regions and specifically the Arctic (Sahlberg, 2001; Hall and Saarinen, 2010; Lück et al., 2010; Stonehouse and Snyder 2010;, Grenier and Müller, 2011; Müller et al., 2013; Lemelin et al., 2013; Viken and Granås, 2014; Lee et al., 2017). Several reviews have also covered the development of the field and outlined future research directions (Stewart et al., 2005, 2017; Demiroglu and Hall, 2020; Müller, 2024). These reviews indicate the maturity of polar tourism research. For future research, Stewart and colleagues (2018) point to issues such as shifting demand, governance, and the influence of new technologies on polar tourism, while Demiroglu and Hall (2020) are more concerned with climate change, which will change Arctic tourism but not turn the region into a region that cannot be visited anymore. This is in line with Lemelin et al. (2010) pointing at the fact that climate change triggers a last-chance tourism, maybe contributing to increasing visitation. However, it is also clear that more nuanced approaches are required to further promote knowledge within the field (Saarinen and Varnajot, 2019; Müller, 2024; Rantala et al., 2024b; Thorsteinsson et al., 2024). This would mean, for example, studying Arctic tourism in relation to overall local and regional development, also acknowledging relevant changes in other sectors of society and environment (Müller, 2024); recognizing the role of creativity in place-making and place-development processes (Jóhannesson et al., 2024); and seeking alternative stories of Arctic tourism futures aside from the grand narratives of tourism growth (Rantala and Höckert, 2024; Tikkanen, 2023).

Today, a variety of perspectives from the social sciences, the humanities as well as from science address tourism in the Arctic from their respective angles, asking new questions and experimenting with new ideas. Still, while many studies in Arctic tourism hitherto have accomplished a baseline knowledge, the rapid development in the (New) Arctic warrants rejuvenated approaches acknowledging the rapid environmental, socio-economic and political changes in the region. In this context, traditional business perspectives are complemented by alternative theoretical approaches highlighting communities, geographical imaginaries and spatial relations, also featuring the application of recent theoretical reasoning within an Arctic context. For example, Arctic tourism scholars highlight the need to revise the research agenda and methodological approaches (e.g. Gren and Huijbens, 2016; Hansen and Ren, 2021; Rantala et al., 2024b; Thorsteinsson et al., 2024) in order to face the crisis of thinking caused by the age of the Anthropocene (Zylinska, 2014; Mol, 2021), which invites us to develop a greater degree of critical reflexivity and imagination (Wright et al., 2018; Valtonen and Rantala, 2020). It should be noted that tourism research has been prevalently dominated by instrumental research interests and a techno-rational agenda aiming for economic growth. The present volume introduces a wider approach to Arctic tourism, acknowledging diverse new conceptualizations that seek to help in addressing the future of the Arctic.

Chapters in this volume

Following this introduction, the first two chapters of the volume approach setting a research agenda for Arctic tourism from the point of view of the possibilities that technology offers for future research activities. In his chapter, Cenk Demiroglu applies a web mapping application to identify the spatial and thematic research gaps and the bibliographic ages in regard to research on Arctic tourism and climate change. Based on the results, he calls for more pan-Arctic research on climate change and tourism in the Arctic, as well as diversification of research, better integrated impact assessment and more systematic examinations. In line with Demiroglu, Patrick Maher and Anne Hardy have a focus on how the use of technology can help in examining timely topics in the context of Arctic tourism. They point out how tourist experiences are mediated by mobile technology and social media, and what kind of implications this has for the research of Arctic tourism in terms of the form of data, use of data and research ethics. Furthermore, they call for a more open discussion regarding the impacts of social media in decision making and tourists' experiences.

In his chapter, Gunnar Thór Jóhannesson moves from discussing the major external phenomenon – such as climate change or digitalization – to an examination of the dynamics emanating from the tourism phenomenon itself. By applying a relational approach, he shows how tourism mobility does not unfold in a pre-defined space but composes space. This kind of research perspective brings forth possibilities to tell alternative stories of tourism development, and to illustrate how tourism is profoundly entangled in various geopolitical interests. According to Jóhannesson, there are multiple narratives to be followed when constructing the futures of Arctic tourism, and the role of researchers is to articulate and disseminate these across different contexts and audiences.

The chapters by Suzanne de la Barre and Trine Kvidal-Røvik, Stein Mathisen and Kjell Olsen focus on cultures and creativity, and follow Jóhannesson in bringing out the worldmaking power of tourism. In her chapter, de la Barre introduces the linkages between Arctic tourism and creative and cultural economies in the Arctic. In particular, she points out how the cultural changes taking place in the Arctic, the intersections of the cultural and creative sector with the tourism sector, and the creativity within locally embedded tourism have possibilities for creating new directions for Arctic tourism. On their part, Kvidal-Røvik, Mathisen and Olsen point out that tourism as a worldmaking process is not detached from other processes shaping the northern societies, and that the outcomes of this worldmaking process are not always positive. This they illustrate with the example of Arctification, which is not always perceived to be beneficial by all and does not necessarily correspond to all local community needs.

In their chapter, Emily Höckert and Outi Rantala conduct a review on post-humanist research on Arctic tourism. They continue the discussion raised in the previous chapters by envisioning alternatives to the distancing and even apocalyptic imaginaries of futures in the Arctic. By focusing on multispecies hospitality, they wish to challenge the normative ways of knowing that dominate current approaches to sustainability and responsibility in Arctic tourism, and to draw attention to questions of multispecies knowing. Carina Ren and Ulunnguaq Markussen continue this discussion for their part by exploring the concept of comparison as a potential tool for collaborative ways of knowing in the Arctic. They frame comparison as a research methodology to explore sameness and difference, as an epistemology to learn, and as an ontology that enables envisioning and worldmaking. For them, it is essential that the comparison takes departure in Arctic realities and desirable futures. In the chapter that follows, Brynhild Granås, June Anthonsen Røsbø and Mats J. Hoel continue the discussion on normative knowing and argue for approaching nature-based tourism as an open relational historic-geographical phenomenon. They illustrate this by attending to nature-based tourism's contingent relations to place processes and ecologies through ethnographic insights, and also suggest that other researchers and institutional actors engage in explorations up-close in order to represent also other voices and connections than those of experts.

Future research needs related to ever-increasing land use modes in the green transition operating environment of the Arctic are discussed by Seija Tuulentie in her chapter. She draws attention especially to questions of justice in tourism landscapes and nature-based tourism land use – issues that should receive more attention if the aim is to build resilient rural areas through the coexistence of various green transition livelihoods. In line with Granås et al., Tuulentie stresses the need for including diverse voices in land use planning in order to better enhance the synergies between tourism and traditional land uses. Dieter K. Müller's examination of the political-economic geographies and ownership of Arctic tourism supplements Tuulentie's chapter. Müller asks whether tourism in the Arctic is an industry to be developed in its own right or as an industry supporting other sectors of the economy. Moreover, he points out how public investments and support for tourism differ among countries, as well as the idea of how embedded tourism should be in the local community. Indeed, according to Müller, larger comparative studies are required in regard to Arctic tourism to understand better the political-economic dimensions – such as the impacts of regulations (see also the chapter by Ren and Markussen).

In his chapter, Alix Varnajot approaches the future of Arctic tourism by introducing adaptation strategies to climate change. According to Varnajot, many of the current adaptation strategies are linked with the Arctification and the associated efforts to maintain the cryospheric gaze, which can be seen in the long run as maladaptation. Moreover, Varnajot considers it critical to change the narratives and aesthetics associated with Arctic tourism. Accordingly, in his chapter, Edward Huijbens calls for countering the predominantly utilitarian perspectives of the Arctic. He suggests that researchers develop a new vocabulary to capture compassion, co-operation and mutual aid, and uses stories of conviviality to counter the predominant individualism and competitive capitalist ethos in the Arctic. Huijbens shows how stories have a capacity for expanding our consciousness and striving for ethical encounters in the North. Thus, he calls for research that acknowledges the plurality of ways of knowing and brings the diverse actors together to foster ecologically sustainable and socially just Arctic tourism.

To conclude the volume, Dieter K. Müller and Outi Rantala discuss the overall development that may affect the future of Arctic tourism, aligning those with the research agendas presented in the previous chapters. All in all, these chapters express both methodological suggestions, theoretical and conceptual directions and research themes that those scholars representing diverse aspects of "tourism" disciplines see as central points if and when we wish to understand the futures of the Arctic.

References

Arbo, P., Iversen, A., Knol, M., Ringholm, T. and Sander, G. (2013). Arctic futures: Conceptualizations and images of a changing Arctic. *Polar Geography, 36*(3), 163–82.

Dawson, J., Johnston, M., and Stewart, E. (2017). The unintended consequences of regulatory complexity: The case of cruise tourism in Arctic Canada. *Marine Policy, 76*, 71–8.

Demiroglu, O. C., and Hall, C. M. (2020). Geobibliography and bibliometric networks of polar tourism and climate change research. *Atmosphere, 11*(5), 498.

Evengård, B., Nymand Larsen, J., and Paasche, Ø. (Eds.) (2015). *The New Arctic*. Cham: Springer.

Ferðamálastofa (2019). *Heildarfjöldi erlendra gesta 1949–2018*. https:// www .ferdamalastofa.is/is/gogn/fjoldi-ferdamanna/heildarfjoldi-erlendra-ferdamanna

Golubchikov, Y. N., Kruzhalin, V. I., and Nikanorova, A. D. (2019). Arctic tourism: State and prospects for Russia. *Geography, Environment, Sustainability, 11*(4), 5–13.

Gössling, S., and Humpe, A. (2020). The global scale, distribution and growth of aviation: Implications for climate change. *Global Environmental Change, 65*. 102194.

Gren, M., and Huijbens, E. (Eds.) (2016). *Tourism and the Anthropocene*. London: Routledge.

Grenier A. A., and Müller, D. K. (Eds.) (2011). *Polar Tourism: A Tool for Regional Development*. Presses de l'Université du Québec.

Hall, C. M. (2005). *Tourism: Rethinking the Social Science of Mobility*. Pearson.

Hall, C. M., and Boyd, S. (2005). Nature-based tourism in peripheral areas: Introduction. In C. M. Hall and S. Boyd (Eds.), *Nature-based Tourism in Peripheral Areas: Development or Disaster* (pp. 3–17). Channel View.

Hall, C. M., and Saarinen, J. (Eds.) (2010). *Tourism and Change in Polar Regions: Climate, Environments and Experiences*. Routledge.

Hansen, A. M. and Ren, C. (2021). *Collaborative Research Methods in Arctic Research. Experiences from Greenland*. Routledge.

House of Lapland (2019). *Helsinki ja Lappi vetävät Suomen matkailun kasvuun*. https:// www.lapland.fi/fi/business-2/nousukayralla-blogi/helsinki-ja-lappi-vetavat-suomen -matkailun-kasvuun/.

James, L., Olsen, L. S., and Karlsdóttir, A. (2020). Sustainability and cruise tourism in the arctic: Stakeholder perspectives from Ísafjörður, Iceland and Qaqortoq, Greenland. *Journal of Sustainable Tourism, 28*(9), 1425–41.

Jóhannesson, G. Þ., Welling, J., Müller, D. K., Lundmark, L., Nilsson, R., de la Barre, S., Granås, B., Kvidal-Rovik, T., Rantala, O., Tervo-Kankare, K., and Maher, P. (2022). *Arctic Tourism in Times of Change: Uncertain Futures – From Overtourism to Re-starting Tourism*. Nordic Council of Ministers.

Jóhannesson, G. T., Lund, K., Thorsteinsson, B., and Jóhannesdóttir, G. R. (2024). Introduction. In B. Thorsteinsson, K. A. Lund, G. T. Jóhannesson, and G. R. Jóhannesdóttir (Eds.), *Mobilities on the Margins: Arctic Encounters*, 1–13. Palgrave Macmillan.

Klöwer, M., Allen, M. R., Lee, D. S., Proud, S. R., Gallagher, L., and Skowron, A. (2021). Quantifying aviation's contribution to global warming. *Environmental Research Letters, 16*(10), 104027.

Kulusjärvi, O. (2019). *Towards a Poststructural Political Economy of Tourism: A Critical Sustainability Perspective on Destination Development in the Finnish North*. Nordia Geographical Publications. Oulu.

Larsen, J. N. and Petrov, A. N. (2020). The economy of the Arctic. In K. S. Coates and C. Holroyd (Eds.), *The Palgrave Handbook of Arctic Policy and Politics*,79–95. Palgrave Macmillan.

Lasserre, F., and Têtu, P. L. (2015). The cruise tourism industry in the Canadian Arctic: Analysis of activities and perceptions of cruise ship operators. *Polar Record*, *51*(1), 24–38.

Lee, Y. S., Weaver, D., and Prebensen, N. K. (Eds.) (2017). *Arctic Tourism Experiences: Production, Consumption and Sustainability*. CABI.

Lemelin, H., Dawson, J., Stewart, E. J., Maher, P., and Lueck, M. (2010). Last-chance tourism: The boom, doom, and gloom of visiting vanishing destinations. *Current Issues in Tourism*, *13*(5), 477–93.

Lemelin, R.H., Maher, P., and Liggett, D. (Eds.) (2013). *From Talk to Action: How Tourism is Changing the Polar Regions*. Lakehead University Centre for Northern Studies.

Lück, M., Maher, P. T., and Stewart, E. J. (Eds.) (2010). *Cruise Tourism in Polar Regions: Promoting Environmental and Social Sustainability?* Earthscan.

Lundgren, J. O. (1982). The tourist frontier of Nouveau Quebec: Functions and regional linkages. *Tourist Review*, *37*(2), 10–16.

Lundgren, J. O. J. (1995). The tourism space penetration processes in northern Canada and Scandinavia: a comparison. In C. M. Hall and M. Johnston (Eds.), *Polar Tourism: Tourism in the Arctic and Antarctic Regions*, 43–61. Wiley.

Maher, P. T., Jóhannesson, G. T., Kvidal-Røvik, T., Müller, D. K., and Rantala, O. (2022). Touring in the Arctic: Shades of grey towards a sustainable future. In D. C. Natcher and T. Koivurova (Eds.), *Renewable Economies in the Arctic*, 82–98. Routledge.

Marjavaara, R., Nilsson, R. O., and Müller, D. K. (2022). The Arctification of northern tourism: A longitudinal geographical analysis of firm names in Sweden. *Polar Geography*, *45*(2), 119–36.

Mol, A. (2021). *Eating in Theory*. Duke University Press.

Müller, D. K. (2011). Tourism development in Europe´s "last wilderness": An assessment of nature-based tourism in Swedish Lapland. In A. A. Grenier and D. K. Müller (Eds.), *Polar Tourism: A Tool for Regional Development*, 129–53. Presses de l'Université du Québec.

Müller, D. K. (2015). Issues in Arctic tourism. In B. Evengård, J. Nymand Larsen, and Ø. Paasche (Eds.), *The New Arctic*, 147–58. Springer.

Müller, D. K. (2016). On the location of tourism: An outlook from Europe's northern periphery. In M. Mayer and H. Job (Eds.), *Naturtourismus: Chancen und Herausforderungen*, 113–24. Meta GIS Systems.

Müller, D. K. (2021). Tourism in national Arctic strategies: A perspective on the tourism-geopolitics nexus. In M. Mostafanezhad, M. Córdoba Azcárate, & R. Norum (Eds.), *The Geopolitics of Tourism: Assemblages of Power, Mobility and the State*, 91–111. University of Arizona Press.

Müller, D. K. (2024). Polar tourism and the changing geographies of the Arctic and the Antarctic regions. *Tourism Geographies* (forthcoming).

Müller D. K., Lundmark L., and Lemelin, R. H. (Eds.) (2013). *New Issues in Polar Tourism: Communities, Environments, Politics*. Springer.

Müller, D. K., Carson, D. A., de la Barre, S., Granås, B., Jóhannesson, G. T., Øyen, G., Rantala, O., Saarinen, J., Salmela, T., Tervo-Kankare, K., and Welling, J. (2020). *Arctic Tourism in Times of Change: Dimensions of Urban Tourism*. Nordic Council of Ministers.

Nieminen, J., and Tolonen, S. (2023). *Alueelliset kehitysnäkymät syksyllä 2023. Työ- ja elinkeinoministeriön julkaisuja.* Alueelliset kehitysnäkymät 2023:45. Ministry of Economic Affairs and Employment in Finland.

Olsen, K. O., Abildgaard, M. S., Brattland, C., Chimirri, D., de Bernardi, C., Edmonds, J., Grimwood, B. S. R., Hurst, C.E.; Höckert, E., Jæger, K., Kugapi, O., Lemelin, R. H.; Lüthje, M., Mazzullo, N., Müller, D. K., Ren, C., Saari, R., Ugwuegbula, L., and Viken, A. (2019). *Looking at Arctic Tourism through the Lens of Cultural Sensitivity: ARCTISEN – A Transnational Baseline Report.* Multidimensional Tourism Institute. Rovaniemi, Finland: LUC Tourism.

Pashkevich, A., and Stjernström, O. (2014). Making Russian Arctic accessible for tourists: Analysis of the institutional barriers. *Polar Geography, 37*(2), 137–56.

Rantala, O., Hallikainen, V., Ilola, H., and Tuulentie, S. (2018). The softening of adventure tourism. *Scandinavian Journal of Hospitality and Tourism, 18*(4), 343–61.

Rantala, O., de la Barre, S., Granås, B., Jóhannesson, G. Þ., Müller, D. K., Saarinen, J., Tervo-Kankare, K., Maher, P. T., and Niskala, M. (2019). *Arctic Tourism in Times of Change: Seasonality.* Nordic Council of Ministers.

Rantala, O., and Höckert, E. (2024). Multispecies stories from the margins. In B. Thorsteinsson, A. K. Lund, G. T. Jóhannesson, and G.R. Jóhannesdóttir (Eds.), *Mobilities on the Margins*, 61–79. Palgrave Macmillan.

Rantala, O., Kinnunen, V., and Höckert, E. (2024a). *Researching with Proximity: Relational Methodologies for the Anthropocene.* Palgrave Macmillan.

Rantala, O., Kinnunen, V., Höckert, E., Grimwood, B. S. R., Hurst, C. E., Jóhannesson, G. T., Jutila, S., Ren, C. Stinson, M. J., Valtonen, A., and Vola, J. (2024b). Staying proximate. In O. Rantala, V. Kinnunen, and E. Höckert (Eds.), *Researching with Proximity*, 1–19. Palgrave Macmillan.

Ren, C., James, L., Pashkevich, A., and Hoarau-Heemstra, H. (2021). Cruise trouble. A practice-based approach to studying Arctic cruise tourism. *Tourism Management Perspectives, 40.* 100901.

Ren, C., Jóhannesson, G. T., Ásgeirsson, M. H., Woodall, S., and Reigner, N. (2024). Rethinking connectivity in Arctic tourism development. *Annals of Tourism Research, 105.* 103705.

Saarinen, J., and Varnajot, A. (2019). The Arctic in tourism: Complementing and contesting perspectives on tourism in the Arctic. *Polar Geography, 42*(2), 109–24.

Sahlberg, B. (2001). *Going North: Peripheral Tourism in Canada and Sweden.* Etour.

Scott, D., Hall, C. M., and Gössling, S. (2016). A report on the Paris Climate Change Agreement and its implications for tourism: Why we will always have Paris. *Journal of Sustainable Tourism, 24*(7), 933–48.

Stewart, E. J., Draper, D., and Johnston, M. E. (2005). A review of tourism research in the polar regions. *Arctic, 58*(4), 383–94.

Stewart, E., Dawson, J., and Johnston, M. (2015). Risks and opportunities associated with change in the cruise tourism sector: Community perspectives from Arctic Canada. *The Polar Journal, 5*(2), 403–27.

Stewart, E.J., Liggett, D., and Dawson, J. (2017). The evolution of polar tourism scholarship: Research themes, networks and agendas. *Polar Geography, 40*, 59–84.

Stonehouse, B., and Snyder, J. (2010). *Polar Tourism: An Environmental Perspective.* Channel View.

Suopajärvi, L., Nygaard, V., Edvardsdóttir, A. G., Iversen, A., Kyllönen, K. M., Lesser, P., Lidestav, G., Moioli, S., Nojonen, M., Ólafsdóttir, R., Bergström, D., Bjerke, J. W., Bogadóttir, R., Elomina, J., Engen, S., Karkut, J., Koivurova, T., Leppiaho, T., Lynge-Pedersen, K., Paulsen Strugstad, M., Rantala, O., Rautio, P., Siikavuopio, S.,

Skum, M., Tuulentie, S., and Tømmervik, H. (2022). *Global Economic Drivers in the Development of Different Industrial Hubs in the European Arctic*. ArcticHubs-project, University of Lapland. https:// projects .luke .fi/ arctichubs/ wp -content/ uploads/ sites/ 47/ 2022/ 09/ d1 .2 -global -economic -drivers -in -the -development -of -different -industrial-hubs_submission-1.pdf.

Thorsteinsson, B., Lund, K. A., Jóhannesson, G. T., and Jóhannesdóttir, G. R. (2024). *Mobilities in Margins. Creative Processes of Place-Making*. Palgrave Macmillan.

Tikkanen, J. (2023). *To Grow or to Degrow? Discourse Analysis on Degrowth and Socio-ecological Justice in the Futures of Arctic Tourism*. Master Thesis. University of Lapland. https://urn.fi/URN:NBN:fi-fe2023061656143.

Timothy, D. J. (2010). Contested place and the legitimization of sovereignty through tourism in polar regions. In C. M. Hall and J. Saarinen (Eds.), *Tourism and Change in Polar Regions*, 306–18. Routledge.

Valtonen, A., and Rantala, O. (2020). Introduction: Re-imagining ways of talking about the Anthropocene. In A. Valtonen, O. Rantala and P. Farah (Eds.), *Ethics and Politics of Space for the Anthropocene*, 1–15. Edward Elgar.

Viken, A., and Granås, B. (2014). *Tourism Destination Development. Tourism Destination Development. Turns and Tactics*. Ashgate.

Wright. C., Nyberg, D., Rickards, L., and Freund, J. (2018). Organizing in the Anthropocene. *Organization, 25*(4), 455–71.

Zelenskaya, E. (2018). Geopolitics and tourism in the Arctic: The case of the national park 'Russian Arctic'. *Journal of Policy Research in Tourism, Leisure and Events, 10*(1), 33–47.

Zylinska, J. (2014). *Minimal Ethics for the Anthropocene*. Open Humanities Press.

2 When POLTOUR app meets generative AI: A walkthrough of research output and outreach on Arctic tourism and climate change

O. Cenk Demiroglu

Introduction

The Arctic is a major hot spot in the exposure to anthropogenic climate change, with warming there taking place four times faster than the global average (Rantanen et al., 2022). The region is also a rapidly emerging destination in the global tourism industry, fueled by the "Arctification" trend (Müller and Viken, 2017), with imaginaries of the North increasingly associated with the Arctic in political and commercial realms – sometimes even extending the border beyond its conventional lineation such as the Arctic Circle – and the concept of "Last Chance Tourism (LCT)" (Carson, 2020). Indeed, LCT is a compact example of how Arctic tourism is paradoxically interrelated with the climate crisis: While the negative impacts of climate change, for instance the loss of charismatic fauna like polar bears, increase publicity regarding the region, its direct positive impacts (in the narrowest sense), such as improved maritime accessibility due to less sea ice, also assist tourism development. This, in turn, results in more greenhouse gas emissions, especially due to the increased carbon-intensive long-haul trips, along with other combined impacts of the increasing human footprint; all these aspects together contribute to a vicious cycle. Unsurprisingly, the combination of Arctic tourism and climate change has become a hot topic for research, yielding various publications from diverse disciplines, especially over the last two decades (Demiroglu et al., 2024). This chapter utilizes the latest techniques, such as "geobibliography," generative Artificial Intelligence (AI) and "altmetrics," to understand both the scholarly and popular volumes of Arctic tourism and climate change literature and to identify research and outreach gaps in relation to a future agenda.

Navigating the POLTOUR geobibliography

The chapter initially walks through the Arctic tourism and climate change literature by navigating the POLTOUR Geobibliography. A "geobibliography" is a methodological concept for mapping spatially oriented studies within a certain research domain by locating them according to their case regions with symbologies based on their thematic and publication attributes using Web GIS (geographical information systems). This enables both an interactive display for users and opportunities for efficient data collection and analytics (Demiroglu et al., 2024). POLTOUR's research thematization is based on the climate-tourism systems' interrelationships framework (Figure 2.1), in which climate change affects and is affected by the tourism system and tourism responds (or does not) to the impacts and its footprint through adaptation and mitigation, respectively. POLTOUR identifies the main themes of studies on impacts and adaptation as "climate risks" and those focusing on emissions and mitigation issues as "carbon risks," in line with the taxonomy adopted by the latest macroregional reviews on climate change and tourism (Fang et al., 2022; Higham et al., 2022; Rutty et al., 2022; Wolf et al., 2022; Dube et al., 2023; Navarro-Drazich et al., 2023; Steiger et al., 2023). Moreover, as exemplified by the LCT case in the introductory section, a third main thematic category of "climate and carbon risks" is also introduced to the app in order to account for the rebound effects and combined impacts (see Figure 2.1) that may result as knock-on effects of adaptation and mitigation efforts.

The first application of a geobibliography was developed for the topic of ski tourism and climate change (Demiroglu et al., 2013), and was later applied to the topic of polar tourism and climate change (Demiroglu and Hall, 2020) through the launch of POLTOUR 1.0 (available at tiny.cc/poltour1). In this chapter, we visit POLTOUR 2.0 (Demiroglu et al., 2024). This version is much more sophisticated than the first, which was developed on the Google My Maps platform with limited capabilities, whereas the new version is based on more advanced Esri platforms such as Experience Builder, Survey123 and 360 VR under the ArcGIS Online (AGOL) ecosystem, allowing for more customized designs and interactions with a variety of widgets.

POLTOUR 2.0 is publicly available (poltour.geo.umu.se). The user is initially greeted by a splash screen providing brief information about the app. The default map view is set to Svalbard in order to engage the user with the app's 3D perspective and high granularity. With one click on the Arctic bookmark in the upper right corner the user can view all Arctic tourism and climate change research cases at once on a global scale. As POLTOUR's underlying dataset

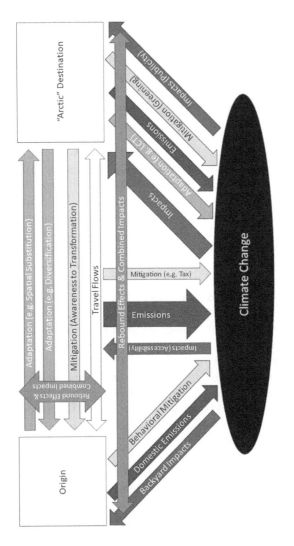

Source: Demiroglu (2020: 277).

Figure 2.1   A framework of climate-tourism systems' interrelationships

contains the Antarctic cases as well, the "Region" filter can be set for the Arctic and to thereby trigger an update of the indicators for the total number of cases/ publications and the thematic (regional, climate/carbon risks, tourism types) aggregations. Further filters, such as a certain time period, can further limit the cases that are displayed and update the aggregate indicators. Last but not least, the user can switch to the "Table" view and export the list of selected publications/cases and their attributes in different file formats. The Table view also lets the user zoom into a particular case, whereas the "Map" view will let the user interact with popups that further link to the original publications, search locations of interest, change basemaps, turn the layers on/off, and zoom/tilt. A proof-of-concept is also available for viewing the scene in a Virtual Reality (VR) environment.

Looking at the results of the Region/Pole filter applied to the Arctic, we find that 114 (83%) of the 137 publications on polar tourism and climate change, surveyed by Demiroglu et al. (2024), are focused on the Arctic. These publications are displayed through 225 case points on the Map view. The multiple representations of the publications are due to the architecture of the geobibliography, whereby studies with more than one case location and/or one theme are populated. Yet one should also note that identifying both the exact case locations and mutual agreements on the coded themes has not always been precise, due to the spatial nature of some publications and the agreement levels among the theme-coding authors who developed POLTOUR 2.0 (Demiroglu et al., 2024). At any rate, the state-of-the-art shows a major dominance of the Arctic in polar tourism and climate change research, but with an uneven distribution among the Arctic regions and the climate themes, with case coverage being the highest for Canada (n: 64), Norway (n: 45) and Finland (n: 35); moderate for Greenland (n: 24), the US (n: 19), Russia (n: 18) and Iceland (n: 15); and the lowest for Sweden (n: 4). Thematically, it is "climate risks" cases (n: 163) involved with "impacts" (n: 84) and "adaptation" (n: 79) that are dominant, followed by "climate & carbon risks" (n: 43) and the "carbon risks" (n: 19) of "emissions" (n: 6) and "mitigation" (n: 13).

In addition to the spatial and thematic gaps identified above, a research agenda for Arctic tourism and climate change should also be temporally informed. The literature is not old, with a publication track dating back to just 2004 (Berman et al., 2004; Kruse et al., 2004). When filtered for the most recent five-year period, 2019–2023, compared to the 2004–2018 period less research is found for Canada (n: 57 vs 7), Finland (n: 31 vs 4) and the US (n: 15 vs 4), whereas Russia (n: 9 vs 9), Norway (n: 23 vs 22) and Iceland (n: 7 vs 8) register similar volumes of spatial research coverage. Interest in Greenland (n: 7 vs 17), on the other hand, has more than doubled between the two periods. It is also worth mentioning that the thematic pattern has remained more or less the same, with most research focusing on climate risks in the Arctic, with the exception of Iceland, where in the last five years carbon risk cases (e.g. Czepkiewicz et al., 2019; Árnadóttir et al., 2021; Raudsepp et al., 2021; Saviolidis et al., 2021) have outnumbered climate risk ones (Welling et al., 2019, 2020; Welling and Abegg, 2021).

In order to statistically confirm the spatiotemporal patterns and trends of Arctic tourism and climate change research, an Emerging Hot Spots Analysis (EHSA) is applied based on the space-time cubes of case points (Figure 2.2a), following Demiroglu and Hall (2020), along with a case density map (Figure 2.2b) that disregards the temporal aspect. Both analyses are carried out on ArcGIS Pro 3.2, which is better software than the AGOL software-as-a-service when it comes to geoprocessing. Spatially speaking, case points form hot spots (Figure 2.2b) around Arctic Fennoscandia, Iceland, West Greenland, and as southerly as Churchill, Canada, due mainly to polar bear tourism. Thanks to the Getis-Ord Gi* statistics and the Mann-Kendall tests run by the EHSA on the space-time cubes of the POLTOUR 2.0 case dataset (Figure 2.2a), statistically significant spatiotemporal patterns and trends are also visible (Figure 2.2b): There is, for instance, a clear division between the Eurasian-Greenlandic oscillating hot spots (i.e. hot spots that have converted from cold spots) on the one hand and the Canadian-Alaskan sporadic (i.e. on-again off-again) and oscillating cold spots (i.e. cold spots that have converted from hot spots) on the other, reflected in the older age of the literature on the latter and the emerging research on the former.

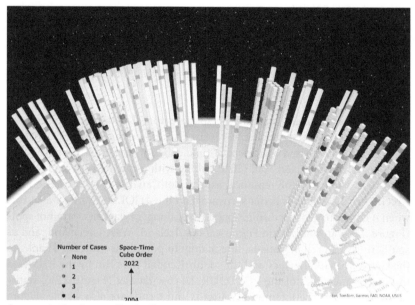

Source: Author's own illustration.

Figure 2.2a   Spatiotemporal patterns and trends of Arctic tourism and
climate change research, represented by space-time cubes
that cluster case locations on a vertical-temporal axis

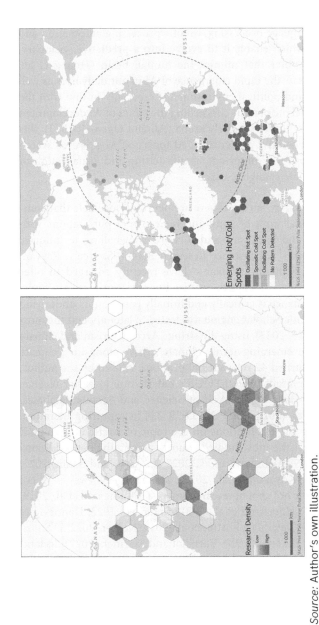

Source: Author's own illustration.

Figure 2.2b   Spatiotemporal patterns and trends of Arctic tourism and climate change research, represented by 2D hexbins (left), and statistically tested hot and cold spots (right)

Extending POLTOUR with Generative AI

Since its first introduction in the 1950s, Artificial Intelligence (AI) has grown into a "composite concept" based on machine learning, deep learning, computer vision, natural language processing, robotic processing automation and expert systems, all of which enable it to evolve into a predictive, visionary, semantic machine/computer that mimics the human brain (Huang et al., 2022). The early 2020s saw the rapid emergence of AI in our daily lives as well as business, academic and political environments, especially in line with the rise of big data. While debate persists concerning the ethics of AI development and utilization, not least in the scholarly arena (Ali and OpenAI, 2023), this chapter dares to visit generative and creative AI tools and AI-powered search engines to assist/improve the surveying, agenda-setting and visualization of Arctic tourism and climate change research.

In order to improve literature surveys, there are new tools available that complement the conventional ways of searching for research publications with certain search strings and backward and forward snowballing techniques. As such, certain AI apps – for instance Research Rabbit, Sourcely, Rayyan, Scite, Iris, Lateral and Semantic Scholar – have recently emerged to offer innovative and comprehensive ways to acquire literature on a certain topic. As POLTOUR's performance is critically and initially based on its underlying literature list, the Semantic Scholar engine was tested to later append the most recent publications (2019–2023), using the string "Arctic tourism and climate c*" to account for the emerging term "climate crisis" alongside "climate change". The query returned 42 relevant publications, chosen by the author, 18 of which were not present in POLTOUR's dataset due to either recency or the relative lack of skills of the Web of Science and Scopus databases, used by Demiroglu et al. (2024) for POLTOUR 2.0, in capturing literature. In total, there are now 132 publications on the topic of Arctic tourism and climate change. Russia is the most studied country among the new additions (Marsadolov et al., 2019; Aleinikova et al., 2020; Mosalev and Sanin, 2022; Grigorieva et al., 2023; Knyazeva et al., 2023), along with Norway – where Svalbard still remains the hot spot of research interest (Holmgaard et al., 2019; Helgadóttir et al., 2021; Hovelsrud et al., 2021; Andersen, 2022; Dannevig et al., 2023) – followed by Canada (Johnston et al., 2019; Kerber, 2022; D'Souza et al., 2023), Finland (Kähkönen, 2020; Varnajot and Saarinen, 2022), Iceland (Helgadóttir et al., 2021; Remer and Liu, 2022), Greenland (Hall, 2021), the US (Grigorieva et al., 2023) and Sweden (Nilsson and Demiroglu, 2024). Also worth noting is the dominance of climate risk papers (n: 11), with only D'Souza et al. (2023) delving into the carbon risks of polar bear tourism in

Churchill, Canada. Figure 2.3 displays how the publications on Arctic tourism and climate change are regionally and thematically distributed for the entire, AI-enriched dataset over the 2004–2023 period. It clearly illustrates the persisting spatial research gaps, especially for Sweden, and the need for more research on carbon risks. Such a thematic gap was also confirmed for Africa (Dube et al., 2023), Asia (Fang et al., 2022), Europe (Steiger et al., 2023) and North America (Rutty et al., 2022), whereas, regarding the Antarctic, research is much more balanced between climate and the carbon risks (Demiroglu et al., 2024). Thus, besides the regional gaps and the relative outdatedness of research in the North American Arctic (see Figures 2.2a and 2.2b), the systematic emissions and mitigation issues of Arctic tourism need more research in the future.

The future of Arctic tourism and climate change as well as the research agenda in this regard were also investigated using AI – through both scientific and artistic means. ChatClimate (Vaghefi et al., 2023), a conversational AI trained to respond by basing its answers on the latest reports by the Intergovernmental Panel on Climate Change (IPCC, 2021, 2022a, 2022b) and the world-renowned GPT-3.5 Turbo model (GPT-4 was not available at the time of writing) were asked "what is the research agenda for Arctic tourism and climate change from both vulnerability and mitigation perspectives?", in "hybrid" mode to ensure references to both the IPCC and the GPT. In summary, the priority areas were stated as the positive impacts (owing to the improved maritime accessibility and the extended warm season), LCT, governance and adaptive capacity (Figures 2.4a and 2.4b). While such AI inputs can enhance the use of POLTOUR in identifying research gaps, it should also be noted that ChatClimate was rather biased/limited in talking about the carbon risks (see also the disclaimer note on Figure 2.4b). Last but not least, the DeepAI.org image generator was used with the prompt "future of Arctic tourism and climate crisis." The image output was worth a thousand words: A bus/train-like vehicle travels on a dead-end road near the edge of a melted (?) glacier within a spectacular landscape (Figure 2.4a), reflecting in a nutshell concepts like the LCT, the paradoxical footprints and the need for transformative mitigation.

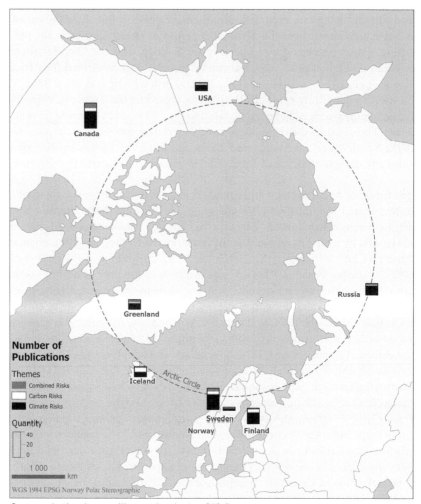

Source: Author's own illustration in ArcGIS Pro.

Figure 2.3   Regional and thematic distribution of research publications
                 on Arctic tourism and climate change (2004–2023)

Source: DeepAI.org.

Figure 2.4a   Future of Arctic tourism and climate change, as illustrated
by DeepAI.org

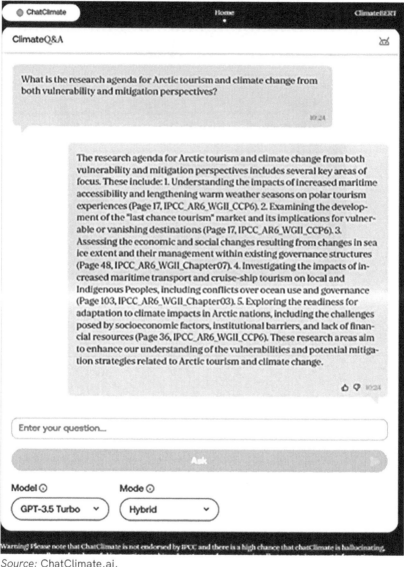

Source: ChatClimate.ai.

Figure 2.4b   Future of Arctic tourism and climate change and its research
agenda, as explained by ChatClimate.ai

What about outreach? An Altmetric perspective

Understanding the popular outreach of Arctic tourism and climate change research, beyond its scholarly output, could provide us with more realistic indicators to confirm the efficacy of academic efforts. Here, altmetrics – an emerging method that is complementary to traditional bibliometrics in quantifying research impact – can assist with measurements of policy and (social) media coverage of research. This chapter presents the aggregate outreach results of all 132 of POLTOUR's publications, referring to the leading altmetrics services, PlumX (Elsevier) and Altmetric.com. In addition, we also check the academic readership of the publications through Mendeley's database (Elsevier), to reveal the levels of multidisciplinarity and seniority among the audience. As can be seen in Table 2.1, the 132 papers have reached a total of 7940 academic fellows at mostly junior levels (students and "researchers") within social and environmental sciences, followed by agricultural and biological sciences, business management and accounting, and Earth and planetary sciences.

The figures above should be read with caution, as such statistics are only as reliable as the quality of the services provided by the aforementioned databases. Nonetheless, the topic of Arctic tourism and climate change emerges as a crossroads of the hard and soft sciences, with the most interest coming from younger researchers (which, however, is a certain common bias found in Mendeley readership counts – see Thelwall and Sud, 2016). Moreover, active popular outreach is also present, and (probably more importantly) policy coverage is also evident – albeit highly skewed. Some 98% of the Facebook posts and 86% of X posts/tweets concern only 15 of the 132 publications, and policy and news/blog coverage is available for only 24 and 17 publications, respectively. The most read papers on Mendeley (Berman et al., 2004; Dawson et al., 2010, 2011; Lambert et al., 2010; Lemelin et al., 2010; Hovelsrud et al., 2011; Hansen et al., 2014; Tolvanen and Kangas, 2016), with more than 200 unique views each, do not necessarily reflect a strong outreach but most probably owe such high metrics to their ages, with the exception of Hansen et al.'s (2014) paper on the future of the Arctic with warmer and wetter winters, which has received the second-highest number of policy citations (n: 10) as well as 51 X posts/tweets. Regarding the most popular papers on Facebook, an interesting cluster forms around carbon risk studies on Iceland (Raudsepp et al., 2021; Árnadóttir et al., 2021; Abrahams et al., 2022; Czepkiewicz et al., 2019), on which a total of 343 posts have been made.

Table 2.1   Outreach audience and outlets of Arctic tourism and climate change research

Readers' Seniority	n	%*	Publications' Multidisciplinarity	n	%*	Communications	n
Professor/Associate Professor	513	8	Social Sciences	1227	29	Facebook posts	841
Lecturer/Post-doc	405	7	Environmental Science	1226	29	Tweets (X posts)	480
Researcher	2348	38	Agricultural & Biological Sciences	627	15	News/blog sites	85
PhD/Post grad/ Masters	2861	47	Business, Man. & Accounting	493	12	Policy citations	74
			Earth & Planetary Sciences	264	6	Wikipedia citations	5

Notes: *of a total excluding the category "unknown"

Conclusion

This chapter departed from the POLTOUR 2.0 Geobibliography – a web mapping application that helps identify the spatial and thematic research gaps and the bibliographical ages of literature on the topic of Arctic (and Antarctic) tourism and climate change. POLTOUR's underlying publication set was further extended with the help of AI, yielding 132 studies. At first glance, the lack of research on some Arctic nations, such as Sweden, as well as the dominance of research on climate vs carbon risks, are very apparent. Moreover, the research on some well covered regions, such as Canada, has aged, indicating a need for more up-to-date studies; meanwhile, the EHSA results (see Figures 2.2a and 2.2b) confirm an opposite trend in most of the Arctic, with more recent studies. Nonetheless, balancing such spatial gaps should aim for more pan-Arctic studies for more consistent and comparable results, and in order to help aid mutual learning at a time when capacity-building is of utmost importance for engaging actors and stakeholders in climate action involving both a mitigation of carbon risks and an adaptation to climate risks.

Using POLTOUR's interface, it is also possible to dig further into the gaps, for instance checking studies based on climatic subtheme and tourism type. Especially regarding tourism types, research should move beyond its major focus on cruise tourism and diversify its scope for other activities and attractions, including those that may not have manifested yet (e.g. "cool weather tourism"). Moreover, more integrated impact assessments, in addition to a pan-Arctic perspective as suggested above, are needed in order to build a more comprehensive understanding of the climate risks and adaptation needs. Likewise, carbon risks also require more systematic approaches, as business-/destination-scale footprint assessments will typically not reflect the actual contributions of the tourism system to global warming, and could even be misleading regarding urgently needed mitigation actions.

In the future, an integration of altmetric indicators – especially those on policy coverage – into POLTOUR will also be useful for understanding the efficacy of research, particularly at a time when high-level climate policies in the Arctic lack diligent reference to tourism-related climate and carbon risks. This is also in line with the call by the TPCC's recent Tourism and Climate Change Stocktake report (Tourism Panel on Climate Change, 2023), which concludes that "[a]t present, no country [...] ha[s] achieved meaningful reductions in tourism greenhouse gas emissions" and that "the intensification of observable impacts of climate change on tourism destinations is unmistakable," with "[f]ew tourism authorities hav[ing] focused adequately on the potentially massive impacts of climate hazards and the paradigm shift that will be required in the transition to climate resilient tourism development" (p. 2). While not in the Arctic, in the polar regions or even on a global scale, only Chile has been found to serve as a role model for national-level climate-tourism policies (Demiroglu et al., 2024; Navarro-Drazich et al., 2023), while less is known about their prospective practical outcomes.

References

Abrahams, Z., Hoogendoorn, G., and Fitchett, J. M. (2022). Glacier tourism and tourist reviews: An experiential engagement with the concept of "Last Chance Tourism". *Scandinavian Journal of Hospitality and Tourism, 22*(1): 1–14.

Aleinikova, A. M., Byashkin, M., Gaivoron, T., Mainasheva, G., and Marsheva N. (2020). The role of specially protected natural areas in solving environmental problems of the Russian Arctic (using the example of Vaygach Island). *E3S Web of Conferences, 169*, 02019.

Ali, F., and OpenAI, Inc, C. (2023). Let the devil speak for itself: Should ChatGPT be allowed or banned in hospitality and tourism schools? *Journal of Global Hospitality and Tourism, 2*(1), 1–6.

Andersen, T. B. C. (2022). Negotiating trade-offs between the environment, sustainability and mass tourism amongst guides on Svalbard. *Polar Record, 58*, e9.

Árnadóttir, Á., Czepkiewicz, M., and Heinonen, J. (2021). Climate change concern and the desire to travel: How do I justify my flights? *Travel Behaviour and Society, 24*, 282–90.

Berman, M., Nicolson, C., Kofinas, G., Tetlichi, J., and Martin, S. (2004). Adaptation and sustainability in a small arctic community: Results of an agent-based simulation model. *Arctic, 57*, 401–14.

Carson, D. (2020). Urban tourism in the Arctic: A framework for comparison. In D. K. Müller, D. A. Carson, S. de la Barre, B. Granås, G. Þ. Jóhannesson, G. Øyen, O. Rantala, J. Saarinen, T. Salmela, K. Tervo-Kankare and J. Welling (Eds.), *Arctic Tourism in Times of Changes: Dimensions of Urban Tourism*, 6–17. Nordic Council of Ministers.

Czepkiewicz, M., Árnadóttir, Á., and Heinonen, J. (2019). Flights dominate travel emissions of young urbanites. *Sustainability, 11*(22), 6340.

D'Souza, J., Dawson, J., and Groulx, M. (2023). Last chance tourism: A decade review of a case study on Churchill, Manitoba's polar bear viewing industry. *Journal of Sustainable Tourism, 31*(1), 14–31.

Dannevig, H., Søreide, J. E., Sveinsdóttir, A. G., Olsen, J., Hovelsrud, G. K., Rusdal, T., and Dale, R. F. (2023). Coping with rapid and cascading changes in Svalbard: The case of nature-based tourism in Svalbard. *Frontiers in Human Dynamics, 5*, 1178264.

Dawson, J., Johnston, M. E., Stewart, E. J., Lemieux, C. J., Lemelin, R. H., Maher, P. T., and Grimwood, B. S. R. (2011). Ethical considerations of last chance tourism. *Journal of Ecotourism, 10*, 250–65.

Dawson, J., Stewart, E. J., Lemelin, R. H., and Scott, D. (2010). The carbon cost of polar bear viewing tourism in Churchill, Canada. *Journal of Sustainable Tourism, 18*, 319–36.

Demiroglu, O. C. (2020). What happens in the Arctic does not stay in the Arctic. In L. Lundmark, D. Carson and M. Eimermann (Eds.), *Dipping in to the North*, 277–79. Springer.

Demiroglu, O. C., Dannevig, H., and Aall, C. (2013). The multidisciplinary literature of ski tourism and climate change. In M. Kozak and N. Kozak (Eds.), *Tourism Research: An Interdisciplinary Perspective*, 223–37. Cambridge Scholars Publishing.

Demiroglu, O. C., and Hall, C. M. (2020). Geobibliography and bibliometric networks of polar tourism and climate change research. *Atmosphere, 11*(5), 498.

Demiroglu, O. C., Bohn, D., Dannevig, H., Hall, C. M., Hehir, C. Lundmark, L., Nilsson, R. O., Olsen, J., Tervo-Kankare, K., Vereda, M., and Welling, J. (2024). A virtual geo-bibliography of polar tourism and climate change. *Journal of Sustainable Tourism.* 10.1080/09669582.2024.2370971.

Dube, K., Nhamo, G., Kilungu, H., Hambira, W. L., El-Masry, E. A., Chikodzi, D., Chapungu, L., and Molua, E. L. (2023). Tourism and climate change in Africa: Informing sector responses. *Journal of Sustainable Tourism*, DOI: 10.1080/09669582.2023.2193357.

Fang, Y., Trupp, A., Hess, J. S., and Ma, S. (2022). Tourism under climate crisis in Asia: Impacts and implications. *Journal of Sustainable Tourism*, DOI: 10.1080/09669582.2022.2112204.

Grigorieva, E., Alexeev, V., and Walsh, J. (2023). Universal thermal climate index in the Arctic in an era of climate change: Alaska and Chukotka as a case study. *International Journal of Biometeorology, 67*, 1703–21.

Hall, D. (2021). *Tourism, Climate Change and the Geopolitics of Arctic Development: The Critical Case of Greenland.* CABI.

Hansen, B. B., Isaksen, K., Benestad, R. E., Kohler, J., Pedersen, Å. Ø., Loe, L. E., Coulson, S. J., Larsen, J. O., and Varpe, Ø. (2014). Warmer and wetter winters: Characteristics and implications of an extreme weather event in the High Arctic. *Environmental Research Letters, 9*, 114021.

Helgadóttir, G., Renssen, H., Olk, T. R., Oredalen, T. J., Haraldsdóttir, L., Skúlason, S., and Thorarensen, H. Þ. (2021). Wild and farmed Arctic charr as a tourism product in an era of climate change. *Frontiers in Sustainable Food Systems, 5*, 654117.

Higham, J., Loehr, J., Hopkins, D., Becken, S., and Stovall, W. (2022). Climate science and tourism policy in Australasia: Deficiencies in science-policy translation. *Journal of Sustainable Tourism*, DOI: 10.1080/09669582.2022.2134882.

Holmgaard, S. B., Thuestad, A. E., Myrvoll, E. R., and Barlindhaug, S. (2019). Monitoring and managing human stressors to coastal cultural heritage in Svalbard. *Humanities, 8*(1), 21.

Hovelsrud, G. K., Poppel, B., van Oort, B., and Reist, J. D. (2011). Arctic societies, cultures, and peoples in a changing cryosphere. *Ambio, 40*, 100–110.

Hovelsrud, G. K., Veland, S., Kaltenborn, B., Olsen, J., and Dannevig, H. (2021). Sustainable tourism in Svalbard: Balancing economic growth, sustainability, and environmental governance. *Polar Record. 57*, e47.

Huang, A., Chao, Y., de la Mora Velasco, E., Bilgihan, A., and Wei, W. (2022). When artificial intelligence meets the hospitality and tourism industry: An assessment framework to inform theory and management. *Journal of Hospitality and Tourism Insights, 5*(5), 1080–1100.

IPCC (2021). *AR6 Climate Change 2021: The Physical Science Basis.* Cambridge University Press.

IPCC (2022a). *AR6 Climate Change 2022: Impacts, Adaptation and Vulnerability.* Cambridge University Press.

IPCC (2022b). *AR6 Climate Change 2022: Mitigation of Climate Change.* Cambridge University Press.

Johnston, M., Dawson, J., and Stewart, E. (2019). Marine tourism in Nunavut: Issues and opportunities for economic development in Arctic Canada. In R. Koster and D. A. Carson (Eds.), *Perspectives on Rural Tourism Geographies. Geographies of Tourism and Global Change*, 115–36. Springer.

Kähkönen, J. A. (2020). Climate resilience of Arctic tourism: A Finnish perspective on the post-Paris Agreement era. In L. Heininen, H. Exner-Pirot and J. Barnes (Eds.), *Arctic Yearbook 2020.* Arctic Portal.

Kerber, J. (2022). Tracing one warm line: Climate stories and silences in Northwest Passage tourism. *Journal of Canadian Studies, 56*(2), 271–303.

Knyazeva, G. A., Porotnikova, N. A., Antipov, V. V., and Makukha, V. V. (2023). Arctic tourism as a driver of sustainable development of the territory: Research of the interest of local stakeholders in the Komi Republic. *Arctic and North, 52,* 152–67.

Kruse, J. A., White, R. G., Epstein, H. E., Archie, B., Berman, M., Braund, S. R., Chapin III, F.S., Charlie Sr, J., Daniel, C. J., Eamer, J., Flanders, N., Griffith, B., Haley, S., Huskey, L., Joseph, B., Klein, D. R., Kofinas, G. P., Martin, S. M., Murphy, S. M, Nebesky, W., Nicolson, C., Russell, D. E., Tetlichi, J., Tussing, A., Walker, M. D., and Young, O. R. (2004). Modeling sustainability of Arctic communities: An interdisciplinary collaboration of researchers and local knowledge holders. *Ecosystems, 7,* 815–28.

Lambert, E., Hunter, C., Pierce, G. J., and MacLeod, C. D. (2010). Sustainable whale-watching tourism and climate change: Towards a framework of resilience. *Journal of Sustainable Tourism, 18,* 409–27.

Lemelin, R. H., Dawson, J., Stewart, E. J., Maher, P. T., and Lueck, M. (2010). Last-chance tourism: The boom, doom, and gloom of visiting vanishing destinations. *Current Issues in Tourism, 13,* 477–93.

Marsadolov, L. S., Paranina, A., Grigoryev, A. A., and Sukhorukov, V. D. (2019). Problems of preservation of prehistoric cultural heritage objects in the Arctic. *IOP Conference Series: Earth and Environmental Science, 302,* 012149.

Mosalev, A., and Sanin, A. Y. (2022). Tourism management in the Arctic coastal zone of Northern Eurasia. *AUC GEOGRAPHICA, 57*(2), 122–30.

Müller, D. K., and Viken, A. (2017). Indigenous tourism in the Arctic. In A. Viken and D. K. Müller (Eds.), *Tourism and Indigeneity in the Arctic*, 3–15. Channel View Publications.

Navarro-Drazich, D., Christel, L. G., Gerique, A., Grimm, I., Rendón, M.-L., Schlemer Alcântara, L., Abraham, Y., del Rosario Conde, M., and De Simón, C. (2023). Climate change and tourism in South and Central America. *Journal of Sustainable Tourism,* DOI: 10.1080/09669582.2023.2210783.

Nilsson, R. O., and Demiroglu, O. C. (2024). Impacts of climate change on dogsledding recreation and tourism in Arctic Sweden. *International Journal of Biometeorology,* https://doi.org/10.1007/s00484-023-02542-z.

Rantanen, M., Karpechko, A. Y., Lipponen, A., Nordling, K., Hyvärinen, O., Ruosteenoja, K., Vihma, T., and Laaksonen, A. (2022). The Arctic has warmed nearly four times faster than the globe since 1979. *Communications Earth and Environment, 3,* 168.

Raudsepp, J., Árnadóttir, Á., Czepkiewicz, M., and Heinonen, J. (2021). Long-distance travel and the urban environment: Results from a qualitative study in Reykjavik. *Urban Planning, 6*(2): 257–70.

Remer, M., and Liu, J. (2022). International tourism in the Arctic under COVID-19: A telecoupling analysis of Iceland. *Sustainability, 14*(22), 15237.

Rutty, M., Hewer, M., Knowles, N., and Ma, S. (2022). Tourism and climate change in North America: Regional state of knowledge. *Journal of Sustainable Tourism*, DOI: 10.1080/09669582.2022.2127742.

Saviolidis, N. M., Cook, D., Davíðsdóttir, B., Jóhannsdóttir, L., and Ólafsson, S. (2021). Challenges of national measurement of environmental sustainability in tourism. *Current Research in Environmental Sustainability, 3*, 100079.

Steiger, R., Demiroglu, O. C., Pons, M., and Salim, E. (2023). Climate and carbon risk of tourism in Europe. *Journal of Sustainable Tourism*, DOI: 10.1080/09669582.2022.2163653.

Thelwall, M., and Sud, P. (2016). Mendeley readership counts: An investigation of temporal and disciplinary differences. *Journal of the Association of Information Science and Technology, 67*, 3036–50.

Tolvanen, A., and Kangas, K. (2016). Tourism, biodiversity and protected areas – Review from northern Fennoscandia. *Journal of Environmental Management, 169*, 58–66.

Tourism Panel on Climate Change (2023). *Tourism and Climate Change Stocktake 2023*. https://tpcc.info/.

Vaghefi, S., Wang, Q., Muccione, V., Ni, J., Kraus, M., Bingler, J., Schimanski, T., Colesanti Senni, C., Webersinke, N., Huggel, C., and Leippold, M. (2023). *ChatClimate: Grounding Conversational AI in Climate Science*. Swiss Finance Institute Research Paper No. 23-88, https://ssrn.com/abstract=4414628 or http://dx .doi.org/10.2139/ssrn.4414628.

Varnajot, A., and Saarinen, J. (2022). Emerging post-Arctic tourism in the age of Anthropocene: Case Finnish Lapland. *Scandinavian Journal of Hospitality and Tourism, 22*(4–5), 357–71.

Welling, J., and Abegg B. (2021). Following the ice: Adaptation processes of glacier tour operators in Southeast Iceland. *International Journal of Biometeorology, 65*, 703–15.

Welling, J., Ólafsdóttír, R., and Árnason, Þ. (2020). Implications of climate change on nature-based tourism demand: A segmentation analysis of glacier site visitors in southeast Iceland. *Sustainability, 12*(13), 5338.

Welling, J., Ólafsdóttir, R., Árnason, Þ., and Guðmundsson, S. (2019). Participatory planning under scenarios of glacier retreat and tourism growth in Southeast Iceland. *Mountain Research and Development, 39*, D1–D13.

Wolf, F., Moncada, S., Surroop, D., Shah, K. U., Raghoo, P., Scherle, N., Reiser, D., Telesford, J. N., Roberts, S., Hausia Havea, P., Naidu R., and Nguyen, L. (2022). Small island developing states, tourism and climate change. *Journal of Sustainable Tourism*, DOI: 10.1080/09669582.2022.2112203.

3 "Justin Bieber posted it on IG, so why can't I visit?" – Understanding the future of the Arctic tourist experience using social media and mobile technologies

Patrick T. Maher and Anne Hardy

Introduction

In 2016, Canadian pop music superstar Justin Bieber, shot two music videos in Iceland. Both were posted to YouTube, and other social media platforms, with controversial results. The first video, for the song "I'll Show You," was shot largely in the Fjaðrárgljúfur Canyon and has been viewed by 517 million viewers. The second video, for the song "Cold Water" by American band Major Lazer featuring Justin Bieber, showcases dancers on fragile moss landscapes on the Eldhraun lava field (Iceland Review, 2016) and has been viewed 335 million times on YouTube.

Prior to their release, from 2016–2020, tourism in Iceland was on a hugely upward trajectory (Maher et al., 2022). Moving beyond what is commonly labelled as overtourism, visitation quickly paused entirely due to the COVID-19 pandemic (see Maher et al., 2022; Jóhannesson et al., 2022 for more details).

The locations featured in the videos were not off limits to Mr. Bieber, and the production companies involved were reputable (see Iceland Review, 2016). However, since their release hordes of "Beliebers" (Justin Bieber's fans) have since descended on the areas shown in the videos. In the 4 years following their release, visitation to the Fjaðrárgljúfur Canyon alone increased by one million visitors (Daley, 2019). This massive rise in numbers caused the temporary closure of the sites (see The Guardian, 2019; As It Happens, 2019), and eventually, extensive hardening was required to deal with the increased numbers (see Backpackers in the World, 2023). This has caused profound changes to the tourist experience in these locations. Justin Bieber is not to blame for all of the resulting visitation and impacts to the Fjaðrárgljúfur Canyon or the Eldhraun lava field; even if the former location is now popularly referred to as "Bieber's Canyon." However, the reach and scope of social media influencers such as Mr. Bieber does create challenges and concerns; as well as altering the tourist experience moving forward. But is this a new phenomenon?

It may be argued that little has changed between what was happening decades ago (or even centuries ago) – individuals going on holiday and then sharing their stories and photographs – and what occurs today. However, the issue now, and moving into the future, is the sheer scope and reach. In the past, not even the distant past when we used analogue film cameras, but even in the near past – tourists would take their digital photos on a separate device and then return home before sharing them with friends and neighbours. But now, tourists can take hundreds of top-quality pictures on their iPhone and share them instantaneously with the entire world. This is where mobile technology and social media collide – and the real-time capabilities of digital technology allow for the inundation of the digital landscape with these artefacts at almost the exact moment they were produced. Moving beyond this, new products such as drones and wearable technology (iWatches and Go-Pros); plus new platforms such as Hootsuite allow for simultaneous posting on multiple platforms (e.g. X, Instagram, Facebook, YouTube, etc.). Arguably this has propelled the sharing of tourism experiences into a hyper-influence stage, where the possibilities to collect, share and disseminate mobility, experience and footage, or see and be influenced by others, are infinitely higher.

As we move to discussing the tourist experience, we need to remember that, as Jandrić et al. (2018) have explained, digital technology and media are no longer separate from typical human and social activity. We are no longer in a human/technology binary state; rather, we exist in a state termed the postdigital. Postdigital does not discuss a future "after" the digital; simply, as Maher and Beames (2024) share, a "digital [that] is just so ubiquitous, so 'every day' and normalized, that it just is."

This constantly connected tourist is a new experience, and as such there are new behavioural patterns. For researchers, the almost ubiquitous use of social media and cell phones offers new opportunities for data collection. This opportunity forms the basis for this chapter and will be explored in the following sections.

Tourist experience/behaviour

As early as the 1960s (see Clawson and Knetsch, 1966), the tourist experience has been viewed as having phases – a before, a during, and an after. This linear and temporal process has been disrupted by mobile technology and social media. What may have been something disconnected from one's everyday life (Uriely, 2005) is now distinctly connected with it due to the advent of mobile technology. In addition, one's own experience on site (the during, the truly "experiential" component of such tourism) is now a reflection of the during/after components of others – those you know, those you don't know, and actual celebrities or "influencers" (see Canavan, 2023). The impact of social media on tourism has been documented as having both positive and negative impacts (see Teles da Mota and Pickering, 2020). It has been recognized as allowing destination management organizations to connect with visitors and market to them, and giving consumers enhanced material to review and choose their experiences. However, the hyper presence that real-time social media connections create also detracts from tourists' ability to be disconnected from home and be present in the moment. There are also impacts to the environment, which occur when a mass of tourists, following one particular route, are involved – as per the Justin Bieber example used to start this chapter.

Larsen et al. (2007) discussed this issue of experience in an increasingly mobile world, but one that largely pre-dated the current state of expansive smartphone and social media usage. Larsen et al. (2007) brought focus to how tourism had moved into assisting with people's friendships and reproducing their social relations. Maher (2010) and Kriwoken and Hardy (2017) explored social connections amongst visitors to the Antarctic, and this could be equally true of Arctic exoticism. In this instance, Uriely's (2005) notion of de-differentiation with everyday life showed promise in changing conceptualizations of the tourist experience. Tourism does not happen for a specific time and place, separate to one's everyday social world. Larsen et al. (2007) state that tourists are not searching for lost difference, but rather distant connections. There is much research completed specifically on aspects of the Arctic Tourist experience (see Lee et al., 2017; Haanpää and García-Rosell, 2020).

The importance of networking tools in tourism is specifically noted by Larsen et al. in 2007. Maher (2010) advanced this conversation in a remote destination such as Antarctica (a scenario that could be mirrored in the Arctic), but much has changed in tourism in the past 15 years. The work of Wang et al., (2012), Kim and Fesenmeier (2017) and Varnajot (2019) offer examples of the shifts in tourist experience in our new mobile technology and social media age. The notion of Larsen et al. (2007) that tourists are experience producers and not just passive consumers has never been more true, and thus their roles shape the experience for others. The possibilities arising from this interconnectivity are a shift in what may be possible with stewardship and ambassadorship (actual behaviour change in tourists). Hehir et al. (2021) and Varnajot (2024) have advanced this conversation in the Polar context, both empirically and theoretically. Furthermore, the interconnectivity and digital traces that tourists use when on holiday, present exciting opportunities for researchers who wish to understand more about the experiences and mobility of visitors to remote regions such as the Arctic.

Using technology to understand mobility and experiences

The rise of social media and mobile technologies offer researchers an opportunity to understand the tourism experience, mobility, tourism impacts and even visitor numbers to locations in several different ways. In this section we explore these possibilities.

Understanding experiences through social media

The rise in social media has presented many exciting opportunities for social media researchers to understand how tourists are experiencing locations. Recent research by Gretzel and Hardy (2019), and Vorobjovas-Pinta and Hardy (2020) explored how tourists experienced vanlife and events. More recently, Blackwood and Ooi (2023) used social media posts to understand how tourists were experiencing and interpreting locations following a bushfire event. While social media platforms most commonly prohibit automated scraping of data, manual scraping may be employed, where researchers search for terms, geotags and hashtags and analyze the wording within the post, or the photo, to gain insight into how tourists are interpreting destinations, transport and tourism experiences (Hardy, 2020). The use of data such as this is often referred to as crowd-sourcing, information generated by a number of individuals, as defined by Walden-Schreiner et al. (2018). Analyzing this form of data is now most commonly undertaken using netnography – the qualitative use of traditional ethnographic techniques in an online context. Initially developed by Kozinets (1998) and refined through the early 2000s (see Kozinets, 2010) it has become a popular method across tourism and other aligned fields (see Andkjær and Højbjerre Larsen, 2024, Björk and Kauppinen-Räisänen, 2012; Tavakoli and Wijesinghe, 2019), and more specifically Arctic tourism (see Varnajot, 2024, Hutton, 2024, Hutton and Rantala, 2024). Netnography provides great flexibility because it acknowledges that online research does not deal only in words, but also assesses "images, drawings, photography, sound files, edited audiovisual presentations, website creations and other digital artefacts" (Kozinets, 2015, p.5). Quantitative tools may also be used to analyze tourist's experiences; recent examples include work by Gretzel and Hardy (2019) who analyzed the frequency of words within hashtags, to gain a sense of significant experiential themes.

The difficulty in using social media data to understand how visitors to a region experience it, is that social media posts are not always a true reflection of one's reality, but rather a curated version of how individuals would like to be seen (Gretzel and Hardy, 2019). Caution is also needed as the impacts of the tourist celebrity gaze, as noted by Canavan (2020), are yet to be researched in detail. Perhaps, moving forward, understanding how places are experienced via netnographic methods is best as a means to triangulate other ways of under-standing Arctic tourist experiences (see Varnajot, 2024).

Understanding mobility

Technology has led to the emergence of two new forms of data: continuous data where tourists' entire travel paths may be sought, and non-continuous data, where their locations at specific points in time can be assessed. Typically, data sourced from social media platforms is non-continuous data, as the digital traces of social media users exist only when individuals have posted images, geotags or text. This form of data can be used to understand which locations are visited, visitor density and directionality. When sourced auto-matically, large amounts of data can be procured; this is possible on platforms such as Twitter/X and Flickr, which allow researchers to use a conduit, called an automated programming interface (API) to access vast amounts of data. When vast volumes of data can be sought through automated means, it has been argued that some social media data can be a proxy for actual visitation numbers (Kádár, 2014; Levin et al., 2015; Spalding et al., 2017; Tenkanen et al., 2017; Walden-Schreiner et al., 2018). In other examples, Ramasco (2016) and Hawelka et al. (2014) assessed tourists' places of residence against places they visited, while Chua et al. (2016) used geotagged Twitter data to assess directional flow of tourists in Italy.

In addition to social media, vast volumes of non-continuous data can also be sourced from mobile phone data, Bluetooth and Wi-Fi functionality – the process of this extraction is discussed in detail in Hardy (2020). While this method produces vast amounts of data that can determine crowding and directionality, like social media data it is limited in its ability to identify the socio-demographic characteristics of its users.

Continuous data may be sourced via global positioning system (GPS) technology which is now embedded within many mobile phones and apps, allowing researchers to use the data of tourists' movement through time and space (Hardy, 2020). Well-known examples of this include Strava and MapMyFitness, whose GPS data can provide precise and continuous mobility patterns to researchers, on tourists' spatial and temporal movement (Hardy, 2020). This form of data has been used with great success by Norman et al. (2019) in Australia, and Korpilo et al. (2017) in Finland.

In addition to this, bespoke research apps with GPS capabilities have been developed to track the mobility of tourists through time and space, producing continuous data. One of the first of this type is Tourism Tracer, an app developed by the University of Tasmania with embedded survey and GPS functionality within it. This app was the first to track tourists' movement through whole destinations for their entire vacation, while also recording their demographic and psychographic characteristics. It resulted in unique insights into the factors that influence dispersal, tourist movement through protected areas, the speed at which they travelled and the way in which specific groups of tourists, such as wine and cruise ship passengers travel (McKercher et al., 2019; Hardy, 2020; Hardy et al., 2020; Hardy and Aryal, 2020; Hardy et al., 2022a; Lewis et al., 2021). Recently, exciting research has used this technology to track cruise ship tourists in Greenland, and particularly the efficacy of behavioural interventions upon their mobility (as mentioned in Cooper, 2023).

Ethical consideration

One of the most significant concerns regarding the use of mobile technology and social media for research purposes is the ethics of tracking tourists' mobility, en masse. Bespoke apps and non-automatically scraped social media data involve researchers making direct contact with research participants and requesting use of their data. However, with data that is sourced from social media via APIs, or data that is collected from Bluetooth, Wi-Fi or via mobile phone companies, the sheer volume of the data renders contact with those who have produced the data impossible. This means that the consequences of data breaches or a lack of consent are far more wide-reaching. Where possible, it is important for researchers to seek consent, and when using social media posts, great care should be taken. For example, Hardy (2020) articulates that while posts on social media may have been set up to appear "public" and therefore be able to be used by researchers, this may not be the case. Kozinets (2019, p. 195) argues that "… a significant number of people – very likely a majority – would prefer that researchers should not use their social media data and information in their investigations."

Similarly, Gretzel (2017, p. 119) notes that "the ease with which observations can occur without participants' knowledge", as well as the concern that the researcher has "the means of extracting and archiving large quantities of often very personal data" are problematic. Consequently Kozinets (2019) recommends that researchers should use opportunities to gain permission and consent whenever possible.

Conclusions: A research agenda for the future of Arctic tourism

Creating a research agenda for the use of technology such as social media and bespoke apps to explore, understand and evaluate Arctic tourism, with so many variables, is difficult. We can be certain that along with technological improvements, the Arctic tourist experience will continue to evolve. There will be new destinations, new activities, a changing climate and operators always seeking to innovate and differentiate. However, what technology offers is the ability to track changes in the Arctic tourism environment quickly, en masse and in real-time. Furthermore, the use of social media and technology as a data source allows researchers to evaluate how destinations are experienced from afar. Climate-conscious research that supports, rather than adds to the causes of climate change, has rarely been evaluated within tourism research, yet is desperately needed; research that supports, rather than detracts from communities has been recently advocated for (Hardy et al., 2022b).

To this end, we argue that the following considerations should be made when using technology to explore the Arctic tourism experience:

- Does the research question centre around a desire to understand tourists' experiences, mobility or visitation numbers?
- Does the technology adequately assess the core research questions?
- How will the data be sourced and is the collection ethical?
- What are the impacts of the data collection on the environment, destination host community and research participants?

Importantly, further research is urgently needed to explore the role that social media plays in influencing decision making and tourists' experiences. For example, one of the key considerations is how we, as individuals, choose to navigate this ever-changing landscape in this time of Technofeudalism, the title of the latest book by Greek economist Yanis Varoufakis (2023). If our everyday thoughts, habits, and actions are shaped by influencers such as Justin Bieber and the owners of big tech corporations (the Googles, the Apples, the Metas among others) what does this mean for the way in which we interpret tourist locations? Furthermore, as Rosenberg (forthcoming) notes, we may seem distracted, having our experiences mediated by a smartphone, or we may be organizing ourselves differently as the "digital tourist" (Sharpley, 2018). With that said, perhaps we are now the post-digital tourist.

The recently published "Routledge Handbook of Mobile Technology, Social Media and the Outdoors" (Beames and Maher, 2024) offers many examples of possible research avenues. They cover many related fields of outdoor recreation, outdoor education, and leisure, but keeping Arctic tourism front and centre, we would expand on three specific ideas.

1. If we are in a post-digital world where we pay "cloud rent" (Varoufakis, 2023, p. xii) and engage with digital social networks that are neither inherently good nor bad; how do we as Arctic tourism researchers, particularly those who often come from the South, change the balance, particularly in a region on the periphery, whereby we could be walking a path as "simultaneously, potential liberators and enslavers" (Varoufakis, 2023, p. 10)?
2. For those outside the Arctic, does mobile technology and social media offer a better glimpse of the region? What if a region has poor cell coverage or non-existent wifi (such as many swaths of Arctic Canada)?
3. What is our role as researchers, generally, if we can't see the entire future, to speculate exactly what platforms and possibilities exist even 5 years down the road? There is an Arctic tourism imperative here if one looks to where the next waves of tourists may come from – China, India, etc. and some of the vast differences in platform availability, surveillance, etc.

Larsen et al. (2007, p. 259) stated that future research should decipher "the interconnections among place, events, and sociabilities, where experiences of place are complexly multifaceted. Their interconnections set out a new agenda so as to examine the multiple ways in which places and performances are elaborately intertwined." From 2007 to 2024, technology has changed greatly, but the substance of what we need to do in the future has largely stayed the same; innovate our research thinking globally, regardless of the hardware or the software, yet not forget the uniqueness of place – in this case the Arctic.

References

Andkjær, S., and Højbjerre Larsen, S. (forthcoming). "Check out my campfire, see my big catch – I am an outdoor person!": Communication and cultural significance in two Danish Outdoor Facebook groups. In S. K. Beames and P. T. Maher (Eds.), *The Routledge Handbook on Mobile Technology, Social Media and the Outdoors*. Routledge.

As it Happens (2019, May 21). *Justin Bieber fans try to bribe their way into Icelandic canyon featured in music video* [Radio broadcast]. https://www.cbc.ca/radio/asithappens/as-it-happens-monday-edition-1.5142627/justin-bieber-fans-try-to-bribe-their-way-into-icelandic-canyon-featured-in-music-video-1.5142631.

Backpackers in the World (2023). *Fjadrargljufur Canyon in Iceland – A Complete Guide*. https://backpackersintheworld.com/fjadrargljufur-canyon-in-iceland-a-complete-guide/.

Beames, S. K., and Maher, P. T. (Eds.) (2024). *The Routledge Handbook on Mobile Technology, Social Media and the Outdoors*. Routledge. https://www.routledge.com/Routledge-Handbook-of-Mobile-Technology-Social-Media-and-the-Outdoors/Beames-Maher/p/book/9781032434766.

Björk, P., and Kauppinen-Räisänen, H. (2012). A netnographic examination of travelers' online discussions of risks. *Tourism Management Perspectives, 2–3*, 65–71.

Blackwood, G., and Ooi, C. S. (2023). Social media, destination image and natural disaster: A Netnographic analysis of #tasfires Instagram posts during the 2018-2019 Tasmanian fires. *Annals of Tourism Research Empirical Insights, 4*(1), 100082.

Canavan, B. (2020). Let's get this show on the road! Introducing the tourist celebrity gaze. *Annals of Tourism Research, 82*, 102898.

Canavan, B. (2023, December 27). Selfies and social media: How tourists indulge their influencer fantasies. *The Conversation*. https://theconversation.com/selfies-and-social-media-how-tourists-indulge-their-influencer-fantasies-214681.

Chua, A., Servillo, L., Marcheggiani, E., and Vande Moere, A. (2016). Mapping Cilento: Using geotagged social media data to characterize tourist flows in Southern Italy. *Tourism Management, 57*, 295–310.

Clawson, M., and Knetsch, J. L. (1966). *Economics of Outdoor Recreation*. John Hopkins University Press.

Cooper, E. (2023). *Tourists on the Edge: Understanding and Encouraging Sustainable Tourist Behaviour in Greenland*. Copenhagen Business School.

Daley, J. (2019, May 20). Justin Bieber ruined this idyllic Icelandic canyon. *Smithsonian Magazine*. https://www.smithsonianmag.com/smart-news/justin-bieber-ruined-idyllic-icelandic-canyon-180972241/.

Gretzel, U. (2017). #travelselfie: A netnographic study of travel identity communicated via Instagram. In S. Carson and M. Pennings (Eds.), *Performing Cultural Tourism: Communities, Tourists and Creative Practices*, 115–27. Routledge.

Gretzel, U. and Hardy, A. (2019). #VanLife: Materiality, makeovers and mobility amongst digital nomads. *E-Review of Tourism Research, 16* (2/3), 1–9.

Haanpää, M. and García-Rosell, J. C. (2020). Understanding performativity and embodied tourism experiences in animal-based tourism in the Arctic. In S. K. Dixit (Ed.), *The Routledge Handbook of Tourism Experience Management and Marketing*. Routledge.

Hardy, A. (2020). *Tracking Tourists. Movements and Mobility*. Goodfellow.

Hardy, A., Birenboim, A., and Wells, M. (2020). Using geoinformatics to assess tourist dispersal at the state level. *Annals of Tourism Research*, *82*, 102903.

Hardy, A. and Aryal, J. (2020). Using innovations to understand tourist mobility in national parks. *Journal of Sustainable Tourism*, *2*(2) 263–83.

Hardy, A., Vorobjovas-Pinta, O., Wells, M., Grimmer, L., and Grimmer, M. (2022a). Measuring cruise passenger dispersal through technology. *Annals of Tourism Research*, *93*, 103319.

Hardy, A., Young, T., Cheer, J., Scheyvens, R., and Movono, A. (2022b). Humanising research: A citizen social science agenda. *Annals of Tourism Research*, *96*, 103468.

Hawelka, B., Sitko, I., Beinat, E., Sobolevsky, S., Kazakopoulos, P. and Ratti, C. (2014). Geo-located Twitter as proxy for global mobility patterns. *Cartography and Geographic Information Science*, *41*, 260–71.

Hehir, C., Stewart, E. J., Maher, P. T., and Ribeiro, M. A. (2021). Evaluating the impact of a youth polar expedition alumni programme on post-trip pro-environmental behaviour: A community-engaged research approach. *Journal of Sustainable Tourism*, *29*(10), 1635–54.

Hutton, E. (forthcoming). *Outdoors Goes Online: Tourist Gaze in Social Media for Visitor Monitoring and Management*. Unpublished PhD-dissertation. University of Lapland.

Hutton, E., and Rantala, O. (2024). Sharing the epic: The absence of everydayness in social media images from hiking trips. In S. K. Beames and P. T. Maher (Eds.), *The Routledge Handbook on Mobile Technology, Social Media and the Outdoors*. Routledge.

Iceland Review (2016, Sept. 16). Moss Abuse in Bieber's Video Criticized. https://www.icelandreview.com/news/moss-abuse-in-biebers-video-criticized/.

Jandrić, P., Knox, J., Besley, T., Ryberg, T., Suoranta, J., and Hayes, S. (2018). Postdigital science and education. *Educational Philosophy and Theory*, *50*, 893–99.

Jóhannesson, G. T., Welling, J., Müller, D. K., Lundmark, L., Nilsson, R. O., de la Barre, S., Granås, B., Rantala, O., Tervo-Kankare, K., and Maher, P. T. (2022). *Arctic Tourism in Times of Change: Uncertain Futures – From Overtourism to Re-starting Tourism*. Nordic Council of Ministers.

Kádár, B. (2014). Measuring tourist activities in cities using geotagged photography. *Tourism Geographies*, *16*(1), 88–104.

Kim, J., and Fesenmaier, D. R. (2017). Sharing tourism experiences: The posttrip experience. *Journal of Travel Research*, *56*(1), 28–40.

Korpilo, S., Virtanen, T., and Lehvävirta, S. (2017). Smartphone GPS tracking—inexpensive and efficient data collection on recreational movement. *Landscape and Urban Planning*, *157*, 608–17.

Kozinets, R. V. (1998). On netnography: Initial reflections on consumer research investigations of cyberculture. In J. W. Alba and J. W. Hutchinson (Eds.). *Advances in Consumer Research*, *25*, 366–71.

Kozinets, R. V. (2010). *Netnography: Doing Ethnographic Research Online*. Sage.

Kozinets, R. (2015). *Netnography: Redefined*. London: Sage.

Kozinets, R. (2019). *Netnography: The Essential Guide to Qualitative Social Media Research*. 3rd ed. SAGE.

Kriwoken, K., and Hardy, A. (2017). Neo-tribes and Antarctic expedition cruise ship tourists. *Annals of Leisure Research*, *21*(2), 161–77.

Larsen, J., Urry, J., and Axhausen, K. W. (2007). Networks and tourism: Mobile social life. *Annals of Tourism Research*, *34*(1), 244–62.

Lee, Y.-S., Weaver, D. B., and Prebensen, N. K. (Eds.) (2017). *Arctic Tourism Experiences: Production, Consumption and Sustainability.* CABI.

Levin, N., Kark, S. and Crandall, D. (2015). Where have all the people gone? Enhancing global conservation using night lights and social media. *Ecological Applications, 25,* 2153–67.

Lewis, G. K., Hardy, A., Wells, M. P., and Kerslake, F. L. (2021). Using mobile technology to track wine tourists. *Annals of Tourism Research Empirical Insights, 2*(2), 100022.

Maher, P. T. (2010). *Footsteps on the Ice: Visitor Experiences in the Ross Sea Region, Antarctica.* Unpublished PhD-dissertation. Lincoln University, New Zealand.

Maher, P. T., and Beames, S. K. (2024). Introduction: Where did we start and where will this book take us? In S. K. Beames and P. T. Maher (Eds.), *The Routledge Handbook on Mobile Technology, Social Media and the Outdoors.* Routledge.

Maher, P. T., Jóhannesson, G. T., Kvidal-Røvik, T., Müller, D. K., and Rantala, O. (2022). Touring in the Arctic: Shades of grey towards a sustainable future. In D. C. Natcher and T. Koivurova (Eds), *Renewable Economies in the Arctic,* 81–98. Routledge.

McKercher, B., Hardy, A., and Aryal, J., (2019). Using tracking technology to improve marketing: Insights from a historic town in Tasmania, Australia. *Journal of Travel and Tourism Marketing, 36*(7) 823–34.

Norman, P., Pickering, C. M., and Castley, G. (2019). What can volunteered geographic information tell us about the different ways mountain bikers, runners and walkers use urban reserves? *Landscape and Urban Planning, 185,* 180–190.

Ramasco, J. J. (2016). Touristic site attractiveness seen through Twitter. *EPJ Data Science, 5*(1), 12.

Rosenberg, A. (2024). Connected disconnections in the Arctic: Reflections on the impact of the digital shift in nature-based adventure tourism. In S. K. Beames and P. T. Maher (Eds.), *The Routledge Handbook on Mobile Technology, Social Media and the Outdoors.* Routledge.

Sharpley, R. (2018). *Tourism, Tourists and Society.* 5th ed. Routledge.

Spalding, M., Burke, L., Wood, S.A., Ashpole, J., Hutchison, J., and zu Ermgassen, P. (2017). Mapping the global value and distribution of coral reef tourism. *Marine Policy, 82,* 104–113.

Tavakoli, R., and Wijesinghe, S. N. (2019). The evolution of the web and netnography in tourism: A systematic review. *Tourism Management Perspectives, 29,* 48–55.

Teles da Mota, V., and Pickering, C. (2020). Using social media to assess nature-based tourism: Current research and future trends. *Journal of Outdoor Recreation and Tourism, 30,* 100295.

Tenkanen, T., Di Minin, E. Heikinheimo, V., Hausmann, A., Her, M., Kajala, L., and Toivonen. T. (2017). Instagram, Flickr, or Twitter: Assessing the usability of social media data for visitor monitoring in protected areas. *Scientific Reports, 7*(1), 1–11.

The Guardian (2019, May 19). *Justin Bieber Effect Leads to Closure of Icelandic Canyon.* https://www.theguardian.com/world/2019/may/19/justin-bieber-effect-leads-to-closure-of-icelandic-canyon.

Uriely, N. (2005). The tourist experience: Conceptual developments. *Annals of Tourism Research, 32*(1), 199–216.

Varnajot, A. (2019). Digital Rovaniemi: Contemporary and future Arctic tourist experiences. *Journal of Tourism Futures, 6*(1), 6–23.

Varnajot, A. (forthcoming). Using social media to examine ambassadorship in tourism. In S. K. Beames and P. T. Maher (Eds.), *The Routledge Handbook on Mobile Technology, Social Media and the Outdoors.* Routledge.

Varoufakis, Y. (2023). *Technofeudalism: What Killed Capitalism.* Penguin.

Vorobjovas-Pinta, O., and Hardy, A. (2020). Resisting marginalisation and reconstituting space through LGBTQI+ events. *Journal of Sustainable Tourism, 29*(3), 1–19.

Walden-Schreiner, C., Dario Rossi, S., Barros, A. Pickering, C., and Leung, Y. (2018). Using crowd-sourced photos to assess seasonal patterns of visitor use in mountain-protected areas. *Ambio, 47,* 781–93.

Wang, D., Park, S., and Fesenmaier, D. R. (2012). The role of smartphones in mediating the touristic experience. *Journal of Travel Research, 51*(4), 371–87.

4   Mobilities and place: Arctic tourism in the making

Gunnar Thór Jóhannesson

Introduction

Two decades ago, Mike Crang described tourism as 'geography writ large', further stating that:

> Tourism is an active agent in the creative destruction of places in what can be a violent, contested, unequal, but sometimes welcomed, transformative and productive process (Crang, 2004, p. 75).

At the risk of oversimplification, it can be argued that tourism research has from very early on been preoccupied with describing this process, that is, the ways in which tourism (re-)makes places and the various repercussions it has for people and nature. Early accounts tended to describe tourism as an external force, as something that happens *to* places, driven by the demand of masses of tourists for the extraordinary and exotic other (see discussion in e.g. Crick, 1989, Shepherd, 2002). While this notion is still held in many corners of tourism research, during the last two decades more varied approaches have emerged, not least through studies on mobilities and performativity that have explored tourism as a performative force that not only impacts spaces but enacts and composes them (Bærenholdt et al., 2004; Sheller and Urry, 2004). That is to say that tourism is something that happens *with* place, people and a wide array of more-than-human actors and elements. As an example of this approach, Franklin describes tourism as an ordering or 'a way of making the world different' (Franklin, 2004, p. 279). Tourism appears then as a 'network that is dynamic: it constantly maps, translates, joins, connects, aestheticizes, exchanges, enrolls, hosts, and courts' (Franklin, 2012, p. 46). Tourism as an ordering thus shapes places through relational encounters and entanglements with diverse mobilities, actors and objects such as people, roads, airports, narratives, finance, menus, buildings, regulations, animals, landscapes, and ships only to name a few (Jóhannesson, 2023, Jóhannesson et al., 2015).

The vision of tourism as a force of creative destruction is without a doubt a part of the reason that tourism development is commonly featured in both policy and public discourse. Tourism has a long history of being promoted as a tool for development. This is not the least the case in the Arctic, where tourism has been promoted as a means of economic diversification for communities traditionally relying on primary industries such as forestry, mining and fisheries (Lundmark et al., 2020). Tourism has indeed grown rapidly in the Arctic in the last two decades (Maher et al., 2014; Maher et al., 2022). The apparent growth has though been uneven both in space, with particularly urban centres becoming tourism hot spots, and in time, as Arctic tourism is in general characterised by stark seasonality (Rantala et al., 2019; Müller et al., 2020). While there are evident success stories of positive changes brought by tourism, such as improved services, more job opportunities and livelier communities, there are many problems related to the fast growth such as overcrowding, environmental degeneration and tourist safety (Sæþórsdóttir et al., 2020; Hild et al., 2023).

The Arctic is increasing in popularity, sometimes marketed as a last-chance destination or the last frontier and commonly associated with images of unspoiled, pure and pristine nature and as the home of authentic and exotic cultures (Dawson et al., 2011; Ren et al., 2020; Huijbens, 2022). It is noticeable that the discourse on tourism development both as a driver of growth and as a force having negative impacts on nature and society is most often based on the idea that tourism mobilities are external forces that impact more or less sedentary and bounded places. Nevertheless, the Arctic is far from static and has been part of global mobilities for centuries, through which many of the aforementioned images of people and landscapes that still are promoted in tourism marketing have been produced and disseminated (Ísleifsson and Chartier, 2011; Huggan and Jensen, 2016). Many of these markers sit uneasily with the realities the residents of this vast region experience on an everyday basis. People living in the Arctic can hardly, however, be described as passive victims of the external (capitalistic) force of tourism. On the contrary, national and regional authorities together with private entrepreneurs and corporations are actively working on enhancing tourism aiming to connect to the lucrative revenue stream it provides. Prominent examples include infrastructure development, such as building airports and upscaling ports, as well as a growing plethora of services and activities on offer. Local and regional actors thus seek to take advantage of and control of tourism mobilities with various effects. Various, as every ordering has its limits, and tourism sometimes takes place in unintended and improvised ways. The question of how tourism writes geographies, or what repercussions it has as 'an agent of creative destruction' therefore remains relevant.

Here I will relate to this question by unpacking some of the ways in which tourism as an ordering of mobilities shapes places. The argument presented in the chapter is that research on mobilities and place making provides fruitful openings to respond to challenges and controversies of tourism development especially as it provides avenues for exploring different registers of power that are in play as tourism geographies of the Arctic take shape. The chapter proposes three focal points for further research, namely to a) trace ordering of tourism mobilities, b) to identify and describe the ways in which power and control are manifested and exerted across time and space and c) more specifically related to current development of tourism in the Arctic, to study infrastructure development and how tourism is entangled with various other geopolitical interests in the region. The following is based on my own positioning and work in the field of tourism research. Advocating a relational approach to tourism mobilities and performance, I understand research as a performative act, which enacts particular versions of reality while it silences or marginalises others. This standpoint entails accepting that the researcher is always in the midst of the things under study and should have a voice and a say in the unfolding tourism realities. The chapter starts with a brief revisit to the concepts of mobilities and ordering before presenting an example of how ordering of tourism mobilities contributes to place making. Based on the example I describe the notions of multiplicity of space and power topologies that serve as building blocks for the future agenda of research I would like to promote.

Tourism mobilities

The concept of mobilities was introduced to tourism research in the early years of the 21st century and was presented by its advocates as a new paradigm as it placed novel issues on the table, transcending disciplinary boundaries and questioned 'the fundamental "territorial" and "sedentary" precepts of twentieth-century social science' (Hannam et al., 2006, p. 2). As Cresswell (2010) notes, it is questionable if the mobility paradigm did mark a break in the history of research as the word paradigm implies. Movement and different sorts of mobilities have indeed been studied before and neither does mobility research negate attention to what slows down or halts mobility, like frictions, boundaries and moorings of various sorts (Cresswell, 2010, 2011). Nevertheless, Cresswell argued that, while movement of people had been dealt with in different disciplines, it often was seen as empty space or dead time that needed to be passed between more meaningful stopping points or destinations. The mobilities approach brought attention to how movement ranging 'from the body [...] to the globe' (Cresswell, 2010, p. 18) becomes meaningful and a source of power (for an example of meaningful travel and waiting see Löfgren, 2008). Mobility 'involves a fragile entanglement of physical movement, representations, and practices' (Cresswell, 2010, p. 18). Cresswell refers to these entanglements as *constellations of mobility*, which have their histories and geographies. At any time, certain arrangements and organisations of movement, representations and narratives of movement, and ways of practising or performing movement are predominant and shape and position places and people's perceptions of the world. Importantly, different constellations may intermingle across time and space and each constellation furthermore entail particular politics as it channels and enacts power in certain ways (Cresswell, 2010). This means for instance that constellations of tourism mobility affect places as they intermingle with other constellations of mobilities, such as transport, industries or patterns of more-than-human mobility, such as fish stocks that are mobile and wax and wane in tandem with changes in ecology, technology and fishery regulations.

As stated above, tourism as an ordering revolves around ordering of a multitude of mobilities. The concept frames tourism as a relational phenomenon that interferes with other things, such as landscapes, animals, material objects and technologies as well as scenarios and ideas about the future (Jóhannesson et al., 2015). Franklin (2012) reminds us that as human efforts to organise and order the world happen in a world where humans and more-than-humans are already entangled in webs of preexisting orderings, such activities are prone to failure and unintended consequences. In his words: 'typically such projects take on a life of their own, as the people and things so ordered respond, block, enable, modify, reconfigure, spread and inspire effects such as continuities, reproductions, refinements, failures, collapses, hybrids' (p. 46). In this sense, tourism as an ordering can be grasped as a program that has been released on the world through various powers and agencies. However, as we will see below, it is often difficult to identify a single choreographer behind ordering attempts and while at times they can be unleashed on the world as full-fledged plans of action by individual actors, they also emerge and grow in an improvisational manner through myriad of relations. Let us move to an example.

Tourism and becoming of place

How does tourism as an ordering of mobilities make place in the Arctic? As an example, I would like to bring you to the Westfjords, a remote region in Iceland. In a small valley, called Skápadalur, which happens to be on the way to

Látrabjarg, the largest bird cliff in Iceland (see Figure 4.1) and one of the main attractions of the region, lies a wreckage of a ship, called Garðar (see Figure 4.2). This is an old fishing vessel that was sailed onto the shore on purpose by its last owner, Jón Magnússon, in the early 1980s and has since been subjected to a more or less constant process of ruination and, somewhat unexpectedly an increasing popularity with tourists. The first time I encountered the wreckage I was on a field trip with a group of researchers working on a study on mobilities in areas that are usually regarded as marginal and remote in one way or another (see Thorsteinsson et al., 2023). As we drove across the valley we decided to stop by the wreckage. We were not alone, some rental cars were parked on the sandbank beside the vessel that served as a car park and tourists were exploring the rusted ship.

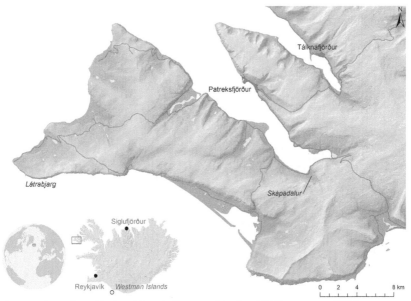

Source: Data from National Lands Survey of Iceland (Jóhannesson 2023; Cartographer: Michaël Virgil Bishop).

Figure 4.1   Map of the location of Garðar and the roads leading to it. Together with Patreksfjörður, it was operated from Siglufjörður, Reykjavík and Westman Islands after being brought to Iceland

We were perplexed by Garðar. We asked ourselves what kind of object this was, and how it would relate to and play a role in the slowly developing tourism in the region?

I later learned that there are different versions of the story behind the reasons Jón sailed Garðar aground. One is that he cherished this ship and valued it as a cultural heritage that he wanted to preserve. Another version of the story is that he simply did not want to pay for the dismantling of the ship and that he saved some money by placing it at the shoreline of Skápadalur, which was, by the way, his own private property. Whatever the reasons were, Jón took some care of the ship, painting it on a regular basis, lighting it up during Christmas time and providing access to it by building a staircase so visitors could freely go on board to have a look on the inside (Morgunblaðið, 1991).

Source: Photo by Gunnar Þór Jóhannesson.

Figure 4.2   Garðar at the shoreline in Skápadalur

The vessel does in fact have an interesting story in the Icelandic context. It is the oldest steel boat in Iceland, built in Oslo in 1912 as a whaling vessel to be used in Antarctic waters. Eventually, it was brought to Iceland in 1945 and used for herring fishing and later, after the collapse of the herring stocks, cod and even lobster fishing, until it was declared unsafe and unseaworthy in 1981. During the almost seventy years it was in operation on the sea, the vessel underwent a series of renovations, upgrading and partial rebuilding in tandem with changes in operations and available technology. As such, Garðar embodies some of the history of use, and often exploitation, of natural resources on which modern societies in the North were built. This is of course only a partial story of the vessel and does not tell about the people whose lives it affected, be it the crew members or the people on land who made a living by processing its catch and neither does it remark on the more-than-human agencies it entwined with, be it fish, radars or weather.

The history of Garðar is not known by many visitors and neither does it seem to matter in terms of its power as an attraction by the roadside (Figure 4.2). Rather it is the physical presence of this metal carcass in the otherwise natural surroundings that attracts. As a site of ruination, Garðar has become meaningful for tourist performance. It immediately grabs the attention of travellers driving the road across the valley and many gravitate towards it like we did, take the turn off the road and start to explore it, photographing it, touching it, peeking through the growing holes on its stern and sides and even crawling on board. Garðar is a popular motif for Instagram photos by travellers in the region, which further attracts more visitors. And that creates concerns. In the recent two decades, without regular maintenance by Magnússon, the vessel has deteriorated, the staircase is long gone, it is easy to cut oneself on the rusty steel and the wooden deck has decayed making it unsafe to embark. Moreover, there are no facilities for visitors at the site, which explains the local expression of it being 'the largest public restroom in the region'.

It is not entirely clear who is responsible and should take care of Garðar since its owner, Jón Magnússon passed away. The municipality has had concerns about the health hazards it poses to visitors and the potential environmental pollution it creates as it slowly disintegrates on the shoreline. Recently, the municipality and the regional Destination Management Office (DMO) have decided to integrate the site into a tourist trail, 'The Westfjord Way' (Vestfjarðaleiðin, 2023). It aims at drawing travellers to the region and directing them to local and regional services and thus slowing people down, getting them to spend more time, and preferably money, in the region (Vestfjarðastofa, 2022). The development of the tourist trail is an effort to advance responsible regional tourism that aligns with the available offerings and capacities in terms of attractions, infrastructure, and services. In practice, the thrust of the effort is to brand the current main road through the region as a tourist experience in and of itself, with a series of designated attractions and sites of service defined along the way. As for the site of Garðar, this involves planning and building basic facilities in the form of a parking lot and restrooms. The tourist representative of the region notes that opinions by locals about the value of Garðar are diverse. She, however, sees it as an important attraction, not the least because it is easily accessible and the fact that it is simple to take good photographs of it means that it may play a significant role in marketing for the region.

Garðar encapsulates diverse constellations of mobilities that connect the past to the present. In a way, its destiny serves as a symbol of broader shifts, reflecting the rising prominence of tourism and the diminishing significance of demersal fishing in the area, the traditional backbone of the regional economy. Rather than capturing whales, herring, and cod it now attracts tourists, many of whom engage with the wreckage in one way or another. Although the region is off the beaten track of tourism mobilities in Iceland, tourism is on the rise and has been heralded as a response to societal change, creating jobs and more diverse employment. The fact that Garðar has been taken on board in an effort to develop more sustainable tourism in the region also underscores the commonly haphazard planning of tourism in sparsely populated and remote areas. Tourism happens, so it seems, somewhat out of control of local or regional actors. Garðar was not thought of as an object of tourism until visitors started to connect with it on their travel through the region. Municipal authorities have been hesitant to embrace the potential role of the shipwreck as an attraction and are in many ways responding to a performance or a choreography started and scripted by visitors taking pictures and sharing them on social media. Clearly, travellers are also responding to the act of sailing the ship on shore, performed by Jón Magnússon in the early 1980s. Of course, it is possible to trace the choreography of place making yet further. That is not the point here, but rather to highlight that tourism is always more than simply tourist consumption of experiences or services. Rather, it is tourism-plus so to say. Tourism mobilities entangle with past mobilities, landscapes, health hazards, municipal politics, infrastructure and ideas and plans of sustainable tourism as in this instance. Tourism as an ordering of mobilities, as the acting out of choreography is never totally orchestrated, there is always room for overflow and excess or simply disorder (Jóhannesson, 2015). To integrate the site of Garðar into the itinerary of the Westfjord Way tourist trail only goes so far. To a certain extent it will formalise a travel pattern already formed but it will hardly stop people from trying to go on board at the risk of injury.

The story of Garðar shows how tourism often takes place in unintended ways as it entwines with multiple other mobilities. This example also underlines that the composition of tourism spaces is far from instrumental, rather it can be done and enacted in many different ways. Tourism may contribute to the

making of places, through unplanned, unintended and improvised configurations of mobility; movement, representation, practice *and* materiality. To
trace orderings of tourism mobilities opens up for critical exploration of how
and why particular spaces of tourism (or tourism realities) are composed and
enacted and brings forth potential alternatives.

Multiplicity of space, valuing of tourism and power

The example discussed above describes how different constellations of tourism
mobility enact and shape space. The idea of reality being performed opens up
the possibility that it can be done and enacted in different ways (Mol, 1999)
and raises thus the (ontological) political question of which realities should
or could be enacted (Law and Urry, 2004) or to paraphrase Crang, what geographies to write. In a similar vein, Massey argued that multiplicity and space
are co-constitutive and described space as 'stories-so-far' (Massey, 2005). This
approach then, underscores the multiplicity of space and raises questions
of the value of tourism, of how and why it comes to matter or which stories
become meaningful to navigate a world in the making. Moreover, it raises
questions of power, that is, by what means and through which processes is it
possible to order constellations of tourism mobilities.

The creation of the tourist trail, The Westfjord Way, and its linking with the
wreckage of Garðar, is intended to create a stronger link between the region
and the tourism mobilities currently affecting Iceland. It does more than
define particular attractions along the trail as it charges the main road running
through the region with a new meaning or a new story to follow. Infrastructures
such as roads can be defined as 'built networks that facilitate the flow of goods,
people, or ideas and allow for their exchange over space' (Larkin, 2013, p. 328).
Although studies frequently highlight the physical existence of infrastructure,
Larkin underlines that infrastructures also embrace various forms of desire,
fantasy, and potential (2013). In a similar vein Easterling (2014) argues that
any form of infrastructure is never entirely ordered but consistently open to
potential alterations or disruptions. Its effects are thus never given in the order
of things but a constant 'matter of concern' (Latour, 2004). With the re-making
of the road as a tourist trail the road not only functions as a line of transportation, connecting points in space, but is now also framed as to offer attractive
experiences to tourists. Moreover, the road, as a tourist trail, orders the relation
between key sites and objects of interests to tourism and thus expands and
shapes the area as a tourist space in a topological sense, in which 'the mutable
quality of relations [...] determines distance and proximity, rather than a sin-

gular and absolute measure' (Harvey, 2012, p. 78). The Westfjord Way tourist trail thus brings particular objects closer together as being part of the regional attractions and keeps some potential attractions out of that group.

The development of the Westfjord Way is a clear attempt to take control of the emergent tourism mobilities in the region. In this case, a certain value proposition of tourism is also evident. The development of the Westfjord Way is an attempt to actualise sustainable tourism in the form of slower travel through the region. It also acknowledges the natural bottleneck created by the sheer distance from the main gateway of international tourists into the country, Keflavík international airport, located on the southwest of the island. The Westfjord region is an unlikely destination for most visitors coming to Iceland, simply because of accessibility and the time it takes to travel there (Thórhallsdóttir et al., 2021). The valuing of responsible growth also fits the public tourism policy currently advocated by national tourist authorities (Stjórnarráð Íslands, 2019). The focus on and valuing of sustainable tourism may thus have equally much to do with the harsh realities of tourism geographies and a convenient fit with current policy objectives as the vision and sustainable ambitions of local residents and stakeholders. What is important in the context of this chapter is that the value base of tourism development is negotiated and shaped through a wide array of relations between people, landscapes, infrastructures, political power centres, policy documents, corporations and objects, like the wreckage of Garðar. Through these relations tourism comes to matter and shapes place.

Tourism mobility, understood as an entanglement of physical movement, representations, and practices, then does not unfold in a pre-defined space but rather, composes space. By tracing this kind of composition or efforts of ordering, tourism research can point to alternative storylines and detect opportunities that could be explored further or interfere in dominant narratives of what is possible and what is not. As we have seen in the examples above, constellations of tourism mobility enact a topological world. According to Allen: 'the driving insight behind topology is that certain characteristics of things retain their integrity despite being twisted or stretched out of shape' (2011, p. 285). He argues that topology challenges a more common understanding of territorial and networked power but does not displace it (ibid.). This is to say that common centres of power, such as government authorities, corporations, interest groups and NGOs surely appear in the process of making tourism geographies. However, their reach and ability to exert control and order are not so much dependent on their position in topographical space as the intensity of the relations they are engaged in. Tourists, roads, airports, cameras, policies, distances, images, landscapes, material objects and various other more-than-human actors also have a say in every becoming ordering.

Tourism research inspired by relational ontology has produced various accounts of such emergent tourism geographies or of how tourism has to be held together by a becoming web of relations linking events and objects of the past, present activities and ideas of future scenarios (see e.g. Jóhannesson et al., 2015). It has to a lesser extent explicitly focused on emergent power geometries of tourism. That is to say, the ways in which more or less distant actors make their presence felt and play a part in shaping the contours of tourism mobilities and places. Following Allen (2011) this means exploring emergent power topologies of tourism, which stresses how actors exert power by 'dissolving, not traversing the gap between "here" and "there" […] through, say, the practices of arms-length manipulation or the mediated leverage of authority and influence' (p. 290). Such effort would include tracing the workings of power, how proximity, distance and reach are enacted and explicitly identifying how power relationships create possible avenues of tourism development and seek to accomplish particular ordering of tourism mobility.

Future directions

This chapter set out from the well-established mobility paradigm that perceives tourism as performed and a performative force. The concept of the constellation of tourism mobility captures the entanglement of physical movement, representations and practice that shape tourism geographies. As the example from the Westfjord region in Iceland illustrates, it is also important to acknowledge the materiality of constellations of mobilities. Tourism mobilities affect places as they entwine with other constellations of mobilities linking the past, the present and the future and this link can be enacted through the presence of a material object, like a ship wreckage. Tourism already has a major influence on the Arctic region and as local stakeholders as well as international corporations seek to relate to a growing demand by travellers for northern experiences the repercussions of tourism activities are bound to grow. It is urgent to follow and describe how tourism composes space. Clearly, this topic is as such, not original at all. The novelty, which the mobility paradigm still provides tourism research today, has to do with the implications of fully integrating relational ontology and performativity of tourism. This approach describes space as multiple, there are, in other words, multiple versions of how tourism 'writes geography' and multiple stories to follow, which calls for research that is able to explore and engage with diverse value propositions of tourism and ontological politics. In practice, this entails that tourism research has to be apt to trace power relations in the making in a mobile and becoming world, as well as being conscious of how research plays into, enacts, resists and advocates particular power dynamics. From a relational perspective, power does not rest inherently with actors but is enacted through relationships (Latour, 1986). While this understanding stresses that the ability to control and order is not confined to particular actors, such as local authorities, corporations or state institutions and their positioning in topographical space it does not preclude the fact that some actors are better equipped to carve out relations to make their presence felt and exert control than others. The concept of power topologies provides a means to explore different registers of power used to shape and direct the emerging configurations of tourism. This is to say, that power is enacted in different ways, sometimes through explicit authority as when public institutions issue and follow up on regulations but sometimes through what Allen (2011) calls *quieter registers*, which stress how leverage and manipulation are practised in order to accomplish the desired results.

To conclude this chapter, I propose three focal points for research on the developing tourism geographies in the Arctic. First, to trace the orderings of tourism mobilities to critically explore how and why particular spaces of tourism (or tourism realities) are composed and enacted and bring forth potential alternatives. Second, to identify and describe emergent power topologies of tourism in the Arctic, the ways in which power and control are manifested and exerted across time and space. This implies to not only describe becoming constellations of tourism mobility in all their diversity, underlining how tourism space is multiple, but to identify different registers of power in play, which works towards certain ends and interests. Third, to focus on infrastructure development and how tourism is entangled with various other geopolitical interests and the rush for scarce natural resources in the Arctic. The third point is more specifically related to the characteristics of the Arctic region. Given the still, somewhat underdeveloped potential of tourism in the Arctic and the fact that it is marked by long distances, weak or limited infrastructure and small populations spread across vast areas this is a highly significant topic of research.

Furthermore, at this point it is fitting to urge researchers to engage and interfere with the ordering of tourism mobility. In order to make tourism research matter it is important to hone the relations through which it becomes meaningful with human and more-than-human actors by enacting careful and collaborative research and staying critically proximate with tourism actors (Jóhannesson et al., 2018). It follows that research on tourism in the Arctic needs to be disseminated and articulated across different contexts, and with actors at different locations and that have different roles. Too often, research is disseminated in confined spaces and is not articulated in the context of the study or along the research process. Dissemination needs to be more than the occasional public presentation or newspaper article, let alone the scientific article even though this is indeed also important. This is often preached but more rarely practised. It demands engagement and often more time and resources than most research projects allow for as well as different kinds of output than what usually has currency within academia.

These are both modest and unsurprising points. They are based on my own position and vision of what I would like to emphasise in the future and thus also serve as reminders for me of what it is that I think is valuable about tourism research. Together these points promote the understanding that tourism research is and should be an integral part of the power topologies that shape tourism in the Arctic. In other words, if tourism composes space, tourism research should contribute to that composition.

References

Allen, J. (2011). Topological twists: Power's shifting geographies. *Dialogues in Human Geography, 1*(3), 283–98.

Bærenholdt, J. O., Haldrup, M., Larsen, J., and Urry, J. (2004). *Performing Tourist Places*. Ashgate.

Crang, M. (2004). Cultural geographies of tourism. In A. Lew, C. M. Hall and A. M. Williams (Eds.), *A Companion to Tourism*, 66–77. Blackwell.

Cresswell, T. (2010). Towards a politics of mobility. *Environment and Planning D: Society and Space, 28*, 17–31.

Cresswell, T. (2011). Mobilities II: Still. *Progress in Human Geography, 36*(5), 645–53.

Crick, M. (1989). Representations of international tourism in the social sciences: Sun, sex, sights, savings, and servility. *Annual Review of Anthropology, 18*, 307–44.

Dawson, J., Johnston, M. J., Stewart, E. J., Lemieux, C. J., Lemelin, R. H., Maher, P. T., and Grimwood, B. S. R. (2011). Ethical considerations of last chance tourism. *Journal of Ecotourism, 10*(3), 250–65. doi:http://dx.doi.org/10.1080/14724049.2011.617449.

Easterling, K. (2014). *Extrastatecraft: The Power of Infrastructure Space*. Verso.

Franklin, A. (2004). Tourism as an ordering: Towards a new ontology of tourism. *Tourist Studies, 4*(3), 277–301.

Franklin, A. (2012). The choreography of a mobile world: Tourism orderings. In R. Van der Duim, C. Ren and G. T. Jóhannesson (Eds.), *Actor-Network Theory and Tourism: Ordering, Materiality and Multiplicity*, 43–58. Routledge.

Hannam, K., Sheller, M., and Urry, J. (2006). Editorial: Mobilities, immobilites and moorings. *Mobilities, 1*(1), 1–22.

Harvey, P. (2012). The topological quality of infrastructural relation: An ethnographic approach. *Theory, Culture & Society, 29*(4/5), 76–92.

Hild, B. O., Jóhannesson, G. T., and Sydnes, A. K. (2023). "Everyone can be a guide until something goes wrong": Adventure guides' competencies and tourist safety in the Arctic. *Scandinavian Journal of Hospitality and Tourism*. Doi:10.1080/1502225 0.2023.2289946.

Huggan, G., and Jensen, L. (Eds.) (2016). *Postcolonial Perspectives on the European High North*. Palgrave Macmillan.

Huijbens, E. H. (2022). The Arctic as the last frontier: Tourism. In M. Finger and G. Rekvig (Eds.), *Global Arctic: An Introduction to the Multifaceted Dynamics of the Arctic*, 129–146. Springer.

Ísleifsson, S., and Chartier, D. (Eds.) (2011). *Iceland and Images of the North*. Presses de l'Université du Québec.

Jóhannesson, G. T. (2015). A fish called tourism: Emergent realities of tourism policy in Iceland. In G. T. Jóhannesson, C. Ren and R. van der Duim (Eds.), *Tourism Encounters and Controversies: Ontological Politics of Tourism Development*, 181–200. Ashgate.

Jóhannesson, G. T., Ren, C., and van der Duim, R. (Eds.) (2015). *Tourism Encounters and Controversies: Ontological Politics of Tourism Development*. Ashgate.

Jóhannesson, G. T., Lund, K. A., and Ren, C. (2018). Making matter in the midst of things: Engaging with tourism imponderables through research. In C. Ren, G. T. Jóhannesson and R. Van der Duim (Eds.), *Co-Creating Tourism Research: Towards Collaborative Ways of Knowing*, 39–54. Routledge.

Jóhannesson, G. T. (2023). Sailing the seas of tourism – Past, present and future mobilities on the margins. In B. Þorsteinsson, K. A. Lund, G. T. Jóhannesson, and G. R. Jóhannesdóttir (Eds.), *Mobilities on the Margins: Creative Processes of Place-making*, 81–98. Palgrave.

Larkin, B. (2013). The politics and poetics of infrastructure. *Annual Review of Anthropology, 42*(1), 327–43.

Latour, B. (1986). The powers of association. In J. Law (Ed.), *Power, Action and Belief: A New Sociology of Knowledge*, 264–80. Routledge & Kegan Paul.

Latour, B. (2004). Why has critique run out of steam? From matters of fact to matters of concern. *Critical Inquiry, 30*, 225–48.

Law, J., and Urry, J. (2004). Enacting the social. *Economy and Society, 33*(3), 390–410.

Löfgren, O. (2008). The secret lives of tourists: Delays, disappointments and daydreams. *Scandinavian Journal of Hospitality and Tourism, 8*(1), 85–101.

Lundmark, L., Carson, D. A., and Eimermann, M. (Eds.) (2020). *Dipping in to the North: Living, Working and Traveling in Sparsely Populated Areas*. Palgrave.

Maher, P. T., Gelter, H., Hillmer-Pegram, K., Hovgaard, G., Hull, J., Jóhannesson, G. T. and Pashkevich, A. (2014). Arctic tourism: Realities & possibilities. In L. Heininen, H. Exner-Pirot, and J. Plouffe (Eds.), *Arctic Yearbook 2014: Human Capital in the North*, 290–306. http://www.arcticyearbook.com/.

Maher, P. T., Jóhannesson, G. T., Kvidal-Røvik, T., Müller, D. K., and Rantala, O. (2022). Touring in the Arctic: Shades of grey towards a sustainable future. In D. C. Natcher and T. Koivurova (Eds.), *Renewable Economies in the Arctic*, 82–98. Routledge.

Massey, D. (2005). *For Space*. Sage.

Mol, A. (1999). Ontological politics: A word and some questions. In J. Law and J. Hassard (Eds.), *Actor Network Theory and After*, 74–89. Blackwell.

Morgunblaðið. (1991, August 28). Elsta stálskipið á sandi í Skápadal: Jón Magnússon, útgerðarmaður, með sitt eigið "sjóminjasafn". *Morgunblaðið*. https://www.mbl.is/gr einasafn/grein/72958/.

Müller, D. K., Carson, D. A., de la Barre, S., Granås, B., Jóhannesson, G. T., Øyen, G. and Welling, J. (2020). *Arctic Tourism in Times of Change: Dimensions of Urban Tourism*. Nordic Council of Ministers.

Rantala, O., de la Barre, S., Granås, B., Jóhannesson, G. T., Müller, D. K., Saarinen, J. and Niskala, M. (2019). *Arctic Tourism in Times of Change: Seasonality*. The Nordic Council of Ministers.

Ren, C., Jóhannesson, G. T., Kramvig, B., Pashkevich, A., and Höckert, E. (2020). Twenty years of research on Arctic and Indigenous cultures in Nordic tourism: A review and future research agenda. *Scandinavian Journal of Hospitality and Tourism, 21*(1), 111–21.

Sheller, M., and Urry, J. (Eds.) (2004). *Tourism Mobilities: Places to Play, Places in Play.* Routledge.

Shepherd, R. (2002). Commodification, culture and tourism. *Tourist Studies, 2*(2), 183–201.

Stjórnarráð Íslands (2019). *Leiðandi í sjálfbærri þróun: Íslensk ferðaþjónusta til 2030.* https://www.stjornarradid.is/lisalib/getfile.aspx?itemid=0bef70be-e109-11e9-944d-005056bc4d74.

Sæþórsdóttir, A. D., Hall, C. M., and Wendt, M. (2020). Overtourism in Iceland: Fantasy or Reality? *Sustainability, 12*(18), 7375.

Thorsteinsson, B., Lund, K. A., Jóhannesdóttir, G. R., and Jóhannesson, G. T. (Eds.) (2023). *Mobilities on the Margins: Creative Processes of Place Making.* Palgrave Macmillan.

Thórhallsdóttir, G., Ólafsson, R., and Jóhannesson, G. T. (2021). A methodology of estimating visitor numbers at an Icelandic destination using a vehicle counter and a radar. *Journal of Outdoor Recreation and Tourism, 35,* 100378.

Vestfjarðaleiðin (2023). *Áhugaverðir staðir.* https://www.vestfjardaleidin.is/is/ahugaverdirstadir.

Vestfjarðastofa (2022). *Áfangastaðaáætlun Vestfjarða: Samantekt* [Westfjords Destination Management Plan: Summary]. Vestfjarðastofa.

5 A future for creative tourism in the Arctic

Suzanne de la Barre

Introduction

The integrity of the Arctic environment, the quality of its natural spaces, and the commitment required to access them, as well as colonial perspectives on human habitation (the "absence of humans") that have defined perspectives on remoteness, have up to now positioned the Arctic as a destination designed for adventure, nature-based, and wilderness tourism. Indeed, while there have been numerous "state of Polar tourism" assessments in the past decades (to name only a few, Hall and Johnston, 1995; Stewart et al., 2005; Hall et al., 2009; Grenier and Müller, 2011; Müller et al., 2013), there has been no Arctic tourism overview research that has focussed on an investigation of cultural tourism – that is beyond those specifically associated with indigenous tourism (see for instance Notzke, 1999; Viken and Müller, 2017; Ren et al., 2020).

The United Nations World Tourism Organization (UNWTO) (2017) defines cultural tourism as "a type of tourism activity in which the visitor's essential motivation is to learn, discover, experience and consume the tangible and intangible cultural attractions/products in a tourism destination" (no pagination). Despite the attention placed on indigenous cultural (change and) tourism, there are other socio-cultural, economic and political transformations in the Arctic that lend themselves to offering different visitor experiences that promise newly diversified destination offerings and impacts. Creative tourism is considered a sub-type of cultural tourism and offers a way for us to investigate cultural tourism development opportunities in a changing Arctic tourism landscape.

Richards and Raymond (2000, p. 18) define creative tourism as a type of tourism which "offers visitors the opportunity to develop their creative potential through active participation in learning experiences which are characteristic of the holiday destination where they are undertaken". Creative tourism relies on the creative industries and the creative economy, which are "knowledge-based creative activities that link producers, consumers and places by utilizing technology, talent or skill to generate meaningful intangible cultural products, creative content or experiences" (OECD, 2014, p. 14). Examples of creative tourism include experiences that incorporate learning and participation in music, the performing and visual arts, gastronomy, design, and film (OECD, 2014).

With an overarching goal of investigating future visions for Arctic tourism – and borrowing inspiration from Yeoman's (2023) editorial insights on tourism futures – the aim of this chapter is to examine creative tourism for the opportunities it offers to ask original questions and gain insight into Arctic tourism development, and support contributions to the development of an Arctic Tourism research agenda. To that end, the following chapter begins with a presentation of creative tourism and its contemporary characterization. A brief overview of past research on creative tourism in the Arctic will follow, and lead to a section that focusses on three trends/issues selected from an analysis of creative tourism scholarship, and for how they facilitate a discussion on a vision for Arctic tourism development and research agenda guidance. They are: 1) cultural change in the Arctic; 2) creative producers and makers ("creatives") and their engagement with tourism; and 3) regenerative tourism as a tourism development approach and goal. A conclusion with recommendations will close the chapter.

Creative tourism

Creative tourism is intertwined with the creative (or cultural) economy. Creative economies broadly understood are creative and cultural activities that form a part of the economy (Comunian et al., 2022). While it is generally agreed upon that the creative sector is difficult to measure (Duxbury and Richards, 2019; Scherf, 2023, 2021), its significance was recently evidenced in two international and global assessment and planning initiatives: a UNESCO (2022) policy-oriented assessment of culture and creativity claimed it to be one of the youngest and fastest growing sectors in the world, accounting for 3.1% of global Gross Domestic Product (GDP) and 6.2% of all employment. Exports of cultural goods and services doubled in value from 2005 to 2019 (US$389.1 billion). Similar findings from a trade-oriented study released by the UNCTD (2022) advanced that the creative economy is a sector of growing importance, and that trade in creative goods and services in 2020 was estimated to represent 3% and 21% of total merchandise and services exports, respectively.

Creative tourism is also shaped by the "experience economy," a type of economy coined by Pine and Gilmore (1999, 2011) which refers to the selling of unique and personalized memorable experiences over products and services. Creative tourism dimensions connected to the experience economy can be examined in association with two critical tourism development factors: First, the more meaningful nature of the visitor experience through experiential engagement, and second, "sense of place" or placemaking elements impacting both the visitor and host experience of tourism.

Creative tourism relies on visitor self-actualization and the co-creative elements of a tourist experience. Richards (2011, 2014) proposed that creative tourism involves leisure time to connect self-development and personal skills enhancement, and that these tenets are at the heart of creative tourism. Duxbury and Richards (2019) continue to emphasize the personal self-expression aspects that are foundational to creative tourism, adding that relational and visitor co-creation aspects in the tourist experience remain important dimensions of the expansion of creative tourism. Revisiting the association creative tourism has to the experience economy, Miettinen et al. (2019, p. 70) claim that creative tourism is not just about consuming experiences, it is about "becoming" more through them. They elaborate this relates to not just becoming more aware of local ways of being, but also because participants are also engaged in the act of becoming as this relates to evolving as an individual through the act of having an experience (Dewey, 1934 [1980]).

Engaging with "local ways of being" through creative tourism enhances the way that creativity can be utilized in placemaking for tourism development (Richards, 2020). Placemaking processes influence the nature of the expectations held by both visitors and locals; for instance, the expectation of enhanced access to the local sphere for visitors ("authenticity"), increased economic benefits for locally-based in-destination entrepreneurs and businesses, and positive "quality of life" impacts for residents. Scherf's explorations of creative tourism (2021) and small tourism (2023) also highlight creative tourism's connection to tourism-related placemaking as it involves residents and visitors as co-creators of "sense of place"; here visitors consciously engage in activities offered by locals, but they also contribute "their own perspective and history to the moment, thus enriching the experience for both sides, and for the community more broadly" (Scherf, 2023, p. 5).

Duxbury and Richards (2019) are among those who believe that creative tourism is likely to increase in the future because of the drive for more engaging culture-based experiences. Supporting this theory are observations about the growing number of creative producers or "creatives" (Petrov, 2008; Richards,

2011). Despite the claims on the value and growth of creative tourism, there is consensus that the characteristics of this type of tourism, and the experiential features it relies upon and that make it distinct from "mass cultural tourism" imply it will likely remain relatively small scale (Richards, 2016; Scherf, 2023).

The value of creative tourism for Arctic tourism relates to the economic and other opportunities it offers to local creatives – with the possibility to attract new migrants to peripheral "remote" regions in the Arctic region. It also depends on small-scale and localized visitor experiences, with an intentional reliance on local creatives working in a co-creation manner with visitors (and other locals). Creative tourism has the potential to engage new market segments, and the place-based community dimensions of the visitor experience can meaningfully engage sustainable and community-based tourism development approaches, which are well-suited to the Arctic tourism context.

Creative tourism in Arctic places

The creative and cultural sector in the Arctic has received growing attention in the last decade or so. Petrov's (2007, 2008, 2014, 2016, 2017; Petrov and Cavin, 2017a, 2017b) extensive assessment of the Arctic's "other economies" provides a compelling story on how creative capital in its widest reading is likely to play a defining role in the regional transformation of the Arctic. Other contributions offer evidence that the cultural economy offers a means for communities to leverage place-based concerns towards desired outcomes, including its ability to strengthen regional and community resilience and to revitalize the economic and cultural life of regions that suffer from economic dislocation and decline (Leriche and Daviet, 2010; Huggins and Clifton, 2011). Its characteristics can also contribute to economic diversification objectives, for instance through entrepreneurship and tourism (Cloke, 2007; Petrov, 2007, 2008). A noteworthy example of what creative tourism looks like in the Arctic is at the entrepreneurial heart of *Creative Iceland* (https://creativeiceland.is). Under the slogan "meet, explore, make, learn with the people that make Iceland a unique place" visitors are invited to book a local experience and co-create with different kinds of creatives, from knitters to potters to photographers and chefs. In so doing, they can participate in "a unique and sustainable form of tourism while at the same time supporting Iceland's cultural and creative community" (Creative Iceland, n.d.).

Public sector organizations are also paying attention. The Nordic Council of Ministers (2018), the official body for inter-governmental cooperation in the

Nordic region, asserts that "although tourism is often not considered a creative and cultural industry, the industry is closely related to Nordic Arctic culture and the promotion of it" (p. 17). Further, they assess that Arctic tourism was growing steadily in the decade leading up to the pandemic, and support the connection between tourism and creative experiences and new sources of income:

> The Nordic Arctic creative and cultural industries of film, tourism, and indigenous cultural businesses are becoming increasingly important platforms through which the Nordic Arctic countries can create value and growth – economically, socially, and culturally (Nordic Council of Ministers 2018, p. 14).

Notwithstanding the potential opportunities, there remain significant issues tied to being able to measure and understand the nature and impacts of creativity and cultural activity generally, and creative tourism more specifically. In communities that exist in remote, sparsely populated areas like those in the Arctic, this challenge has been documented by Petrov (2016, p. 12) who explains that "although instances of cultural economy in Arctic communities are easy to find, there is no systematic knowledge of its volume, characteristics and geography" (see also Brouder, 2012, Petrov, 2014). We also know very little about how creativity interacts with tourism. Still, attempts are being made to better understand the relationship between tourism and the creative and cultural sector.

In north western Canada, the Yukon Government released its first Cultural Sector strategy in 2021 (Yukon Government, 2021). They claim the sector contributed $59.7 million or 2% to the Yukon's Gross Domestic Product (GDP). The vision for the strategy is one that seeks to enable the sector to make a positive contribution to social and economic outcomes; tourism alignments feature prominently in their postulations. In her work, de la Barre (2021) explored innovative ways to gauge the trajectory of the cultural industries and their potential for broad-based positive social and cultural impacts in the Territory. She found evidence that they were increasingly significant in the tourism options on offer in what has been (and remains) a primarily nature-based tourism destination. This statement is widely reflective of nature-based travel motivations to Arctic destinations, notwithstanding the in-progress revisions to this legacy as a result of the growing interest in indigenous cultural tourism. In this regard, tourist motivations for creative tourism experiences in an Arctic context underline the need to better understand intentional and incidental creative tourists/travellers highlighted by Duxbury and Richards (2019).

The circumpolar-wide Arctic Arts Summits held in Harstad (Norway) in 2017, Rovaniemi (Finland) in 2019 followed by the third summit held in Whitehorse (Yukon, Canada) in 2022 all attest to the prospects of a reinvigorated and newly positioned role for creativity in Arctic places. In Huhmarniemi and Jokela's (2019) assessment of the 2019 Arctic Arts Summit in Rovaniemi they assert that responsible tourism and the creative industries are both growing sectors in the Arctic, and that this creates an opening to develop sustainable tourism with artists and creative industries. They point to a number of issues that need to be addressed to successfully consider this potential collaboration including ecological and cultural sensitivities. The former recognizes the fragile Arctic environment, growing climate emergency concerns, and the way tourism is engaged to mitigate (or exacerbate) this state of affairs in the future. For the latter, these include consideration for cultural appropriation and exploitation – which would apply especially, but not exclusively, to collaborations at the foundation of creative tourism with indigenous people.

Shaping a vision and research agenda for creative tourism futures in the Arctic

As presented in the previous section, the creative sector as it intersects with tourism development in the Arctic is widely perceived to be a dynamic force that is increasingly connected to innovative opportunities. Still, there are a number of considerations that must be addressed to support the realization of a vision for creative tourism. These considerations and research gaps are explored using three issues/trends that demonstrate beneficial possibilities for creative tourism, while also exposing challenges that are intertwined with context-significant, if differently experienced and expressed, tourism development realities across the Arctic region: 1) Cultural change in the Arctic; 2) What do creatives want with Creative Tourism?; and 3) Regenerative tourism – complicities and detachments.

1   Cultural change in the Arctic

Indigenous tourism has advanced in earnest over the past four decades. Today it is associated with a sophisticated critique of the development approaches and applied features required for it to have a positive impact on indigenous people and their communities. This critique includes a mature analysis of the potential negative impacts that tourism brings with it, and assessments of many tried and tested mitigation strategies – even if these known strategies are not always or perfectly implemented. Moreover, new knowledge and development innovations are continuously in progress and increasingly determined by the indigenous people who deliver or who stand to benefit from tourism in their communities. Indigenous leaders are voicing their support for an enhanced focus on the transformative values associated with economic development control generally (Hilton, 2017), and tourism specifically (Bunten, 2010; Bunten and Graburn, 2018; Aikau and Gonzales, 2019). It follows that cultural change brought about through indigenous empowerment in the Arctic has presented openings for the development of creative tourism. There is emerging evidence that indigenous empowerment, accompanied by principles of indigenous ownership and control over the tourism development process and outcomes, is a noteworthy influence leading to the increase in creative tourism opportunities in the Arctic (see for instance Hull et al., 2017).

Still, despite the connection that indigenous tourism has towards the growth of creative tourisms in the Arctic, there are other equally interesting and noteworthy aspects of cultural change occurring (differently) across the region that require our attention. These cultural changes are related to global mobilities and migration and the implications these have on cultural diversity and are relevant to the discussion on the future of Arctic creative tourism. These trends point to a glaringly neglected body of knowledge and a lack of applied understanding about the changing and unaddressed questions of non-indigenous cultures in a changing circumpolar north generally (Lempinen, 2019). These also have consequences on the different kinds of creative tourism that are possible in the Arctic.

In their assessment of immigration to the Circumpolar North Yeasmin et al. (2021) describe new settler demographics in the region explained by dynamic push and pull factors. Push factors include the demographic and other pressures (e.g., climate change, food security, conflict) experienced on other continents. Pull factors on the other hand can in part be understood by looking at trends that make the Arctic increasingly attractive for new settlers: for instance, accessibility, employment, and sense of place. Urbanization in the Arctic is another transformation that has received some attention (Müller et al., 2020); it supports cultural change generally, and can foster creative tourism by extension. Taylor et al.'s (2016) collection of case studies on this topic demonstrate the complexity involved in attracting new settlers to sparsely populated areas in different countries (e.g., Australia, Canada, the Nordic countries). Despite the many challenges (i.e., housing, settlement support), the volume presents some evidence that even small numbers of new migrant-born settlers can have an impact on cultural diversity. In particular, Carson et al. (2016) in that volume explore local innovations and the revitalization of sparsely populated areas in relation to temporary and mobile populations, including lifestyle migrants – what they explain as the long-term end of the temporary mobility spectrum. The authors suggest tourism entrepreneurs and the "creative class" are among those who may be attracted to the place and lifestyle-based characteristics that shape perceived economic and other opportunities in remote regions like those of the Arctic. Petrov's (2008) more targeted study of the creative class in northern Canada noted that, despite significant out-migration and depopulation in many resource towns, small cities such as Whitehorse and Yellowknife have benefitted from an influx of artists, singers, and crafters. In Petrov's (2008, p. 165) view:

> It is difficult to argue that the creative capital in peripheral northern communities can make them successful in competing with national and global innovation powerhouses, but it is plausible to suggest that the availability of this factor improves their prospects for future economic transformation and development. This theory, however, remains the subject of ongoing research.

The potential for community reinvention proposed with demographic change bodes well for creative tourism opportunities. A tourism futures lens avails itself to a more robust understanding of cultural change in Arctic regions and how these will influence tourism generally, and creative tourism specifically.

In a similar "peripheries" context, Gibson's (2012, p. 3) exploration of creativity in the remote regions of Australia is relevant. A central geographical question shaped his inquiry:

> If proximity is vital to the creative field, to enabling face-to-face interactions and reducing risk within volatile markets for creative products ("keeping up with trends"), what challenges does remoteness and smallness generate for creative producers – the fact of being a long way from "happening" places and scenes?

Those who live in peripheral or sparsely populated areas may point out that "remote" is also a matter of perspective and is subject to where one is located. Nonetheless, one geographical reality that is generally true of Arctic destinations is that they are far away from central locations which offer more densely populated areas. Distance to visitor markets has influenced how destinations develop.

Despite the significant distance-related deliberations, it may be worth investigating if supporting artists already living in the Artic and attracting new ones to relocate there can actually support the development of creative tourism. To this point, it is important to consider that the presence of creatives alone does not necessarily mean they want or are able to participate in tourism, even if it is "creative tourism." Indeed, there has been little to no research on what motivates creatives to share their creative process with others in a visitor economy context – that is, with tourists be they from far away or close by – including residents who may "behave" like visitors when participating in creative tourism. Indeed, even if cultural change can favour the development of creative tourism, there remain critical assumptions, combined with a lack of knowledge on the contextual features that encourage and support creatives to want to share their creative process or the outcomes of their work.

2   What do creatives want with Creative Tourism?

Given the principles and values associated with creative tourism it is easy to associate the potential benefits for Arctic communities and destinations. Creative Tourism can provide opportunities to attract different visitors and foster more beneficial local level impacts, and is able to influence also innovative and dynamic entrepreneurial initiatives that enable the development or support for small scale economic impacts (Yeasmin et al., 2021). Some attention has been given to the creative capacities of people living in rural areas (Cloke, 2007), the internal capacity of communities (Petrov, 2017), and informal networks that support creatives and lifestyle entrepreneurs (Jóhanneson and Lund, 2018; Prince et al., 2021). Petrov's (2008) Northern Canada study provides some mobility-related motivations (e.g., family reunification, lifestyle and place-related creative inspiration) but fails to examine the specific reasons that entice creatives to share their skills, abilities and passions with anyone, let alone tourists. What seems apparent in a general sense is that, to date, cultural and tourism development strategies appear to widely presume creatives' desire and motivation to participate in tourism. There is little knowledge or understanding available that would support being able to actually determine the feasibility of their engagement in the delivery of tourism experiences, much less understand how to integrate this engagement in the successful planning and management of creative tourism. As Duxbury and Richards (2019) conclude, there is little known about artists – the "creative supply" producers – who collaborate to make creative tourism happen.

The absence of knowledge and understanding that we have about creatives and their desire and ability to participate in tourism stands in contrast to the amount of existing scholarship that assumes artist participation in tourism. There is much that has been presented about the tourist consumption dimensions proposed through the tourism development-oriented focussed perspectives – from industry to academic research. This gap in knowledge is even more pronounced in peripheral tourism destinations like those found in the Arctic. Foremost, a tourism-centric perspective rests on the assumption that artists can easily shift their creative motivations and shape their activities for the purposes of tourism. Similar challenges associated with this assumption have been presented in the decades-long discussions on indigenous tourism. The discussions are intrinsically connected to cultural production and the motivations of cultural producers at the intersection with tourism – which is, after all, a commercial transaction. Depending on the tourism development approach used, results have varied from "best case scenario" to "abominable", Even if community-based/led forms of tourism development offer promising – even "enlightened" – impacts, for instance through cultural exchange and creative producer or community benefits, as may be the case with the creative tourism model, the issue of why artists produce art and what might be required for them to share their process – especially beyond the commercial transaction that tourism intrinsically depends on, remains a bit of a mystery.

With a tourism futures lens, we might investigate emerging trends and assess how they can support artists – for instance, recognition for their work through economic rewards (e.g., the ability to make a living with their art), as well for the more difficult to assess contribution they make to placemaking dimensions that also shape civic engagement and community well-being, for instance. Arctic-wide forums like the Arctic Arts Summit can inform a tourism futures lens and a research agenda (Huhmarniemi & Jokela, 2019, 2020); especially if we anticipate that we will need to better understand why and how artists want to share their art making and the potential processes they can share with visitors – including the role and experience that "visitors" locally situated in their own communities bring to the tourism development discussion.

Environmental art offers some answers, or at least may help to frame some useful tourism development-oriented questions. In their "topography of creative tourism in Lapland", Miettinen et. al. (2019) propose that creative participation in tourism activities in the Arctic context introduces "a polyphonic discussion of the tourism landscape … which expands the landscape into a multi-dimensional and spatial topography" (p. 69). The participative elements – walking in the snow, gazing, and artistic collaboration – are introduced as a way to learn through creative engagement – key tenets of creative tourism. It is through engaging with topographies and winter in Lapland as an act of becoming, of committing to the local, that there is a contribution to sustainable livelihoods in local economies, including the livelihoods of artists (Miettinen et al., 2019). In a similar vein, Huhmarniemi and Jokela (2019,

p. 63) also build a case for a future Arctic tourism that pays attention to the unique contributions of environmental art for sustainability, and claim that:

> [T]he foundations for increasing the use of environmental art in the Arctic region's nature tourism concern both the employment needs of artists and the need to improve the quality of tourism environments and services.

They also advance that creatives and the cultural sector generally, have been largely excluded from the benefits of tourism in the sense that "art and culture are not emphasized in Lapland's tourism marketing" (p. 64). Further, they add that the art and culture sector seeks to expand its funding base, which can increase artists' desire to cooperate with the tourism sector.

As the two examples above demonstrate, there are place-based creative tourism experiences available because of intrinsic characteristics attached to the Arctic's geography and climate. These also point to uniquely available creative tourism prospects (for another example see Shiver Arts Festival in Dawson City, Yukon: https://dawsoncity.ca/event/shiverwinterartsfestival/). By extension, geography and climate-related experiences attend also to a growing awareness of climate change and the tourism-influenced challenges associated with it. It is this topic that informs the issue/trend featured in this chapter.

3   Regenerative tourism – complicities and detachments

As described in the opening sections of this chapter, there is much potential for creative tourism in the Arctic given its intrinsic attention to community and socio-cultural benefits and its positioning as a type of small-scale tourism. Regenerative tourism is advanced as one way to address the climate emergency and, due to its emphasis on "the local," it lends itself well to the development of creative tourism. As Bellato et al. (2022, p. 1026) explain, regenerative tourism "departs from the sustainable development paradigm by positioning tourism activities as interventions that develop the capacities of places, communities and their guests to operate in harmony with interconnected social-ecological systems".

There is an abundance of scholarship on the significant ways that tourism intersects with the climate emergency (see for instance Gössling and Hall, 2006, Weaver, 2011). The 2021 Nordic Council of Ministers' framework to monitor sustainable tourism submits that the carbon footprint of global tourism is a major concern (Nordic Council of Ministers, 2021). They claim that 75% of the World Tourism Organization's estimate of 5% of global emissions stems from the aviation sector. Elsewhere, in their systemic review of climate change and tourism scholarship, Scott and Gössling (2022) conclude that climate change does not appear to be a high priority on the tourism academy's research agenda, nor is there evidence that the tourism industry makes widespread use of the information base that is available. They surmise that: "It is disconcerting that a central finding of this review is that the last 30 years of research have failed to effectively prepare the sector for a climate resilient transformation that must take place over the next 30 years" (Scott and Gössling, 2022, p. 10). They also suggest that tourism's responsiveness to climate change should begin with "a more critical engagement of the implications for tourism of a decarbonized and climate disrupted world, including meaningful challenges to the marketing and development of carbon-intensive destination growth" (p. 11).

Meanwhile, already in 2014 Hollenhorst et al. (2014, p. 305) proposed proximity tourism as a way to support the "de-growth of the high-carbon, distant travel model of tourism and replacement with a low-carbon model that emphasizes local destinations, short distances, lower-carbon transport modes, and capital investment (both financial and social) in local communities". They also advance proximity or "locavist" travel as a way "to remedy a mindset that associates travel with exotic distances from one's place of residence" (p. 305).

Notwithstanding the implications that flight shaming may hold for tourism to the Arctic (Mkono 2019), a tourism futures exercise might at least include an intentional discussion on where the visitors we aim to attract *could* come from? Indeed, despite the central claim made regarding the connection between carbon emissions and aviation made by the Nordic Council of Ministers (2021), there is little mention of the climate-change-related problem of "getting to" the Arctic. Tourism scholarship as well as tourism development and destination management initiatives generally engage the carbon emission opportunities available in the Arctic once visitors are in place – that is, once they get off the plane. Only then can visitors participate in low(er) carbon opportunities, sometimes promoted through place-based "slow tourism" offerings (see for instance, de la Barre, 2012). Of course, there are obvious reasons for this in the Arctic context: Low-density local populations + distance to domestic and international markets + the "boring bits in between" (Koster and Carson, 2019) = a need for carbon-intense travellers.

Given these distance-related challenges, what is perhaps most useful about proximity tourism is that it is not just concerned with questioning the long-held tourism narratives that have almost exclusively valued the stories that arise due to our "distance from" (the exotic). There are unexamined opportunities in a shift that places value on "proximity to" (the familiar). In this sense, proximity tourism is committed to disrupting a tourism narrative that claims the search for the exotic in far-away places, and positions wonder for the familiar of what is in our own backyards. Expressing the sentiment at the foundation of this challenge, Jóhannesson and Ren (2024, p. 76) recognize a need to reflect on the way "proximity may be cultivated as a way to *re-experience and retell* tourism and how research – this powerful, world-building tool – might become more sensitive to modest and mundane tourism practices, particularly to proximity tourism". Central to the exercise is to scrutinize the binary of "nearness" and "farness" that defines the ontology of tourism itself (for discussions see Rantala et al., 2020; Rantala et al., 2024; Salmela et al., 2021). In this context of proximity tourism we find another allegiance to creative tourism because, as Miettinen et al. (2019, p. 69) propose, creative tourism offers a tool for collaboration that positions "community members as visitors in their own topography".

Conclusion: Creative tourism futures in the Arctic

This chapter aimed to examine creative tourism for the opportunities it offers to ask original questions and gain insight into Arctic tourism development, and support contributions to the development of an Arctic Tourism research agenda. Suggestions for a research agenda that might support realizing a future vision for Arctic tourism that can benefit from creative tourism were obtained through an examination of three trends/issues: 1) cultural change in the Arctic; 2) creative producers and makers ("creatives") and their engagement with tourism; and 3) regenerative tourism as a tourism development approach and goal.

The creative tourism investigation highlighted a lack of knowledge about a broad-based and changing Arctic cultural context and its potential to inform and contribute to as yet under-developed tourism opportunities. In addition, research undertaken to date suggests that the impacts of creatives in the periphery may influence different kinds of desirable outcomes, including placemaking initiatives that attract both new visitor markets and new residents, and diversifying the economy to achieve increased local and regional resiliency.

While there are emerging and thoughtful considerations on who creatives are and the positive impacts their presence might have on peripheral places, there are many challenges involved to meet the circumstances that can enable their contributions. Where creative tourism development opportunities are concerned, knowledge gaps in how creatives participate in tourism are lacking, and their inclusion in tourism development strategies is largely based on assumptions aimed at tourism development, and is not informed by perspectives that prioritize creatives. Moreover, current Arctic tourism development initiatives are often not (adequately) informed by emerging or established cultural and creative industries' planning initiatives.

Finally, research agenda suggestions that involve creative tourism might enhance climate change relationships to Arctic tourism. One possibility for this is through the lens of "proximity tourism." The value in examining proximity tourism lies in formulating different questions about what tourism is and what we expect from it – as travellers and as residents of the places that hold tourism. Even devoted proponents of small and creative tourism agree that mass tourism – which is very dependent on carbon intense travel – is not likely going to disappear (Duxbury and Richards, 2019; Scherf, 2021, 2023).

The small-scale nature of creative tourism lends itself well to the geographic and cultural features of the Arctic and its communities: among other things, less densely populated communities, and meaningful engagement in unique natural settings. Combined, these characteristics elevate vibrant resident and visitor interactions, including engagement with increasingly empowered indigenous populations and experiences that also benefit from (and support) the Arctic's growing cultural diversity. In an Arctic tourism development context, there are opportunities for creative tourism to contribute to a type of tourism able to attract different visitors and foster more beneficial local level impacts, influence innovative and dynamic entrepreneurial initiatives that support small scale economic impacts, regional economic diversification, and contribute to tourism development that aims for enhanced resiliency and sustainability.

References

Aikau, H. K. and Gonzales, V. (Eds.) (2019). *Detours: A Decolonial Guide to Hawai'i*. Duke University Press.

Bellato, L., Frantzeskaki, N., and Nygaard, C. A. (2022). Regenerative tourism: A conceptual framework leveraging theory and practice, *Tourism Geographies, 25*(4), 1026–46.

Brouder, P. (2012). Creative outposts: Tourism's place in rural innovation. *Tourism Planning and Development, 9*(4), 383–96.

Bunten, A. (2010). More like ourselves: Indigenous capitalism through tourism. *The American Indian Quarterly, 34*(3), 285–311.

Bunten, A. C. and Graburn, N. (2018). *Indigenous Tourism Movements*. University of Toronto Press.

Carson, D. A., Cleary, J., de la Barre, S., Eimermann, M., and Marjavaara, R. (2016). New mobilities – new economies? Temporary populations and local innovation capacity in sparsely populated areas. In A. Taylor, D. B. Carson, P. Ensign, L. Huskey, R. O. Rasmussen and G. Eilmsteiner-Saxinger (Eds.), *Settlements at the Edge: Remote Human Settlements in Developed* Nations, 178–206. Edward Elgar Publishing.

Cloke, P. (2007). Creativity and tourism in rural environments. In G. Richards and J. Wilson (Eds.), *Tourism, Creativity and Development*, 37–47. Routledge.

Comunian, R., Faggian, A., Heinonen, J., and Wilson, N. (2022). Introduction to a modern guide to creative economies. In R. Comunian, A. Faggian, J. Heinonen and N. Wilson (Eds.), *A Modern Guide to Creative Economies*, 1–19. Edward Elgar Publishing.

Creative Iceland (n.d.). *About Creative Iceland*. https://creativeiceland.is/about-creative -iceland.

de la Barre, S. (2012). Travellin' around on Yukon Time. In S. Fulagar, K. Markwell and E. Wilson (Eds.), *Mobilities: Experiencing Slow Travel and Tourism*, 157–69. Channel View.

de la Barre, S. (2021). Creative Yukon: Finding data to tell the cultural economy story. In K. Scherf (Ed.), *Creative Tourism and Sustainable Development in Smaller Communities: Place, Culture, and Local* Representation, 109–35. University of Calgary Press.

Dewey, J. (1934/1980). *Art as Experience*. Reprinted in 1980. Perigee Books.

Duxbury, N. and Richards, G. (Eds.) (2019). *A Research Agenda for Creative Tourism*. Edward Elgar Publishing.

Gibson, C. (2012). *Creativity in Peripheral Places: Redefining the Creative Industries*. Routledge.

Gössling, S. and Hall, C. (Eds.) (2006). *Tourism and Global Environmental Change*. Routledge.

Grenier, A. and Müller, D. K. (Eds.) (2011). *Polar Tourism: A Tool for Regional Development*. Presses de l'Université du Québec.

Hall, C. M. and Johnston, M. E. (Eds.) (1995). *Polar Tourism: Tourism in the Arctic and Antarctic Regions*. John Wiley and Sons.

Hall, C. M., Müller, D. K., and Saarinen, J. (2009). *Nordic Tourism: Issues and Cases*. Channel View.

Hilton, C. A. (2017). *Indigenomics: Taking a Seat at the Economic Table*. New Society Publishers.

Hollenhorst, S. J., Houge-Mackenzie, S., and Ostergren D. M. (2014). The trouble with tourism. *Tourism Recreation Research*, 39(3), 305–19.

Huggins, R., and Clifton, N. (2011). Competitiveness, creativity, and place-based development. *Environment and Planning A, 43*(6), 1341–62.

Huhmarniemi, M., and Jokela, T. (2019). Environmental art for tourism in the Arctic: From handicraft to integrated art and reform on artists' skills. In M. Huhmarniemi, T. Jokela and T. Hautala-Hirvioja (Eds.), *Arctic Art in the Time of* Change, 63–80. University of Lapland.

Huhmarniemi, M., and Jokela T. (2020). Arctic arts with pride: Discourses on Arctic arts, culture and sustainability. *Sustainability 12*(2), 604.

Hull, J., de la Barre, S., and Maher, P. (2017). Peripheral geographies of creativity: The case for aboriginal tourism in Canada's Yukon Territory. In A. Viken and D. K. Müller (Eds.), *Arctic Indigenous Tourism*, 157–81. Channel View.

Jóhanneson, G. T., and Lund, K. A. (2018). Creative connections? Tourists, entrepreneurs and destination dynamic. *Scandinavian Journal of Hospitality and Tourism*, *18*(1), 560–74.

Jóhannesson, G. T., and Ren, C. (2024). Cultivating proximities: Re-visiting the familiar. In O. Rantala, V. Kinnunen and E. Höckert (Eds.), *Research with Proximity: Relational Methodologies for the Anthropocene*, 75–88. Palgrave Macmillan.

Koster, R. L., and Carson, D. A. (Eds.) (2019). *Perspectives on Rural Tourism Geographies: Case Studies from Developed Nations on the Exotic, the Fringe and the Boring Bits in Between*. Springer.

Lempinen, H. (2019). Indigenous cultures, local lifestyles? 'Culture' in the northern strategies of the eight Arctic states. In M. Huhmarniemi, T. Jokela and T. Hautala-Hirvioja (Eds.), *Arctic Art in the Time of Change*, 13–24. University of Lapland.

Leriche, F., and Daviet, S. (2010). Cultural economy: An opportunity to boost employment and regional development? *Regional Studies*, *44*(7), 807–11.

Miettinen, S., Erikkilä-hill, J., Koistinen, S. M., Jokela, T., and Hiltunen, M. (2019). Stories of design, snow, and silence: Creative tourism landscape in Lapland. In N. Duxbury and G. Richard (Eds.), *A Research Agenda for Creative Tourism*, 69–83. Edward Elgar Publishing.

Mkono, M. (2019). Eco-anxiety and the flight shaming movement: Implications for tourism. *Journal of Tourism Futures*, *6*(3), 223–26.

Müller, D. K., Lundmark, L., and Lemelin, R. H. (Eds.) (2013). *Issues in Polar Tourism: Communities, Environments, Politics*. Amsterdam: Springer.

Müller, D. K., Carson, D. A., de la Barre, S., Granås, B., Jóhannesson, G. T., Øyen, G., Rantala, O., Saarinen, J., Salmela, T., Tervo-Kankare, K., and Welling, J. (2020). *Arctic Tourism in Times of Change: Dimensions of Urban Tourism*. Nordic Council of Ministers.

Nordic Council of Ministers (2018). *Arctic Business Analysis: Creative and Cultural Industries*. Nordiska Ministerråd.

Nordic Council of Ministers (2021). *Monitoring the Sustainability of Tourism in the Nordics*. pub.norden.org/nord2021-033.

Notzke, C. (1999). Indigenous tourism development in the Arctic. *Annals of Tourism Research*, *26*(1), 55–76.

OECD (2014). *Tourism and the Creative Economy*. OECD Studies on Tourism, OECD Publishing.

Petrov, A. (2007). A look beyond metropolis: Exploring creative class in the Canadian periphery. *Canadian Journal of Regional Science*, *30*(3), 359–86.

Petrov, A. (2008). Talent in the cold? Creative capital and the economic future of the Canadian north. *Arctic*, *61*(2), 62–78.

Petrov, A. (2014). Creative Arctic: Towards measuring Arctic's creative capital. In L. Heininen, H. Exne-Pirot and J. Plouffe (Eds.), *Arctic Yearbook* 2014, 149–66. Northern Research Forum.

Petrov, A. (2016). Exploring the Arctic's "other economies": Knowledge, creativity and the new frontier. *The Polar Journal*, *6*(1), 51–68.

Petrov, A. (2017). Human capital and sustainable development in the Arctic: Towards intellectual and empirical framing. In G. Fondahl and G. Wilson (Eds.), *Northern Sustainabilities: Understanding and Addressing Change in the Circumpolar World*, 203–20). Springer.

Petrov, A., and Cavin, P. (2017a). Creating new path creative capital: Theories and evidence in the northern periphery. *The Journal of Rural and Community Development, 12*(2/3), 127–42.

Petrov, A., and Cavin, P. (2017b). Creative Alaska: Creative capital and economic development opportunities in Alaska. *Polar Record, 49*(4), 48–61.

Pine, B. J., and Gilmore, J. H. (1999). *The Experience Economy: Work is Theatre and Every Business a Stage.* Harvard Business School Press.

Pine, B. J., and Gilmore, J. H. (2011). *The Experience Economy.* Updated edition. Harvard Business Review Press.

Prince, S., Petridou, E., and Ioannides, D. (2021). Art worlds in the periphery: Creativity and networking in rural Scandinavia. In K. Scherf (Ed.), *Creative Tourism and Sustainable Development in Smaller Communities: Place, Culture, and Local Representation* 259–82). University of Calgary Press.

Rantala, O., Kinnunen, V., and Höckert, E. (Eds.) (2024). *Research with Proximity: Relational methodologies for the Anthropocene.* Palgrave Macmillan.

Rantala, O., Salmela, T, Valtonen, A., and Höckert, E. (2020). Envisioning tourism and proximity after the anthropocene. *Sustainability, 12,* 12103948.

Ren, C., Jóhanneson, G. T., Kramvig, B., Pashkevich, A., and Höckert, E. (2020). 20 years of research on Arctic and Indigenous cultures in Nordic tourism: A review and future research agenda. *Scandinavian Journal of Hospitality and Tourism, 21*(1) 111–21.

Richards, G. (2011). Creativity and tourism: The state of the art. *Annals of Tourism Research, 38*(4), 1225–53.

Richards, G. (2014). Creativity and tourism in the city. *Current Issues in Tourism, 17*(2) 119–44.

Richards, G. (2016). The challenge of creative tourism. *Ethnologies, 38*(1–2), 31–45.

Richards, G. (2020). Designing creative places: The role of creative tourism. *Annals of Tourism Research, 85,* 102922.

Richards, G., and Raymond, C. (2000). Creative tourism. *ATLAS News, 23,* 16–20.

Salmela, T., Nevala, H., Nousiainen, M., and Rantala, O. (2021). Proximity tourism: A thematic literature review. *Finnish Journal of Tourism Research, 17*(1), 46–63.

Scherf, K. (Ed.) (2021). *Creative Tourism and Sustainable Development in Smaller Communities: Place, Culture, and Local Representation.* University of Calgary Press.

Scherf, K. (Ed.) (2023). *Adventures in Small Tourism: Studies and Stories.* University of Calgary Press.

Scott, D., and Gössling, S. (2022). A review of research into tourism and climate change – Launching the annals of tourism research curated collection on tourism and climate change. *Annals of Tourism Research, 95,* 103409.

Stewart, E. J., Draper, D., and Johnston, M. E. (2005). A review of tourism research in the Polar Regions. *Arctic, 58*(4), 383–94.

Taylor, S., Carson, Dean, B., Ensign, Prescott C., Huskey, L., Rasmussen, R. O., and Saxinger, G. (Eds.) (2016). *Settlements at the Edge: Remote Human Settlements in Developed Nations.* Edward Elgar Publishing.

United Nations Educational, Scientific and Cultural Organization (UNESCO) (2022). *Re-shaping Policies for Creativity: Addressing Culture as a Global Public Good.* https://www.unesco.org/reports/reshaping-creativity/2022/en/download-report.

United Nations Conference on Trade and Development (UNCTD) (2022). *Creative Economy Outlook – The International Year of Creative Economy for Sustainable Development: Pathway to Resilient Creative Industries.* https://europaregina.eu/orga nizations/igos/united-nations/unctad/creative-economy-outlook-2022/.

United Nations World Tourism Organization (UNWTO) (2017). *Tourism and Culture*. https://www.unwto.org/tourism-and-culture#:~:text=According%20to%20the%20defin ition%20adopted%20by%20the%20UNWTO,and%20intangible%20cultural%20attr actions%2Fproducts%20in%20a%20tourism%20destination.

Viken, A., and Müller, D. K. (Eds.) (2017). *Tourism and Indigeneity in the Arctic*. Channel View Publications.

Weaver, D. (2011). Can sustainable tourism survive climate change? *Journal of Sustainable Tourism, 19*(1), 5–15.

Yeasmin, N., Hasanat, W., Jan Brzozowski, J., and Kirchner, S. (Eds) (2021). *Immigration in the Circumpolar North: Integration and Resilience*. Routledge.

Yeoman, I. S. (2023). Editorial: Tourism futures researchers inspiration. *Journal of Tourism Futures, 9*(2), 146–50.

Yukon Government (2021). *Creative Potential: Advancing the Yukon's Creative and Cultural Industries*. November. https://yukon.ca/en/ccis.

6 Tourism, imaginaries, and cultural heritage in the Arctic: The need for studying the particular

Trine Kvidal-Røvik, Stein R. Mathisen and Kjell Olsen

Introduction

Images and discourses about peoples and places are crucial in tourism, and cultural heritages on display as part of contemporary tourism are often rooted in imaginaries formed long ago, under different contexts than today. This chapter explores the interconnection between tourism imaginaries and cultural heritage processes in the North, examining their links with regional development expectations and potentials.

Imaginaries, described as 'socially transmitted representational assemblages that interact with people's personal imaginings', are tools for world- and meaning-making which are 'both a function of producing meanings and the product of this function' (Salazar, 2012, p. 864). The Arctic, as an imaginary, has typically been constructed by people coming from outside, from the 'central' parts of the world, describing what – for them – was seen as the exotic ways of living in local communities labelled as Arctic. These descriptions often emphasized cultural and natural features distinct from what is found in global centres and have later been transformed into heritages put on display in ethnographic museums, art galleries, and tourism. But these imaginaries also encapsulate ideas about the Arctic's prospects and potentials for industries beneficial to development.

This article calls for a *broad* tourism research agenda that recognizes tourism's integral role in other worldmaking processes. Simultaneously, it emphasizes the need for an attention to the specificities and *particular* in Arctic tourism studies, since the Arctic is an imaginary – or more correctly imagin*aries* – imposed from the 'outside' on areas that hold diverse populations with distinct developments, economic and political conditions, histories, and heritages.

Outsiders' imaginaries of the Arctic, when treated as a single entity in theoretical thinking, may oversimplify the complex colonialities in various parts of what from the outside is seen as the Arctic, but are home to those residing there.

The article begins with an exploration of early outsiders' descriptions of the Arctic, before we discuss them as imaginaries of Otherness. We use the concept of Arctification to describe how an imaginary of the Arctic has become localized in places previously regarded as Northern Europe. Using the northern part of Fennoscandia as our focal point, the article underscores the importance of caution and awareness when researchers frame their analysis within the imaginary of the Arctic, as researchers themselves still contribute to perpetuating these 'socially transmitted representational assemblages', as conceptualized by Noel Salazar (2012).

Early northbound itineraries: Descriptions of the Arctic

Stories about traveling to the North are not a recent phenomenon. While travels to the North came first, they were subsequently followed by an abundance of written travelogs, which in turn established these Northern areas as representing a geography of peoples, cultures, and climates completely different from that in Central Europe. Somewhat a forerunner in offering such descriptions of the Scandinavian North were the works of Olaus Magnus (1490–1557), which were – at least partly – based on self-experience. Magnus was the last Catholic archbishop in Uppsala, Sweden and after more or less being forced to live in exile in Italy, he first administered the printing of the map *Carta Marina* (Magnus, 1539) in Venice and then wrote his *Historia de Gentibus Septentrionalibus* (Magnus, 1555), printed in Rome. With fantastic illustrations, both the map and the book presented a creative and ingenious mixture of facts, myths, and legends, and this work continued to influence the imageries of the Northern areas through the next centuries. The Northern area in this way got established, through teaching materials and literature, as the abode of dangerous waters, warriors, and monstrous beings. But also, as a land of riches and possibilities.

As traveling possibilities improved beyond armchair journeys in the world of books and travelogs, new travellers followed suit, enriching the imagery of Northern Scandinavia with fresh descriptions. To highlight a few of the most influential figures: In 1802, the Italian Giuseppe Acerbi (1773–1846) published a two-volume travelogue in London recounting his experiences in Lapland from 1798–1799 (Acerbi, 1802). Only a decade later, an earlier travelogue from 1732 by the renowned Swedish botanist Carl von Linné (1707–1778), previously available only as a manuscript in Swedish, was translated and printed in London (Linnæus, 1811). In 1823 and 1827, the English gentleman, traveller, and adventurer Arthur de Capell Brooke (1791–1858) published a two-volume travelogue documenting his journeys in Northern Scandinavia (de Capell Brooke, 1823, 1827). All these travelogs and diaries were accompanied by printed illustrations. One might argue that these descriptions, rooted in personal experiences, were more ethnographic and conveyed more realistic images of the people and cultures encountered. Simultaneously, newer descriptions often drew on earlier readings, using these older observations and the myths they presented as a starting point for their own narratives.

The publication of these travelogs can be understood as the outcome of a dual mission undertaken by the travellers. Venturing into the world to explore distant places served as a means for affluent young men of means to establish their status as adventurers or to embark on future careers as researchers. However, to distinguish their travels and experiences as genuinely adventurous, the encounters during their travels had to be notably distinct, exotic, and at times even perilous. Even armchair traveling was intended to leave readers in awe and suspense. This implied that deliberate search for real cultural differences, which became a focal point in many travelogs.

In Northern Scandinavia, for instance, this easily positioned the Indigenous Sámi, and their distinctly alien reindeer herding culture at the core of the travelogs. Embarking on a journey to Lapland, after all, necessitated vibrant descriptions of the local Sámi cultures. While discovering exotic cultures on trips to the African or Asian continents was one thing, it was even more peculiar to encounter such unfamiliar ways of living on the European continent itself. Nevertheless, comparatively less attention was given to those inhabitants who did not sharply contrast with the visitors.

Simultaneously, during the early 19th century, London, where the majority of these literary works were printed and published, stood as the epicentre of British empire building. Each of these travelogs, in line with the expectations of their era, also concentrated on the natural resources, economic development prospects, and the demographic makeup of the Indigenous populations in the visited regions. While not always directly associated with colonization efforts, the descriptions were nevertheless closely tied to prevailing forms of coloniality (cf. Mignolo, 2000; Quijano, 2000).

As the number of travellers to the North grew in tandem with knowledge, economic development, and opportunities, so too did the number of books recounting these travels (for extensive overviews see Bring, 1954; Schiötz, 1970). Even for those who could not raise enough money to make the strenuous journey to the far North, it was then still possible to read a book about it, and maybe even dream about visiting these areas once. These descriptions might have influenced later imaginaries and descriptions of the Northern areas, and further on, may also influence understandings of the cultural composition of the area, as well as the valuation of the heritages of importance to be preserved for future knowledge. Such choices can be said to influence the construction of a new tourism industry in the area, and in that way also the contemporary tourists' understanding of Northern Scandinavia's cultural past and future. Simultaneously, such processes have also been at work in other parts of the North, that, contrary to the European part, were imagined as frontiers (Huebner, 2015; Erickson, 2021).

Imaginaries and otherness: The role of tourism

Elements in these old travelogs described above are today easily understood and interpreted as exoticism and myth-creating. Sámi and other Indigenous peoples of the Arctic are increasingly resisting such processes stripping them of agency (Kramvig, 2017; Wright, 2017; Mazzullo, 2022). However, at the time of their printing the travelogs could be read as useful facts about the areas described, and as something that eventually would be helpful for future industry, trade, and commercial activities. In hindsight it is consequently necessary to investigate possible empirical roots in travelogs, as well as prevalent and contemporary imaginaries and myths.

In contemporary tourism industries, one can observe how elements of indigenous heritages have become obvious and recognizable parts of this trade today (Graburn, 1984; Butler and Hinch, 2007; Bunten, 2010; Mathisen, 2010; Bunten and Graburn, 2018; Olsen and Pashkevich, 2023). It is also necessary to identify any policies and colonializing power structures that have enhanced the formation of such products (Viken and Müller, 2017). As the historical contexts of coloniality favored descriptions of cultural Alterity and of Otherness, they also directed the attention of visiting tourists towards the past. Meeting modernity and progress represented by travellers from urban, central Europe, the people and the cultures of the Scandinavian North generally found themselves situated in a past understood to be less developed, and sometimes even primitive. In a tourism context, however, the prospect of experiencing something that could embody a contemporary rendition of the shared history of humankind was naturally more intriguing and challenging for a well-off European and urban public with the means to travel. These feelings are similar to what Renato Rosaldo (1989) terms 'imperialist nostalgia', a form of nostalgia 'where people mourn the passing of what they themselves have transformed' (Rosaldo, 1989, p. 108). It is important to note in this connection that what people are mourning the passing of, is primarily a construction of their own – and hence a mythical and imagined – past that perhaps never existed. Whether these myths and imaginaries have been termed Orientalism (Said, 1978), or Borealism (Broberg 1982) by their critics, they all are based in Occidental or Western ideologies and imaginaries about the Other, whether this Other was to be found in the East or in the North.

It is not surprising that these ideas persist in contemporary tourism. Any concept that can generate widespread interest in the general public is prone to being commodified and subsequently commercialization. 'Seductive images and discourses about peoples and places are so predominant that without them there probably would be little tourism, if any at all' note Noel Salazar and Nelson Graburn in the introduction to their book *Tourism Imaginaries* (Salazar and Graburn, 2014, p. 1). This implies that the imaginaries of peoples and places persist, maintaining a continued existence even when perceived as irrelevant in modern everyday life. Their influence endures through staged performances in tourism and in the experience industry. The question arises whether it is possible to dismantle the 'colonial fictions that still shape our social imaginaries', as suggested by Christina Bacchilega (2007, p. 3), particularly concerning tourism in other parts of the world. Bacchilega explores imaginaries of Pacific cultures, delving into the use of Indigenous myths and narratives in Hawai'i, and says:

> How does colonialism rupture the (narrative) traditions of colonized and/or indigenous peoples? Clearly it others them; at times it violently seeks to erase them; but even in doing so it represents them. In rupturing tradition, colonialism then simultaneously delegitimizes the narratives of the colonized and constructs them as representative of the colonized "culture". Scholars in various disciplines, Edward Said, Johannes Fabian, Gayatri Chakravorty Spivak, have convincingly argued that the "culture" of the colonized people is not, however, the origin of this kind of narrative representation, but its effect. (Bacchilega, 2007, p. 2)

Moreover, the general inclination towards the past plays a crucial role in the production of Indigenous and Northern heritages, necessitating careful consideration of the origins of these ideas. In the contemporary development of the heritage sector, the gaze of the visiting tourist is a vital factor, albeit one that is frequently concealed and unspoken.

In support of the tourists' search for authentic experiences, the line between staged tourism performances in touristic theme parks and museum exhibitions is often thin, porous, and blurred when analyzed in a tourism context. Tourism calls for history to be told in an easily exhibitable way, in what Barbara Kirshenblatt-Gimblett (with an allusion to Disney World) chooses to term 'Distory' (1998, p. 173), or 'about history as it should have happened' (p. 175). The past would in that way be dramatized and adjusted to the imaginaries about these cultures already recognized and purported in the tourism business. To use Barbara Kirshenblatt-Gimblett's phrasing again: 'Where do old ideas go to die? Tourism, a museum of the consciousness industry' (Kirshenblatt-Gimblett 1998, p. 176). Although heritages in tourism are linked to the past, they are always produced in the present, and they are in that way not replicas of the past but represent new modes of cultural production (Kirshenblatt-Gimblett 1998, p. 149).

It is notable that cultures on display in tourism have deep roots and are connected to imaginaries created a long time ago, in very different contexts from the present. Still, these imaginaries tend to re-appear in these new tourism contexts, and this time as transformed, to a heightened status and value as indigenous or local heritage. While the argument for establishing something with a status as heritage most often is linked to needs for preservation, the values calling for this preservation are more vague, and might refer to identity building, age, uniqueness, and authenticity. In tourism, questions of these kinds of values are seldom asked, and they are more or less taken for granted, at least as long as they have been secured in institutions similar to museums. Placing an imagined past on display is often enough to make it worthy of being a tourism attraction, or at least something worth visiting. By being situated in the middle of these more complicated questions of value, the role of tourism as something more than a creator of pure monetary gains emerges. This is also the juncture at which tourism industries reveal their nonindustrial characteristics (Bendix, 2018, p. 20), seeing values beyond purely economic considerations, and occasionally discovering them, for better or worse. Much like the early travellers whose travelogs from the North were not solely driven by an interest in the exotic aspects of the culture, but also intertwined with political and industrial objectives, contemporary notions about the Arctic amalgamate different interests. This became evident when the Northern European mainland became part of the Arctic approximately 30 years ago.

Arctificating the North

As mentioned earlier, tourism and tourism imaginaries have consistently intersected with other worldmaking processes in the Northern part of Europe. For us, at least two recent developments underscore the necessity for new research agendas in future tourism studies. These developments emphasize the importance of conceiving tourism research as integral to worldmaking processes intertwined with the shaping Northern societies.

One such development, present for some time now, is the Arctification of what was formerly the northern part of Europe. The second development stems from the geopolitical tension resulting from the Russian war against Ukraine, currently establishing Northern Fenno-Scandia as a geopolitical borderland.

First, the Arctification of the Northern part of Europe has already been described for some time as a general process as well as a specific development in the tourism industry in the area (Keskitalo, 2003; Keskitalo et al., 2019; Müller et al., 2019; Saarinen and Varnajot, 2019; Marjavaara et al., 2022). According to Keskitalo (2003) an Arctic imaginary of North American origin, where the Arctic has been understood as an undisturbed natural area with an indigenous population with distinct economic adaptations and just recently impacted by extractive industries and new settlers, has been imposed on new areas. Contrary to this imaginary, the northern part of Europe was earlier not regarded as the Arctic, which in a Fenno-Scandian imagination started outside the mainland. And as Keskitalo, Pettersson and Sörlin describe this difference, the northern part of Europe is characterized 'by amongst others a more inte-grated nature interlinkage and more varied population groups, developing in relation to long-term established institutions – state, regional and local munic-ipality, in certain areas since the Middle Ages' (2019, p. 2). As demonstrated by Saarinen and Varnajot (2019) the Arctic is an image that can, and has, spread to places previously outside all definition of what is Arctic. Such a development towards Arctification might not be perceived to be beneficial by all. It does not necessarily correspond to all local community needs (Rantala et al., 2019). Neither do all minorities fit into this settler–native scheme and this has prob-ably consequences for how their heritage becomes a part of tourism imaginar-ies. National minorities in the northern areas, like the Kvens in Norway and Tornedalians in Sweden, seldom appear in the national marketing of tourism in the northern areas (Kvidal-Røvik and Olsen, forthcoming). Destination Marketing Organizations (DMOs) typically reinforce a distinction between settled and nomadic cultures in the North, often rendering minority cultures and heritage invisible. This lack of visibility extends to tourism research, presenting a notable contrast to the well-established literature on Sámi tourism.

Aligned with a broader European trend wherein tourism is perceived as a means of bolstering national peripheries, the field of tourism research has also witnessed a significant growth. The spotlight on the Arctic has intensified due to climate change, not only for the purpose of fostering a more sustainable world but also driven by the Arctic imaginary as a region rich in exploitable natural resources and new routes. Laura Junka-Aikio contends that the 'Arctification of governmental research policies intersects with the neoliberalization of the academy' (2019, p. 8), a trend reflected in the substantial increase in research funding and scientific publications related to Sámi tourism over the past decade. Junka-Aikio (2019, pp. 8–9) demonstrates, particularly for Finland but relevant for other Nordic countries as well, that heightened expectations for regional relevance have led many universities in the northern areas (and beyond) to consider Sámi research as 'highly pertinent for attempts to secure and increase their own relevance'.

Given its association with the broader academic fields and an imaginary of the Arctic and Arctic indigenous people, Sámi tourism aligns well with the needs of Arctic governance and serves both individual and institutional academic objectives. A consequence of this emphasis is that there may be an impression that there are more researchers involved in Sámi tourism *research* than there are Sámi individuals engaged in the tourism *industry*. Conversely, other minority and majority heritages with a longstanding presence in the European Arctic receive less attention from tourism researchers seeking funding for their research and advancing their careers in an increasingly precarious academic environment.

The consequence is that old imaginaries are perpetuated in new forms as worldmaking processes without reflecting the cultural complexity, connections and frictions that are not represented by the tourism industry – and, often, research – as neat categories following long-established categorizations. As Junka-Aikio demonstrates, this is also a continuance of previous research traditions as the travelogs made by men of means, and the Lappology that was 'encouraged by Europe's appetite for exotic difference and also then academic engagement with the "Lapps" offered Scandinavian researchers and institutions a fast track to obtain international prestige and to secure access to the metropolitan centres of science' (2019, p. 9).

Second, the new imaginary of the Arctic is very much indebted to the creation of the Arctic Council, formally established in 1996 by the Ottawa Declaration.

With its eight Arctic States and six Permanent Participants (who are all Indigenous), this body of cooperation is a result of the division caused by the Cold War. Since the Russian war against Ukraine, the previous cooperation between the partners has been split and there is now a divide between Russia and six, soon seven, NATO states. The imaginary of the Arctic as a place for peaceful cooperation might easily be changed to a reminiscence of the Cold War scenario, with closed borders, security risks, and potential conflict. For the Scandinavian part of the Arctic, where NATO now has extended its borders to Russia dramatically at the northern flank, this has already had some consequences. Tourism, tourism education, and research are no longer solely measures legitimized by national policies aimed at developing peripheral regions. In Norway, these endeavors have also become integral to security policies, with the goal of preserving as much of a declining population as possible in the border areas. This shift has resulted in a noticeable trend where discourse on land and sea routes, as well as the development of extractive industries, increasingly rely on security arguments.

Concluding remarks

These developments pose new areas of concern for tourism research in the European Arctic. One significant issue pertains to how new infrastructure will evolve in the region. Accessibility is a key asset for the tourism industry in this area. Unlike other parts of the Arctic region, the Fenno-Scandian area boasts relatively easy accessibility from both external and internal perspectives and is more densely populated. This infrastructure has played a pivotal role in facilitating the rapid growth of tourism in the region. However, it is essential to consider how the evolving geopolitical situation might influence this infrastructure, potentially leading to new winners and losers in a region characterized by unevenly distributed tourism.

Another concern is the proximity of Fennoscandia to the Russian North Fleet with its nuclear weapons, and how this will affect tour operators' and tourists' apprehension of risk in the area. The impact on the already uneven distribution of tourists in the area remains to be seen. A third issue revolves around the so-called policy of Norwegianization, implemented from the mid-19th century until the early post-World War II period. This policy, enacted as a conscious policy targeting the northern minorities, was not only a consequence of nationalism but also a security measure aimed at defending national borders by ensuring a Norwegian population in the borderlands of the north (Eriksen and Niemi, 1981). Eriksen and Niemi highlight a long-standing academic imaginary of the North, claiming that: 'Practically all Norwegian historical accounts that include the northern regions emphasize the "Russian menace", to the exclusion of all else' (1981, p. 352).

This imaginary, in which the northern population, as viewed from the centre, was not considered sufficiently rooted in national cultures, might be seen as a time passed by. However, when reflecting on the enduring elements in the imaginary of the Arctic developed over time, national changes in funding practices for research, investments, and strategies could indeed become a viable subject of study for tourism researchers interested in exploring the type of heritages that can be introduced into a – at the moment – unsecure Arctic, where borders are being reconstructed among previously cooperating states.

Tourism imaginaries and cultural heritage processes are linked. Cultures on display in tourism are connected to imaginaries created a long time ago, in contexts different from those of today, but when the imaginaries re-surface in new tourism contexts, it is in the form of Indigenous or local heritage. Even when they are not considered to have any relevance in modern everyday life, these imaginaries' influence continues from the staged performances in tourism and in the experience industry. This point encourages a call for a wider approach to Arctic tourism, in which cultural heritage perspectives interlinked with economic and political processes are part of an Arctic tourism research agenda. Some of these processes will be of a character that make them into common processes that make the Arctic into one. Anyhow, seen from the inside, from the everyday life of those who live in these areas, they are apprehended differently and often are so, due to the specificity of places, regions, and nation-states. Since not only tourism, but also tourism research is among those worldmaking processes shaping the imaginary of those areas now labelled Arctic, we need a research agenda that develops theories that are able to attend to differences, the particular, and a broader perspective on how the Arctic imaginary are made by processes where tourism is firmly interlinked and interdependent of other policies of a global scale.

References

Acerbi, J. (1802). *Travels through Sweden, Finland, and Lapland, to the North Cape, in the Years 1798 and 1799.* Vols. I–II. Joseph Mawman.

Bacchilega, C. (2007). *Legendary Hawai'i and the Politics of Place. Tradition, Translation, and Tourism.* University of Pennsylvania Press.

Bendix, R. (2018). *Culture and Value. Tourism, Heritage, and Property.* Indiana University Press.

Bring, S. E. (1954). *Itineraria svecana. Bibliografisk förteckning över resor i Sverige fram till 1950.* Almquist & Wiksell.

Broberg, G. (1982). Lappkaravaner på villovägar: Antropologin och synen på samerna fram mot sekelskiftet 1900. *Lychnos* 1981–1982, 27–86.

Bunten, A. C. (2010). More like ourselves: Indigenous capitalism through tourism. *American Indian Quarterly, 34*(3), 285–311.

Bunten, A. C., and Graburn, N. H. (2018). *Indigenous Tourism Movements.* University of Toronto Press.

Butler, R., and Hinch, T. (2007). *Tourism and Indigenous Peoples: Issues and Implications.* Butterworth-Heineman.

de Capell Brooke, A. (1823). *Travels through Sweden, Norway, and Finmark to the North Cape in the Summer of 1820.* Rodwell and Martin.

de Capell Brooke, A. (1827). *A Winter in Lapland and Sweden, with Various Observations Relating to Finnmark and its Inhabitants.* John Murray.

Erickson, B. (2021). The neoliberal tourist: Affect, policy and economy in the Canadian North. *ACME: An International Journal for Critical Geographies, 20*(1), 58–80.

Eriksen, K. E., and Niemi, E. (1981). *Den finske fare. Sikkerhetsproblemer og minoritetspolitikk i nord 1860–1940.* Universitetsforlaget.

Graburn, N. H. H. (1984). The evolution of tourist arts. *Annals of Tourism Research 11,* 393–419.

Huebner, A. (2015). Tourism and cultural encounters in 'the last frontiers'. *International Journal of Heritage Studies, 21*(9), 862–68.

Junka-Aikio, L. (2019). Institutionalization, neo-politicization and the politics of defining Sámi research. *Acta Borealia, 36*(1), 1–22.

Keskitalo, E. C. H. (2003). *Negotiating the Arctic: The Construction of an International Region.* Routledge.

Keskitalo, E. C. H., Pettersson, M. and Sörlin, S. (2019). Introduction: Understanding historical contingencies into the future: Cases from northern Europe. In E. C. H. Keskitalo (Ed.), *The Politics of Arctic Resources. Change and Continuity in the "Old North" of Northern Europe,* 1–17. Routledge.

Kirshenblatt-Gimblett, B. (1998). *Destination Culture. Tourism, Museums, and Heritage.* University of California Press.

Kramvig, B. (2017). Orientalism or cultural encounters? Tourism assemblages in cultures, capital and identities. In A. Viken and D. K. Müller (Eds.), *Tourism and Indigeneity in the Arctic.* Channel View Publications.

Kvidal-Røvik, T., and Olsen, K. (forthcoming). Kvenske forhåpninger på tampen av en vårflom? Kvensk synlighet i den offentlige reiselivsdiskursen. In T. Kvidal-Røvik, K. Olsen and S. R. Mathisen (Eds.), *Tuulessa – I vinden – Kvensk kultur i museer, kulturnæring og familier.* Universitetsforlaget.

Linnæus, C. (1811). *Lachesis Lapponica, or a Tour in Lapland.* Vols I–II. White and Cochrane.

Magnus, O. (1539). *Carta Marina.* Marine map and description of the northern lands and of their marvels, most carefully drawn up at Venice in the year 1539 through the generous assistance of the Most Honourable Lord Hieronymo Quirino. https://no.wikipedia.org/wiki/Olaus_Magnus#/media/Fil:Carta_Marina.jpeg.

Magnus, O. (1555). *Historia de Gentibus Septentrionalibus.* Romae: Iohannem Mariam de Viottis Parmensem.

Marjavaara, R., Nilsson, R. O., and Müller, D. K. (2022). The Arctification of northern tourism: A longitudinal geographical analysis of firm names in Sweden. *Polar Geography, 45*(2), 119–36.

Mathisen, S. R. (2010). Indigenous spirituality in the touristic borderzone: Virtual performances of Sámi shamanism in Sápmi Park. *Temenos. Nordic Journal of Comparative Religion, 46*(1), 53–72.

Mazzullo, N. (2022). Issues of Sámi representation in Finnish tourism: A quest for authenticity. In S. Valkonen, Á. Aikio, S. Alakorva and S.-M. Magga (Eds.), *The Sámi World* 197–213. Routledge.

Mignolo, W. D. (2000). *Local Histories/Global Designs: Coloniality, Subaltern Knowledges, and Border Thinking.* Princeton University Press.

Moyne, E. J. (1981). *Raising the Wind. The Legend of Lapland and Finland Wizards in Literature.* University of Delaware Press.

Müller, D. K., Byström, J., Stjernström, O., and Svensson, D. (2019). Making "wilderness" in a northern natural resource periphery. In E. C. H. Keskitalo (Ed.), *The Politics of Arctic Resources: Change and Continuity in the 'Old North' of Northern Europe*, 99–111. Routledge.

Olsen, K., and Pashkevich, A. (2023). Selling the indigenous in Nordic welfare states: Examples from Norway and Sweden. *Journal of Tourism and Cultural Change.* Doi: 10.1080/13683500.2023.2217352.

Quijano, A. (2000). Coloniality of power, eurocentrism, and Latin America. *Nepantla: Views from the South, 1*(3), 533–80.

Rantala, O., de la Barre, S., Granås, B., Jóhannesson, G. Þ., Müller, D. K., Saarinen, J., Tervo Kankare, K., Maher, P. T., and Niskala, M. (2019). *Arctic Tourism in Times of Change: Seasonality.* Nordic Council of Ministers.

Rosaldo, R. (1989). Imperialist nostalgia. *Representations, 26*, 107–22.

Saarinen, J., and Varnajot, A. (2019). The Arctic in tourism: Complementing and contesting perspectives on tourism in the Arctic. *Polar Geography, 42*(2), 109–24.

Said, E. W. (1978). *Orientalism.* Vintage Books.

Salazar, N. B. (2012). Tourism imaginaries: A conceptual approach. *Annals of Tourism Research, 39*(2), 863–82.

Salazar, N. B., and Graburn, N. H. H. (2014). *Tourism Imaginaries. Anthropological Approaches.* Berghahn.

Schiötz, E. H. (1970). *Itineraria Norvegica. Utlendingers reiser i Norge.* Universitetsforlaget.

Viken, A., and Müller, D. K. (2017). *Tourism and Indigeneity in the Arctic.* Channel View Publications.

Wright, R. (2017). Nå er vi blitt så trygg i oss selv at vi kan selge oss til turister. PhD thesis. UIT Norges arktiska universitet.

7   Multispecies hospitality

Emily Höckert and Outi Rantala

Invitation

For some time now, we have been reimagining more-than-human relations and responsibilities with the notion of multispecies hospitality. Bringing this concept to the Arctic tourism research agenda means expanding the focus beyond human hosts and guests by posing the question of how more-than-human hosts and guests – like plants, microbes, fungi, soil, human and non-human animals, and water in its different forms – welcome and care for each other in tourism settings. The idea of multispecies hospitality challenges us to extend our moral imagination (Caton, 2018) beyond human subjects and address the interdependencies of well-being and survival of all living communities amid ecological crisis. This approach is urgently needed in the Arctic context, where the effects of climate change are creating fundamental challenges for the region's ecosystems, wildlife and livelihoods, including tourism (AMAP, 2021; Varnajot and Saarinen, 2021). In this chapter, we take these thoughts with us to an overnight visit to a neighbouring forest in Rovaniemi, located at the Arctic Circle in Finland, to discuss tourism in more-than-human homes.

Our research agenda on Arctic tourism is grounded on the relational ideas of researching with, staying proximate to, and sharing research stories of lived and embodied multispecies experiences that can welcome further engagement (Rantala et al., 2024). This type of research agenda reflects our aim to envision alternatives to the distancing, and even apocalyptic imaginaries of the ecological crisis (Varnajot and Saarinen, 2022). Our approach joins the multispecies and posthuman research on Arctic tourism that draws attention to human-nature connectedness based on relational ontology as the key research theme in pursuit of sustainability transformations (Huijbens, 2023; Jóhannesson et al., 2024). These streams of discussions share the concern of the prevailing human failure to cognitively recognise our entanglements with other-than-human species (West et al., 2020). The concepts of "multispecies" and "more-than-human", used often interchangeably with "other-than-human" and "non-human", have been taken into use to dismantle

taken-for-granted culture-nature binary and the hegemonic human excep-
tionalism (Guia and Jamal, 2023). These notions are being used to address the
interdependency of our common well-being and survival "within a broader
epoch of eco-social unravelling" (Price and Chao, 2023, p. 178).

Our thinking with multispecies hospitality is guided by multispecies studies in
environmental humanities that experiment with novel ways of engaging with
the world around us (van Dooren et al., 2016; Kirksey and Chao, 2022). These
discussions seek to cultivate the art of attentiveness to the diverse ways that
the lives of different species – such as animals, plants, and microorganisms –
become entangled and constitute worlds. The aim of the multispecies studies
is to open up new understandings, relationships, and accountabilities and,
not least, to craft meaningful responses (Kimmerer, 2013). Thus, conjoining
the multispecies approach with the idea of hospitality as an ethical relation
between self and multiple others means extending the ideas of welcome and
care beyond human hosts and guests. Whilst multispecies hospitality can be
understood in terms of hospitality management, our theoretical exploration is
inspired, most of all, by postcolonial philosophies of hospitality that approach
ethical subjectivity as openness and responsibility to alterity and "the Other"
(Levinas, 1969; see also Höckert, 2018; Höckert and Grimwood, 2024).

Exploration of multispecies hospitality forms part of our collaborative work
within Intra-living in the Anthropocene (ILA) research group. During the past
years, this group of multidisciplinary scholars has been experimenting with
new ways of engaging with the present periods of ecological crisis, known as
the age of the Anthropocene; that is, the Epoch defined by the mass extinc-
tion of species, pollution, climate change and overuse of natural resources
(see Gren and Huijbens, 2014). We have used the notion of "intra-living" to
draw focus on situated, more-than-human ways of relating and co-living, and
thereby co-constituting each other. Intra-living also refers to the symbiotic
relationship and interconnectedness of our mutual well-being and survival
on our shared home planet. We are engaging with the current crisis from
a relational, "down-to-earth" perspective (see also Huijbens, 2023) – and as
Donna Haraway (2016) challenges us to do, to "stay with the trouble" in caring,
sensitive, and thoughtful ways (see also Ren, 2021). We share an interest in
unsettling the distancing, generalising, and even apocalyptic imaginaries of
the Anthropocene by staying proximate with mundane beings, relations, and
places in the Arctic (Rantala et al., 2024).

Instead of setting an agenda for researching for or about multispecies hospitality, the purpose of this chapter is to explore different modes of attuning to
and engaging with more-than-human worlds – with modes such as wonder,

openness, affinity, and uneasiness. Our aim here is to continue experiment-ing with a research approach that is based on relational ontologies and epistemologies as well as a sensitive, caring, and curious orientation towards more-than-human entanglements and multispecies storytelling (Rantala et al., 2024). Furthermore, while the research contexts, theoretical inspirations, and more-than-human "messmates" may vary, the ethico-political interest of "staying with the trouble" (Haraway, 2016) and gathering around common matters of care works as a baseline for our research (van der Duim et al., 2017; Ren, 2021). Hence, by taking these discussions into the forest, we wish to walk – or more rightly ski – this talk: to enact research by positioning ourselves within the phenomenon at hand.

It is early March; the sunshine is starting to feel warm at the Arctic Circle and the forest is calling. We should start packing. Would you like to join us?

Packing for the trip: Post humanist Arctic tourism literature

When commencing a trip to a forest – especially in an Arctic environment – it is important to be prepared. The pre-pandemic growth in tourism made visible problems that relate to the increased amount of unskilled or uninformed tourists visiting the Arctic landscapes (Rantala et al., 2018). Indeed, the unpre-paredness to move about in Arctic environments has led to an increase in rescue situations (Finnish Broadcasting Company YLE, 2023), disturbance of local human and non-human communities (Olsen et al., 2019), and unpleasant holiday memories or even fatal situations (Hild et al., 2023). To avoid these unintended outcomes on our forthcoming ski trip in the forest, we want to take the time to pack our backpacks with care and fill them with relevant readings. Kaya Barry (2017) has approached packing as a hands-on engagement that forms and re-forms relationships and can illustrate "more banal aspects of being a tourist" (p. 335). Hence, the purpose of explaining our packing process for this trip is to make visible how our research builds on previous work conducted by Arctic tourism researchers. Moreover, it also reveals the "banal" aspect of being a researcher; that is, how by proposing a research agenda we are using our worldmaking power of re-forming relationships between previous and ongoing research, as well as future research directions.

Therefore, despite the necessity of bringing along some large items such as a tent, sleeping bags, and mattresses, we want to make sure that there is enough room for previous literature related to more-than-human agencies and encounters in Arctic tourism. These streams of discussions have been emerging and increasing, especially during the past decade, and offer us a nourishing package of knowledge for our trip. This literature has brought, for example, animal agency into the examination of the sustainability of Arctic tourism (Lemelin, 2006; Yudina and Grimwood, 2016; Hoarau-Heemstra and Kline, 2022), Arctic tourism landscapes (Granås, 2018; Äijälä, 2021), and Arctic tourism organisation (Tallberg et al., 2022). The previous literature related to more-than-human agencies and encounters in Arctic tourism has a strong undercurrent of ethical concerns about tourism in the Anthropocene (Kristoffersen et al., 2015), expanding the idea of care to previously overlooked species. For instance, discussions on the roles of insects in Arctic tourism encounters (Lemelin, 2009) call for relational understandings that highlight "the complex, embodied, messy, and contextual nature of ethics and the subsequent tension between violence and care" (Valtonen et al., 2020, p. 8; see also Huijbens, 2023). The literature on more-than-human encounters has also well-illustrated the need for diversifying the methodological repertoire within Arctic tourism research; by developing and applying, for instance, videography (Haanpää et al., 2021), mobile methods (Äijälä, 2021), memory work (Valtonen et al., 2020), and multispecies-based ethnographic methodologies (Yudina and Grimwood, 2016).

Once the largest things are packed, we move on to pack the practical items needed on our visit to the forest, such as the stove, kettles, knife, and axe. Indeed, the second strong direction in the previous posthuman Arctic tourism research has been the examination of the materiality of tourism practices. Tourism researchers have shown that the materiality of the biophysical environment interferes with, and directs the actions of, for example, guides (Valkonen, 2009; Rantala, 2010), tourism entrepreneurs (Valtonen, 2009), and expedition cruise crews (Lamers et al., 2017). Application of actor-network theory and practice theories has also paved the way for the use of other relational approaches, by showing ways to critically investigate socio-material dimensions and by providing toolkits for generating analyses of the heterogeneous relations in tourism (Lamers et al., 2017; van der Duim et al., 2017).

Finally, next to the extra down jackets, headlamps, chocolate bars, and a first aid kit, we pack literature related to the affective atmospheres in Arctic tourism. This literature is essential for us to understand the importance of how bodies and rhythms intertwine with the surroundings, human and more-than-human, creating tourism experiences, and contributing to the affective field of Arctic tourism destinations (Jóhannesson and Lund, 2010). It also visualises how the Arctic seasons afford various lightscapes and soundscapes both for humans and more-than-humans (Rantala and Valtonen, 2014), and how to conduct research *with* these different atmospheres (Hurst and Stinson, 2024).

While there is still space left in the backpack's side pockets, we resolve to bring along some of the critically oriented discussions of how post humanist approaches are being used and to what effect (Guia and Jamal, 2023). The relational and post humanist theories in Euro-Western academia have been critiqued for their erasure of non-European, and especially Indigenous knowledge systems (Todd, 2016). It is thus essential to recognise how the use of meta-categories such as the Anthropocene, climate change, human, and "we", all come with the risk of overlooking alternative ways of attending to multispecies relations and their situated character (Rantala et al., 2024, p. 3). Chris Hurst and Bryan Grimwood (2023) have also raised the concern of the presumed superiority of non-human animals that create new dichotomies of sentient and non-sentient beings and overlook the agency of other non-human subjects. As their writing shows, the post humanist aim of blurring and disrupting dualistic epistemologies whilst avoiding the creation of new dichotomies must be accepted here as an ever-present challenge; not least when playing with the notions of hosts and guests (Guia and Jamal, 2023), tourism and other-than-tourism (Pernecky, 2023), academic and traditional knowledge (Valkonen and Valkonen, 2019), and Arctic and non-Arctic (Marjavaara et al., 2022; Varnajot and Saarinen, 2022; Vola, 2022).

And now, with our backpacks quite full of material and immaterial support, we feel properly prepared to begin our winter skiing trip.

Recognising hospitality

> We drive for twenty minutes or so to reach the point where we wish to start our journey. Kurivaara is quite a popular place to visit, featuring built trails and a shelter. At the same time, it is a place that allows us to experience a glimpse of wilderness and the absence of urban sounds. Although we have been here before, we do not wish to claim to know the place, but rather to visit it with the art of hospitality in mind. (Quote from the authors' field notes.)

As briefly mentioned in the introduction, our interest is not in commercial hospitality products and services as such, but in joining somewhat alternative streams of tourism research where host–guest relationships are perceived as relational and affirmative encounters. This means drawing on philosophical discussions on the ethics of hospitality as compasses that guide our attention, call for critical reflection, and can enable us to expand our moral imaginations (e.g. Höckert, 2014, 2018; Doering and Kishi, 2022; Höckert and Grimwood, 2024; Guia and Jamal, 2023).

Since some time back, we have been drawing particularly on Emmanuel Levinas' (1969) and Jacques Derrida's (1999) writings on hospitality to reflect how both human and other-than-human hosts and guests are making space for otherness and "the Other" (Höckert and Grimwood, 2024). Levinas and Derrida's way of prioritising the relation over individual freedom can be seen as quite radical and unique in the Western spirit of morality and justice. This priority makes it impossible for us to be responsible as detached adventurers or researchers and also reveals the arrogance of taking the welcome of "the Other" for granted. Instead, as Derrida (1999) underlined, it is necessary to recognise how the conditions of hospitality become negotiated between different kinds of hosts and guests. Importantly, this notion of hospitality disrupts the pre-set roles of hosts and guests, both *hôte* in French, and suggests that the agency and responsibility to welcome and care are continuously changing in reciprocal relations (Höckert, 2018).

After unpacking the car, putting the skis on, and lifting our rucksacks to our backs, we head toward the track that will take us to the shelter. While there is no door or gate, it feels like we are about to enter somewhere. When we see a branch of a tree leaning towards another under the weight of snow, forming almost a gate, we decide to stop and perform a symbolic knocking or request to enter. We have heard of kindergarten groups where educators teach the children to ask the forest for permission to enter. Following their example and words, we ask: "Please open the lock, the forest's block". After entering through the gate, we lock it again after us: "Please close the lock, the forest's block".

The purpose of imagining an entrance to this more-than-human Arctic destination is not to reinforce dualistic thinking between human and nature but to provide an example of a practice that recognises and respects the hospitality of multispecies communities. A multispecies approach calls attention to the deprived status of the other-than-humans in Western ontologies and cultural and religious formations and puts in question the anthropocentric urge to conquer and dominate "nature" or treat it as a background to our activities (Schlosberg, 2007; Celermajer et al., 2021). We make a mental note to search for inspiration from already existing practices of multispecies recognition that might take place in tourism settings. We know that, for instance, Frida Marie Omma's (2023) ongoing research within the context of Northern Norway is providing these kinds of inspiring examples (see also Äijälä, 2021).

The relational idea of multispecies hospitality and transcendence between "two worlds" has obvious linkages with indigenous worldviews that recognise and respect the agency and vitality of matter (Kimmerer, 2013; Todd, 2016). Along with wider streams of tourism research in the Arctic, this kind of conceptual development poses the risk of neglecting or appropriating Indigenous philosophies (Viken et al., 2021). Not least, the increasing Western efforts to "reconnect with nature" tend to overlook the spiritual dimensions of Indigenous cosmologies or to reinforce problematic dualism between material and spiritual (Celermajer, et al. 2021). Indeed, the multispecies approach sets out to replace the homogenising and generalising conceptions of the "human" by emphasising how human lives unfold differently in particular situations and places.

Respecting everyone's right to roam

From the perspective of the Nordic "everyone's rights" or *allemansrätten*, this kind of cordial entering manoeuvre appears unnecessary, as there is no need to ask for permission to enter or move about in Arctic forests. It is only when hunting and fishing (aside from angling), starting a campfire outside designated areas, or staying in a tent for more than one night, that permission must be asked from the forest owner. Also, permission to collect the young tips of a spruce tree or cones must be asked from the human who owns the land – not from the tree.

Recently, the concept of "everyman's rights" has been altered into *everyone's* right to remove the gendered aspect of it. In the Finnish context, we can thank Ilma Lindgren whose experience of injustice in 1914 led to a battle in court and finally to the eventual creation of everyone's rights (Laari, 2023). Today's formulations of everyone's rights include metaphors of hosts and guests, and, for instance, Visit Finland (2023) reminds us that "When you're on private land, remember that you're not just a guest of nature but a guest of the landowner." Whilst the notion of everyone's right refers clearly to humans, it is worth asking whether the re-conceptualisation could lead to a broader multispecies understanding of the right to roam (Granås, 2024; Nousiainen et al., 2024) – and asking for permission.

When the track takes us deeper into the forest, we lean to the side so as not to break the branches of the trees. Next to the ski track, we see traces of a rabbit and a fox on the soft snow. While we hear a woodpecker at work or playing music somewhere close by, it is clear that our presence also frightens away some of the local hosts.

Source: Photo by Tapio Nykänen.

Figure 7.1   Skiing visitors in Kurivaara, Rovaniemi

The emerging discussions on multispecies justice are seeking to alter the anthropocentric understandings of rights by cultivating arts of attentiveness and noticing especially in the sites of abandonment and extraction (Kirksey and Chao, 2022). Rather than taking individual entities or species as units of research, the multispecies lens trains our attention to ways in which human and non-human communities interact with and depend on one another. This approach is fruitful especially in the Arctic region, characterised by long distances and relatively scarce human population. By focusing on particularities, the multispecies hospitality lens offers a chance to address how environmental impacts, risks, and injustices are unequally divided between kinds, species, and regions. At the same time, there is also a need to recognise small acts of justice that are occurring in our multispecies relations.

All of a sudden, we encounter a reindeer 20 metres from us, barely seeming to notice us while bending its head to eat. We whisper to each other, negotiating the best way to proceed – should we take a detour in deeper snow in order not to scare the reindeer away, or should we continue on the track? We wish we could somehow tell the reindeer that we are here only for a visit, without the wish to make a mess or disturb them. At the same time, we ponder that in this place both military planes fly over with a horrendous sound and hunters shoot their guns, so our visit with skis and whispers is maybe not the most threatening act.

Encounters like the one described above show how pre-set codes of conduct often fall short in situated "face-to-face" encounters in the North. Despite the written guidelines or recommendations, we are thrown as guests into relations with constant hesitation about whether to lean in or step back, engage, or give space. Whilst everyone's rights in the Nordic countries offer general instructions on how to be a responsible guest, the conditions of hospitality tend to become negotiated in situated relations between self and the other that require the preparedness to be unprepared (Derrida, 1999). In theory, we can put up our tent anywhere in the woods – as long as there are no houses nearby – without asking permission from any human owners of that land. Yet, what about the favourite sleeping places of the willow grouse, common paths of the reindeer, or the striving communities of mosses? How to make sure not to overstay our welcome? Or even more, how to make kin in a place where many humans visit to hunt and cut down trees?

The idea of multispecies justice also unsettles the predominant idea of categorising certain animals or plants as unwanted guests, or as pests – such as the mosquito during the Arctic summer season (Valtonen et al., 2020; Paredetes, 2022; Pashkevic and Hoarau-Heemstra, 2023). Aligned with multispecies studies, Lynx Vilden (2023) underlines how all beings have something to share and teach us when we know how to listen. Listening in forests like these can mean, for instance, becoming attentive to the changes of colours in lichens and rabbits, and paying attention and respect to paths chosen by a marten. Instead of accepting our limited ability as social scientists to listen and translate multispecies voices, we can choose to see this as an ethico-political provocation to explore alternative more-than-human methodologies. For instance, Szymanski (2023) suggests that the human desire to speak *with* other creatures, instead of speaking *for, about,* or *around* them, "requires drawing a distinction between capacities to affect/be affected and assumptions about any creature's internal state of mind" (p. 138). Along with Despret's (2016) wonderful book "What would animals say if we asked the right questions?", expanding our circles of care to multispecies worlds requires revision of research questions and the curiosity to follow more-than-human signs of hospitality (see also Pyyhtinen, 2022).

Reciprocity of care

When we arrive at the shelter, we add a layer of warm clothes and make a fire. Camping in winter in the North is very much about keeping warm, so we start right away to prepare our guest house for the night in the forest. We stamp the snow behind the shelter with our skies, making it more solid. Once we have put up the tent and unpacked our rucksacks, we place the air-filled winter mattresses and thick sleeping bags in there. We hang a headlamp to the ceiling of the tent for the night, and decide to crawl inside, since it all looks so cosy. How privileged are we – lying here, next to each other, feeling safe, wrapped inside our expensive winter camping gear. We do not have to dig our food under icy snow like many animals do in the changing climate but have our snacks easily available. Something at this moment invites us to talk about Monica Nadegger's (2023) analyses of the agency of snow in the ruins of alpine skiing; that is, how alpine skiing is troubled by its capitalist, extractive, and exploitative relations. All the messiness of this makes us silent. We end up just lying still here in our guesthouse in the forest, pondering how our search for multispecies hospitality from this forest is also inherently entangled with capitalist consumerism and the exploitative use of nature.

It seems like our consumption-driven societies are currently facing the challenge of changing the prevailing mindsets of owning and surviving towards belonging and striving (Vilden, 2023; Vlasov, 2023). This would require, for instance, replacing the questions of "What is in it for me?" and "Who benefits?" with reflection on reciprocal well-being in multispecies communities. It also requires problematising the tendency of treating "nature" as a resource or background for human economic activities, which has been an increasing tendency in the Arctic recently and seeking ways of recognising and respecting the intrinsic value of more-than-human communities. Perhaps by widening the idea of being social beyond humans, as our colleague Neal Cahoon would say?

In addition to making space for the other, the idea of multispecies hospitality boils down to the multiple ways in which care occurs in more-than-human worlds. As our outdoor gear materials provide us with the needed help to stay warm during this visit in the forest, the willow grouse survives in the Arctic winter by diving into an air pocket in the snow. The layers of snow also give protection to mosses and other plants that rest for the next intensive season of providing care for multiple hosts and guests in this forest (Grimwood and Höckert, 2023). Indeed, as Robin Wall Kimmerer (2013) states, the term for plants translates to "those who take care of us" in some Native languages.

Future inquiries with multispecies hospitality

Next day, while skiing back to the car, we discuss how trips like these are guided by a paradoxical urge, on the one hand, to get lost and encounter something yet unknown, and on the other, to return to something that we have actually all come from. There is a desire to re-find connection, knowledge and skills that we have lost somewhere along the way. It feels as if trips like these offer a glimpse of the promise of re-discovering the ecological knowledge that we have had in us since the beginning. As if the multispecies communities of the forest were inviting us to remember, reconnect – to belong. And then there is an almost-too-difficult-to-talk-about feeling of melancholy about the uncertainty of the winters to come. Will there be enough snow to carry the weight of our skis in the future? Will the rabbits keep their coats that act as white camouflage?

We have written this chapter as an invitation and provocation to think, imagine and act tourism and research with the notion of multispecies hospitality. Instead of strengthening dualist thinking between hosts and guests, self and the other, culture and nature, home and away, our wish is to cultivate the relational and reciprocal idea of hospitality where the roles between multispecies hosts and guests are continuously changing. While in this chapter we enjoyed the local forests' hospitality as guests and felt occasionally at home, we actually do not need to travel far to experience this kind of symbiotic care between more-than-human hosts and guests. In effect, the fruitfulness of the notion of multispecies hospitality lies in the way it can be thought of on multiple scales and in different kinds of metaphorical homes. On a planetary level, this approach sparks questions of conviviality (see chapter 13 in this book) on this shared home called Earth or the changes in local habitats brought about by the rapidly warming climate in the Arctic. At the same time, as our dear colleague Veera Kinnunen often reminds us, these kinds of multispecies relations can be found in ourselves, as the well-being of human bodies depends on the vibrant multispecies host-guest relations that occur in our "guts" – that is, in our bodies that simultaneously host and are cared for by millions and billions of micro-organisms (Pyyhtinen, 2014).

On our short trip, we stayed in the forest with posthumanist Arctic tourism readings that guided our attention to the agencies of non-human animals, plants resting under the snow (Yudina and Grimwood, 2016; Grimwood and Höckert, 2023), and especially the soundscapes in this supposedly quiet place (Hurst and Stinson, 2024). We attuned our attention to how we were re-shaping the winter landscape by following and crossing paths with local hosts who were most likely intimidated by our presence (see Äijälä, 2021). While trips like these are often filled with a desire to feel at home and become part of the place, our high-tech clothing, skis, food, and camping equipment underline how privileged we are as guests. And again, none of this equipment can protect us from the affective atmosphere that has emerged from the omnipotent uncertainty of the accelerating ecological crisis (Varnajot and Saarinen, 2022).

Supported by the previous and ongoing post humanist discussions in tourism and beyond, we find it important to couple the idea of multispecies hospitality with post-rational epistemologies to unsettle the boundaries of "normative ways of knowing" that dominate current approaches to sustainability and responsibility in Arctic tourism. Hence, we return from our trip with a dedication to continuing with the multispecies hospitality approach as an onto-logical, epistemological, and methodological disposition that calls for radical openness toward difference and otherness and invites scholars from different backgrounds to gather around the common matters of concern amidst climate change and biodiversity loss. By inscribing openness into the epistemological feature of our multispecies approach, we have wished to question the deeply rooted assumption of humans as the only beings capable of producing and sharing knowledge (Guia and Jamal, 2023).

In more concrete terms, this chapter proposes questions that could be lifted to the future agenda of Arctic tourism research. Firstly, our research has been driven by curiosity about how the metaphors of hospitality and visiting others' homes might shape visitors' behaviour at Arctic tourism destinations. That is, whether the hope of being a good guest who would be welcomed for a re-visit might enhance the feeling of responsibility among different kinds of tourists? Second – and this is a question that we have posed to ourselves while skiing in Kurivaara – what does it mean to approach the idea of freedom to roam from the perspective of multispecies justice and rights in the tourism context, and beyond? Finally, the notion of multispecies hospitality encourages asking how we make space for the Other and otherness, and how spaces are being open and kept for "us." This means drawing focus and recognising how the conditions of hospitality become negotiated between species and on the diverse ways that the negotiations are taking place. As the main souvenir from the trip, this chapter has aimed to draw attention to questions of knowledge in multispecies settings and has sought to underline the importance of cultivating the art of attentive-ness in both tourism and research relations.

References

Äijälä, M. (2021). Mobile video ethnography for evoking animals in tourism. *Annals of Tourism Research, 89,* 103203.

AMAP (2021). *Arctic Climate Change Update 2021: Key Trends and Impacts. Summary for Policy-makers.* Arctic Monitoring and Assessment Programme (AMAP), Tromsø, Norway.

Barry, K. (2017). *Everyday Practices of Tourism Mobilities: Packing a Bag.* Routledge.

Caton, K. (2018). Conclusion: In the forest. In B. S. R. Grimwood, K. Caton, & L. Cooke (Eds.*), New Moral Natures in* Tourism, 194–205. Routledge.

Celermajer, D., Schlosberg, D., Rickards, L., Stewart-Harawira, M., Thaler, M., Tschakert, P., Blanche V., and Winter C. (2021). Multispecies justice: Theories, challenges, and a research agenda for environmental politics. *Environmental Politics, 30*(1–2), 119–40.

Despret, V. (2016). *What Would the Animals Say if We Asked the Right Questions?* University of Minnesota Press.

Derrida, J. (1999). *Adieu to Emmanuel Levinas.* Stanford University Press.

Doering, A., and Kishi, K. (2022). "What your head!": Signs of hospitality in the tourism linguistic Landscapes of rural Japan. *Tourism, Culture & Communication, 22*(2), 127–42.

Finnish Broadcasting Company, YLE (2023). *Turistit aiheuttavat sesonkina usein valtaosan Lapin pelastuslaitoksen hälytyksistä – "Pitää vain yrittää sinnitellä.* https://yle.fi/a/74-20010446.

Granås, B. (2018). Destinizing Finnmark: Place making through dogsledding. *Annals of Tourism Research, 72,* 48–57.

Granås, B. (2024). Sensing morally evocative spaces. In O. Rantala, V. Kinnunen and E. Höckert (Eds.), *Researching with Proximity,* 89-104. Palgrave Macmillan.

Gren, M., and Huijbens, E.H. (2014). Tourism and the Anthropocene. *Scandinavian Journal of Hospitality and Tourism, 14*(1), 6–22.

Grimwood, B. S. R., and Höckert, E. (2023). Cultivating relations with plant stories. *Annals of Tourism Research, 103,* 103661.

Guia, J. and Jamal, T. (2023). An affective and posthumanist cosmopolitan hospitality, *Annals of Tourism Research, 100,* 103569.

Haanpää, M., Salmela, T., García-Rosell, J. C., and Äijälä, M. (2021). The disruptive 'other'? Exploring human-animal relations in tourism through videography. *Tourism Geographies, 23*(1-2), 97–117.

Haraway, D. J. (2016). *Staying with the Trouble: Making Kin in the Chthulucene.* Duke University Press.

Hild, B. O., Jóhannesson, G. T., and Sydnes, A. K. (2023). "Everyone can be a guide until something goes wrong": Adventure guides' competencies and tourist safety in the Arctic. *Scandinavian Journal of Hospitality and Tourism.*

Hoarau-Heemstra, H., and Kline, C. (2022). Making kin and making sense of human-animal relations in tourism. *Ecological Economics, 196,* 107396.

Höckert, E. (2014). Unlearning through hospitality. In S. Veijola, J. G. Molz, O. Pyyhtinen, E. Höckert and A. Grit (Eds.), *Disruptive Tourism and its Untidy Guests: Alternative Ontologies in Future Tourism Hospitalities,* 96–121. Palgrave Macmillan.

Höckert, E. (2018). *Negotiating Hospitality: Ethics of Tourism Development in the Nicaraguan Highlands.* Routledge.

Höckert, E., and Grimwood, B. S. R. (2024). Inquiring with hospitable methodologies. In O. Rantala, V. Kinnunen and E. Höckert (Eds.), *Researching with Proximity: Relational Methodologies for the Anthropocene*, 21–41. Palgrave Macmillan.

Huijbens, E. H. (2023). Tourism earthly attachments in the Anthropocene. *Tourism Geographies*, DOI: 10.1080/14616688.2023.2269534.

Hurst, C. E., and Grimwood, B. S. R. (2023). Posthumanism and the sentient elephant in the room. *Annals of Tourism Research, 101*, 103604.

Hurst, C. E., and Stinson, M. J. (2024). Inviting engagement with atmospheres. In O. Rantala, V. Kinnunen and E. Höckert (Eds.), *Researching with Proximity*, 165–87. Palgrave Macmillan.

Jóhannesson, G. T., and Lund, K. A. (2010). Aurora Borealis: Choreographies of darkness and light. *Annals of Tourism Research, 37*(1), 249–64.

Jóhannesson, G. T., Lund, K. A., Thorsteinsson, B., and Jóhannesdóttir, G. R. (2024). Introduction. In B. Thorsteinsson, K. A. Lund, G. T. Jóhannesson and G. R. Jóhannesdóttir (Eds.), *Mobilities in Margins. Creative Processes of Place-Making*, 1–13. Palgrave Macmillan.

Kimmerer, R. W. (2013). *Braiding Sweetgrass: Indigenous Wisdom, Scientific Knowledge and the Teachings of Plants*. Milkweed Editions.

Kirksey, E., and Chao, S. (2022). Introduction: Who benefits from multispecies justice? In S. Chao, K., Bolender, and E. Kirksey (Eds.), *The Promise of Multispecies Justice*, 1–22. Duke University Press.

Kristoffersen, B., Norum, R., and Kramvig, B. (2015). Arctic whale watching and Anthropocene ethics. In M. Gren and E. Huijbens (Eds.), *Tourism and the Anthropocene*, 94–110. Routledge.

Laari, S. (2023, September 1). Tämä nainen hankki suomalaisille oikeuden liikkua metsissä ja poimia sieniä: "Tosi kova muija". *Helsingin Sanomat*.

Lamers, M, van der Duim, R., and Spaargaren, G. (2017). The relevance of practice theories for tourism research. *Annals of Tourism Research, 62*, 54–63.

Lemelin, R. H. (2006). The gawk, the glance, and the gaze: Ocular consumption and polar bear tourism in Churchill, Manitoba, Canada. *Current Issues in Tourism, 9*(6), 516–34.

Lemelin, R. H. (2009). Goodwill hunting: Dragon hunters, dragonflies and leisure. *Current Issues in Tourism, 12*(5–6), 553–71.

Levinas, E. (1969). *Totality and Infinity: An Essay of Exteriority*. Duquesne University Press.

Marjavaara, R., Nilsson, R. O., and Müller, D. K. (2022). The arctification of northern tourism: A longitudinal geographical analysis of firm names in Sweden. *Polar Geography, 45*(2), 119–36.

Nadegger, M. (2023). Carving lines through melting lands: A diffractive engagement with troubled and troubling relations of alpine skiing in the Anthropocene. *Leisure Sciences*, DOI: 10.1080/01490400.2023.2269159.

Nousiainen, M., Rantala, O., and Tuulentie, S. (2024). Rush hour in a national park: Mobile encounters in a peripheral tourism landscape. In B. Thorsteinsson, K. A. Lund, G. T. Jóhannesson and G. R. Jóhannesdóttir (Eds.), *Mobilities in Margins. Creative Processes of Place-Making*, 225–43. Palgrave Macmillan.

Olsen, K. O., Abildgaard, M. S., Brattland, C., Chimirri, D., de Bernardi, C., Edmonds, J., Grimwood, B. S. R., Hurst, C. E.; Höckert, E., Jæger, K., Kugapi, O., Lemelin, R. H., Lüthje, M., Mazzullo, N., Müller, D. K., Ren, C., Saari, R., Ugwuegbula, L., and Viken, A. (2019). *Looking at Arctic Tourism through the Lens of Cultural Sensitivity*.

ARCTISEN – A Transnational Baseline Report. Multidimensional Tourism Institute. Rovaniemi, Finland: LUC Tourism.

Omma, F. M. (2023). *Sustainable tourism and non-human ethics: Nature guides' beliefs and practices.* Paper presented in the 31st Nordic Symposium on Tourism and Hospitality Research, Östersund, Sweden.

Pashkevich, A., and Hoarau-Heemstra, H. (2023). *Is there a dark side of (wild)life encounters in the Arctic?* Paper presented in the 31st Nordic Symposium on Tourism and Hospitality Research, Östersund, Sweden.

Paredetes, A. (2022). "We are not Pests". In S. Chao, K. Bolender and E. Kirksey (Eds.), *The Promise of Multispecies Justice,* 77–102. Duke University Press.

Pernecky, T. (2023). Kinmaking: Toward more-than-tourism (studies). *Tourism Recreation Research, 48*(4), 558–68.

Price, C., and Chao, S. (2023). Multispecies, more-than-human, non-human, other-than-human: Reimagining idioms of animacy in an age of planetary unmaking. *Exchanges: The Interdisciplinary Research Journal, 10*(2), 177–93.

Pyyhtinen, O. (2014). Paradise with/out parasites. In S. Veijola, J. G. Molz, O. Pyyhtinen, E. Höckert and A. Grit (Eds.), *Disruptive Tourism and its Untidy Guests: Alternative Ontologies in Future Tourism Hospitalities,* 42–67. Palgrave Macmillan.

Pyyhtinen, O. (2022). Lines that do not speak: Multispecies hospitality and bug-writing. *Hospitality and Society, 12*(3), 343–59.

Rantala, O. (2010). Tourist practices in the forest. *Annals of Tourism Research, 37*(1), 249–64.

Rantala, O., and Valtonen, A. (2014). A rhythmanalysis of touristic sleep in nature. *Annals of Tourism Research, 47,* 18–30.

Rantala, O., Hallikainen, V., Ilola, H., and Tuulentie, S. (2018). The softening of adventure tourism. *Scandinavian Journal of Hospitality and Tourism, 18*(4), 1–19.

Rantala, O., Kinnunen, V., Höckert, E., Grimwood, B. S. R., Hurst, C. E., Jóhannesson, G. T., Jutila, S., Ren, R., Stinson, M. J., Valtonen, A., & Vola, J. (2024). Staying proximate. In O. Rantala, V. Kinnunen and E. Höckert (Eds.), *Researching with Proximity,* 1–19. Palgrave Macmillan.

Ren, C. (2021). (Staying with) the trouble with tourism and travel theory? *Tourist Studies, 21,* 133–40.

Schlosberg, D. (2007). *Defining Environmental Justice: Theories, Movements, and Nature.* OUP Oxford.

Szymanski, E. A. (2023). Conversations with other-than-human creatures: Unpacking the ambiguity of "with" for multispecies rhetorics. *Rhetoric Society Quarterly, 53*(2), 138–52.

Tallberg, L., García-Rosell, JC., and Haanpää, M. (2022). Human–animal relations in business and society: Advancing the feminist interpretation of stakeholder theory. *Journal of Business Ethics, 180,* 1–16.

Todd, Z. (2016). An Indigenous feminist's take on the ontological turn: "Ontology" is just another word for colonialism. *Journal of Historical Sociology, 29*(1), 4–22.

Valkonen, J. (2009). Acting in nature: Service events and agency in wilderness guiding. *Tourist Studies, 9*(2), 164–80.

Valkonen, J. & Valkonen, S. (2019) On local knowledge. In T. Hylland Eriksen, S. Valkonen, & J. Valkonen (Eds.), *Knowing from the Indigenous North: Sámi Approaches to History, Politics and Belonging,* 12–26. Routledge.

Valtonen, A. (2009). Small tourism firms as agents of critical knowledge. *Tourist Studies, 9*(2), 127–43.

Valtonen, A., Salmela, T., and Rantala, O. (2020). Living with mosquitoes. *Annals of Tourism Research, 83*, 102945.

van der Duim, V. R., Ren, C., and Jóhannesson, G. T. (2017). ANT: A decade of interfering with tourism. *Annals of Tourism Research, 64*, 139–49.

van Dooren, T., Kirksey, E., and Münster, U. (2016). Multispecies studies: Cultivating arts of attentiveness. *Environmental Humanities, 8*(1), 1–23.

Varnajot, A., and Saarinen, J. (2021). "After glaciers?" Towards post-Arctic tourism. *Annals of Tourism Research, 91*, 103205.

Varnajot, A., and Saarinen, J. (2022). Emerging post-Arctic tourism in the age of Anthropocene: Case Finnish Lapland. *Scandinavian Journal of Hospitality and Tourism, 22*(4–5), 357–71.

Vilden, L. (2023). *Return: A Journey Back to Living Wild.* Harper One.

Viken, A, Höckert, E., & Grimwood, B. S. R (2021). Cultural sensitivity: Engaging difference in tourism, *Annals of Tourism Research, 89*, 103223.

Visit Finland (2023). Finnish everyman's rights – the right to roam & enjoy nature. Retrieved December 15, 2023, available at https://www.visitfinland.com/en/articles/finnish-everyman-rights-the-right-to-roam/.

Vlaslov, M. (2023). *Rewild, survive, thrive – How ancestral survival skills education reaffirms the relevance of friluftsliv in the Anthropocene.* Paper presented in the 31st Nordic Symposium on Tourism and Hospitality Research, Östersund, Sweden.

Vola, J. (2022). HOMUNCULUS Bearing Incorporeal Arcticulations. PhD Dissertation. Acta electronica Universitatis Lapponiensis 334. https://urn.fi/URN:ISBN:978-952-337-309-9.

West, S., Haider, J. L., Stålhammar, S., and Woroniecki, S. (2020). A relational turn for sustainability science? Relational thinking, leverage points, and transformations. *Ecosystems and People, 16*(1), 304–25.

Yudina, O., and Grimwood, B. S. R. (2016). Situating the wildlife spectacle: Ecofeminism, representation, and polar bear tourism. *Journal of Sustainable Tourism, 24*(5), 715–34.

8   A comparative advantage? Using situated comparison for collaborative ways of knowing in Greenlandic tourism

Carina Ren and Ulunnguaq Markussen

Introduction – Finding new grounds for Arctic comparison

Going back centuries, the Arctic has been compared with and valued against models of "the South." Most often, this way of seeing and acting upon the Arctic has not turned out to its advantage. Speaking of infrastructure, Exner-Pirot et al. (2017) explain how the Arctic has consequently been framed as "a global periphery, [...] in relation to, and as a poorer version of, the South: terrible internet connections, bad roads, no services" (Exner-Pirot et al., 2017, p. 2). In blunt comparison to more Southern societies, places and communities in the Arctic have been outlined as colder, wilder and voider antipodes (through what Ryall et al. (2010) refer to as "Arcticism") or even in some cases, as its inferior, distant and backwards relative in need of help to raise morality or living standards. To "fix" this, many solutions conceived elsewhere have been attempted implemented far North, most often with little or no success or even with grave repercussions.

In Greenland, this way of planning and developing "in comparison to 'the South'" has been most visible in the controversial and disputed so-called G50 and G60 development policies that aimed at centralizing, modernizing, and industrializing its society in the 1950s and 1960s following a Danish welfare state ideology. Subsequent development plans encompassed among others the building of new housing, schools, a fishing industry, and a new health care system, all of which were later criticized for transferring Danish or Western models one-to-one into a completely different and unprepared environment (Rud, 2017). In their critique, opponents of the Danish modernization plans have argued that imported solutions to modernize Greenland and its communities were unsuited because Greenland and Denmark are in fact *incomparable*.

As Greenland moves towards independence and seeks to secure a responsible and sustainable future development, this argued incomparability has led to outspoken demands and work to find "other others" besides Denmark to learn and develop from and new ways of implementing solutions beyond usual cookie-cutter approaches. This reflects broader calls, for instance within Arctic regionalism (Knecht, 2013), to replace old discourses and practices of geopolitical alliances, national identity, and postcolonial relationships as well as routes of development, trade, and collaboration with new partners. This demands that novel ways of thinking and learning be nurtured and has led to questions of how to learn from whom. One answer to this question is through comparison, learning and doing as – or in contrast to – other comparable societies, communities, or sectors.

For research, this entails revisiting and reflecting upon comparison in its many forms and to ponder what avenues for comparison may be moving forward. In this chapter, we explore and discuss the concept of comparison as a potential tool for collaborative ways of knowing in the Arctic. We zoom in on tourism which as a *field of study* has received little comparative attention (with notable exceptions in the series of Arctic tourism publications by Rantala et al., 2019; Müller et al., 2020 and Jóhannesson et al., 2022); although as a sector, many facets of comparison are being deployed and experimented with, as is shown in this chapter. We also argue that tourism is a productive field to see and explore the opportunities as well as caveats of comparison, as some marginalized positions are gaining a voice in the new Arctic, while others continue to be silenced.

In proceeding, we will first define comparison beyond a positivist knowledge regime, arguing for (at least) three modes of comparison. We unfold and illustrate these, first showing comparison as a "learning lens" *within research* that invokes or amplifies difference and sameness across places of tourism, before venturing into an approach defined as a *politics of comparison* (Gad, 2021), which explores what is and what is not compared or deemed suitable for comparison by actors on the ground. The chapter continues by proposing comparison not only as an epistemological tool but also as an ontological device, which enables the probing and deliberation of, in our case, what tourism is and what it *should or could be about*. Finally, the idea of "situated comparison" is proposed as a fruitful heuristic towards an inquiry of desirable Arctic tourism futures.

Comparison in Arctic tourism – how and why?

In this chapter, comparison is framed in three distinct ways. Firstly, comparison is understood as a research methodology in the way that researchers select, study, and compare destinations based on their own selection of various criteria. As within tourism studies more generally (Tribe and Airey, 2007) comparisons between or across destinations have rarely been used in Arctic tourism research (with the exception of quantitative benchmark studies). There are naturally exceptions, such as the work of Pashkevich et al. (2015) on Norwegian and Russian governance practices in Arctic cruises and the doctoral work of Stewart (2009) on community perceptions of tourists in three Arctic communities. Most often, however, destinations are researched through single case studies, whether local, regional, or national. Larger, more comprehensive studies of international regions, such as the European Arctic, have also been undertaken. However, comparative studies that seek to draw together or contrast tourism development across the Arctic have been rare up until today. In the following section, we exemplify and discuss the pros and cons of using comparison as a fruitful heuristic device in tourism learning and research.

A second way to understand and study comparison is through what Gad (2021) describes as the politics of comparison and which in the context of tourism refers to how Greenland compares itself, or is being compared by others, to other destinations. Although many of these categories sit uneasily, "Greenlandic political debate and policy formulation, but also scientific studies of Greenland, implicitly and explicitly compare Greenland with other Indigenous Peoples in the Arctic, with Nordic welfare states, with other post-colonial societies, with non-sovereign overseas territories and even at times with Danish municipalities" (our translation, p. 100). In this context and as we later show, comparison operates both as a way of learning from what others are or do, but also as a political and strategic proposition of who "we are" in comparison to others.

The last mode of comparison is ontological and proposes comparison as a way of "worlding," that is mundane, unfinished, and often fragile ways of imagining and enacting how other worlds – other "tourisms" – could be possible and how these are always already in the making as a process of becoming-with (Ren and Jóhannesson, 2018). As we show in the section on the ontological mode of comparison, such comparative practices are performative and as such also expressions of ontological politics (Mol, 1999), which ultimately according to Law and Urry (2004) seek to address "which realities might we try to enact?"

(p. 396) by deliberating on what should count as relevant, important, or valuable.

In each their way, these modes of comparison add to knowing Arctic tourism in new and productive ways. First, *methodologically* as a fruitful way to explore sameness and difference. Second, *strategically* to build new (or cut old) models, relations, and conversations and lastly, *ontologically* by enacting new ways of being with(out) others. Regardless of which mode of comparison we draw on in our research, it is important to stress that none are innocent and that all operate far beyond a positivist regime stipulating neutral or value-free engagement. By selecting certain rather than other destinations for comparison, some views or voices disappear or are muted. However, even taking this into consideration, there is still value in uncovering and comparing "other others" in Arctic tourism, as we shall now see.

Comparison as "learning lens" – differences and sameness

Conducting research on the ground through fieldwork is time-consuming and expensive; the Arctic, where distances, lack of infrastructure and sparse population render travels and longer stays within communities difficult and costly, is no exception. Perhaps this is the simple or practical explanation for why most Arctic tourism research publications have up until recently been based on single case studies. It is simply too resource-demanding to conduct cross-case analysis, not to mention multi-site ethnographies in Arctic tourism research. Edited volumes on Arctic tourism have sought to remedy this by compiling studies from across the Arctic on indigeneity (Viken and Müller, 2017), governance and policy (Maher et al., 2011; Müller et al., 2013) or destination development (Viken and Granås, 2014). Nevertheless, comparison as a research methodology is underdeveloped.

This seems, however, to change due to funding schemes by intergovernmental bodies such as NordForsk and the European Commission allow larger pan-Arctic (or at least Nordic Arctic) consortia to be built for tourism research and development. Often, these allow for or even require cross-case synthesis as in many EU research projects or cross-destination product development, as in the Destination Arctic Europe. A noteworthy illustration of such work are the three reports commissioned by the Nordic Council of Ministers on seasonality (Rantala et al., 2019), urbanization (Müller et al., 2020) and the impacts of COVID (Jóhannesson et al., 2022) in Arctic tourism. In projects such as these, international teams of researchers and practitioners find themselves working together across vast distances around common themes and challenges, that often take on completely different meanings and expressions in often variegated contexts.

An example of this is ARCTISEN, a project funded by the EU Northern Periphery Arctic program aimed at developing culturally sensitive tourism in Finnish, Swedish, and Norwegian Sapmi and Greenland. During the project, researchers and practitioners worked around issues and controversies pertaining to indigenous tourism, certification and labelling, commercialization of culture and digital storytelling. Within a Norwegian, Swedish and Norwegian context, much research had already addressed some of these issues at a national level or across Sapmi (spanning across Norway, Sweden and Finland, and Russia). However, in the introduction of and later comparison to a new emerging "Other" in Arctic tourism, namely Greenland, some of these "well-rehearsed" issues took on a different meaning by way of showing similarities and differences, that not only "reflected" well-rehearsed views and relations but also diffracted and challenged them.

One instance is the way of using indigenous markers in tourism, such as the common use of the Gákti attire in Sami tourism while taking tourists for reindeer sledge rides or Lavvu tent visits. During a trip to Sisimiut and Nuuk in Greenland, Sami tourism entrepreneurs were invited on a backcountry tour with fellow Greenlandic operators to prepare, cook and eat birds. After their return to the town, an entrepreneur mentioned his surprise at how the Greenlanders had not worn any "Greenlandic" attire during the trip, "only Fjällräven (trek pants) and a sweater", as he noted. What had struck him was how the whole experience had felt very "everyday like" but still felt authentic and profoundly Greenlandic to him even though indigenous markers had not been displayed. This left him to reflect on whether he could also rethink, tone down or even omit Sami symbols and markers in his product and still be able to offer a perceived authentic experience to his guests.

Comparison across Arctic destinations offers new ways to discern sameness and differences within destinations. As seen in ARCTISEN, encountering and comparing destinations to "new others" can be productive for researchers as well as for practitioners as it "lifts" issues and practices into new contexts, bringing forth new ways of relating and reflecting. Comparison serves as a mirror to showcase similarities (such as being Arctic, indigenous and nature-based destinations) and differences (such as catering for different clienteles, offering tourism products based on different material cultures or living with different colonialism pasts and presents). Also, as seen in the example from above, the comparative encounter may work as a kaleidoscope, rather than a mirror, offering new ways of approaching and seeing long-standing truths (such as the necessity to wear indigenous attire in tourism encounters), thus diffracting, rather than reflecting what is already known.

The politics of comparison – comparing what with whom?

Another way to work with comparison is through the empirical exploration of comparisons "on the ground" through what Gad (2021) has termed the politics of comparison, using the example of Greenland and how the nation compares itself to others in its way to self-determination. According to Gad, wider and more drastic geopolitical transformations in the Arctic have necessitated a better understanding of how Greenland is imagining itself towards independence. While full independency might not be the end goal elsewhere in the Arctic, this analytical lens is relevant to apply to cases, where nations, territories and communities currently imagine and create new, meaningful ways of developing beyond those of an often Southern or distant state.

A productive way to explore local politics of comparison is to look at the way actors, in this case Greenland, select "comparative companions" in different contexts, such as diplomacy, mining, fisheries and tourism. Tourism is especially interesting seeing its connections to nation-building. In his work, Franklin (2003) has pointed to the close connections between modern tourism and the forging of a national identity, he points to how citizens of the nation-state performed citizenship in the late 1900s through "nation-state tourism" to newly identified important national sights/sites, he suggests viewing tourism as a tool for ordering modernity and the nation.

Ren and Abildgaard (2021) build on this work to explore the current and overlapping nation (state) building and "destinization" (Granås, 2018) in Greenland, where tourism is currently experiencing growing political and societal interest and investments, for instance in the shape of two new transatlantic airports set to open in Nuuk in 2024 and in Ilulissat in 2025. Looking at the recent airport projects and their connected political discourses as well as campaigns such as "Nunarput Nuan," which urged domestic travellers to "know their country" during and after COVID, authors identify the ongoing development of national sites/sights. They argue that Greenland slowly builds itself as an attractive and recognizable (desti)nation through marketing initiatives and funding that shape and enable desirable domestic travel practices. Building the (desti)nation not only happens from within but also in comparison to other neighbouring destinations such as Iceland, as we shall now see.

Ren and Jóhannesson (2023) explore Greenland's comparative (desti) nation-building as they look at ways in which Greenlandic tourism actors compare Greenlandic tourism development and Greenland as a destination similar or in contrast to that of Iceland. Authors show how Iceland and Greenland are deemed comparable by tourism actors in regard to their structural challenges, but also – on a more positive note – as both being part of a new, attractive North Atlantic region for present and future tourists: "Through the comparison of sameness, Greenland and Iceland are brought closer together within and into a new North Atlantic region, where things can be learnt from one another (but mostly from Iceland to Greenland) based on common challenges and advantages" (Ren and Jóhannesson, 2023, p. 5). In this comparison, we also see how Iceland, while deemed comparable or similar in some regards, is sometimes seen as "ahead" in Greenland.

In other instances, actors address differences rather than comparability or sameness, pointing for instance at Greenland's insular structure and massive size that create very specific challenges for tourism development that are deemed incomparable to those in Iceland. Contrasts made to the rapid tourism development and massive number of tourists in Iceland also made "Greenland stands out as the alternative, sustainable (and less travelled) choice on the North Atlantic or adventure tourism scene." In this perspective, Iceland becomes a trope for what Greenland *did not* wish to develop into. For tourism actors, comparison helps to make sense of regional and global positioning and offering them an occasion to delimit Greenlandic challenges and strengths. Thus, analytically, "politics of comparison serve as an epistemological tool to explore how stakeholders imagine, discuss, prepare and plan for a Greenlandic tourism future" (Ren and Jóhannesson, 2023, p. 2).

Politics of incomparability? What tourism actors overlook

The exploration of the politics of comparison of Arctic destinations – that is with what, with whom and how destinations and tourism actors compare themselves – not only functions as a way to identify emerging comparative companions in a new Arctic tourism landscape but may also help shed light on what is *not* identified and addressed as suitable, relevant, or strategic to compare. In other words, what fails to be seen or recognized as comparable in these comparisons? In her doctoral work in East Greenland, in which she explores the overlooked internal cultural consequences and downsides of Greenlandic nation-building, Markussen (2023, p. 19) notes that: "The notion that Greenlanders are a homogeneous people with common cultural identity, history and language, creates challenges in relationships to include all citizens in Greenlandic society as equal and active citizens" (our translation).

As Markussen continues, a West Greenland hegemony in national, media and municipal domains means a continuation of "an unacknowledged national homogenization manifested through language politics, uneven power relations and inequalities between West Greenlanders and East Greenlanders" (Markussen, 2023, p. 19, our translation). In the process of building a "whole" Greenland catering to the dominant discourse of independence, internal heterogeneity such as cultural differences and language barriers between West and East Greenland become overlooked. As we shall see, this is also the case for tourism.

In their study of tourism development in Tasiilaq in East Greenland, Markussen and Ren (2024) explore the barriers and lack of access within areas such as funding, guidance and education identified by local tourism entrepreneurs. In bringing forward discriminatory and exclusionary practices in East Greenland they demonstrate how "a national wish to develop itself towards *one* Greenlandic destination overlooks the particularities, challenges and possibilities of East Greenland." As Greenland compares itself to new regional or global "others" - most predominantly Iceland, the Nordic Arctic and increasingly the Faeroe Islands, internal differences, for instance between Western and Eastern indigenous cultures and languages are overshadowed or neglected, as are the subsequent lack of representation and equal opportunities within a system based on Western Greenlandic and Danish languages and norms. This bears resemblance to debates and lack of internal reconciliation in a Sami context, where some Sami groups have felt overshadowed by more dominant and more conspicuous Sami groups both within a broader context of nation building (for lack of a better word) and within tourism. The question is how we may become more aware of and better prepare for preventing such injustices by studying and learning from the politics of comparison in Arctic tourism.

Comparison as ontological tool for tourism world making

Having now established two productive ways of researching *by comparison* and researching *politics of comparisons*, we now turn to the performative capacities of comparing. This ontological mode of comparison looks at how comparison is not only a passive tool to reflect, contrast or juxtapose fix(ed) destinations but rather "has to do with what kind of tourism should or could be created, made accessible and attractive; what kind of stories of and about tourism in a given destination are enacted" (Ren and Jóhannesson, 2013, p. 4). As a force or an ordering (Franklin, 2004), comparison enacts things that are in motion and do not rest still – turbulent, potential, and emerging tourism realities. In their analysis of the comparison between Iceland and Greenland, Ren and Jóhannsson (2023) note how Iceland is not only used as a benchmark, but also as a "deliberative other" which actors use to bring forward contradictory trajectories of tourism development and contrasting views on the values and meaning of tourism development between the two destinations. In this way of comparing, "stakeholders no longer deliberate around the question of 'who Greenland compares itself to and how' but rather 'what kinds of "tourisms" are compared(able?) and valued(able?)?' Should tourism be framed as an economic or political tool? Should tourism policy be growth-oriented or value-based in the future development of tourism in Greenland?" (Ren and Jóhannsson 2023, pp. 6–7).

This way of imagining new ways of developing and valuing tourism through ontological comparison is retrieved in Wright's 2017 doctoral dissertation on Sami tourism, where a study trip to New Zealand allowed Sami tourism entrepreneurs not only to "compare" tourism practices but rather to generate new insights through moments of productive friction, hereby opening for more place-based and inclusive ways to define and develop indigenous tourism in a Sami context. Wright demonstrates how it gradually becomes clearer for travellers during their journey to New Zealand that the development of Sami tourism will not only require clearer protection and demarcation of the "real" Sami, but rather a strengthening of cultural resources, knowledge, and expertise.

In the second part of her dissertation, Wright illustrates how this could be done somewhat surprisingly by following Sea Sami women in a wide range of everyday practices that at first glance are about cooking and food. By offering yet another ontological comparison of "Saminess" (in the kitchen and in tourism) Wright shows that despite clear Sami "markers," these everyday practices unfold as Sami world-making through knowledge about and care for nature and place. It is argued that the women's knowledge, characterized by entangled relationships between humans and more-than-humans, creates new stories and conversations about the Sami which, she argues, may be used in a tourism context to expand the repertoire of cultural expressions in tourism and counter a simplification of Saminess. By linking seemingly disconnected life worlds, Wright firstly shows that tourism contains the opportunity to challenge and co-create identity in complex configurations through the complex socio-material network in the work of creating Sami cultural awareness and knowledge. Secondly, she shows that new narratives and world-creating practices between everyday life, culture and market can interfere in tourism in caring and response-able ways.

Ontological comparison, in which new worlds are enacted rather than merely reflected or described in research, links to the question posed by Law and Urry (2004) of "which realities might we try to enact?" (p. 396). For tourism, this means that comparison "shapes and disrupts tourism realities, moving beyond Euclidean location and opening new horizons to discuss and reflect on tourism's value and how it may come to matter" (Ren and Jóhannesson, 2023, p. 6). In ontological comparison, research is also an active co-producer of tourism realities in the way of framing and juxtaposing some, rather than other destinations, tourism actors or tourism landscapes in specific ways. This is illustrated by Chimirri and Ren (2022), who show the entanglements of tourism wording by way of comparing life maps drawn by tourism entrepreneurs in East Greenland. The life maps were used to collaboratively explore relations in tourism in other ways than through conversation. In the article, two maps are shown drawn by two tour operators (Figure 8.1). As close collaborators, their maps should ideally showcase a similar tourism landscape but were surprisingly different from each other. One drew a broken mirror to illustrate what he explained as a fragmented tourism landscape, while the other displayed a well-managed business environment of multiple actors resembling a tourism management textbook.

Discussing the drawing, the first actor elaborated on his "broken" life map, seeing local collaboration as damaged. Yet, the glue shows that there is still a possibility to fix it, but as he adds, "the cap is still on. That means that something prevents it from working [...] there are still some connecting points, not a lot, but we do work with quite a lot of people." Thus, he points to the awaiting difficult but necessary steps of mending pieces, illustrated by the still-connected mirror pieces. In contrast to the first actor, the second gives the impression of a smooth situation, depicting structure and order. While he talks of also facing challenges during the interview, he is motivated to develop his business and the local community, which he illustrates through plans of expanding and engaging with even more local suppliers.

Source: Chimirri and Ren, 2022.

Figure 8.1   Two life map drawings

By comparing the two maps, authors (Chimirri and Ren, 2022, p. 4) argue that:

> At first sight, the life maps show despair and frustration on one side, and on the other, an organised, well-structured business. Two different worlds, side by side. By looking closer and tying additional conversations and contexts to the life maps, we discover new details and new concerns. What unites the tourism stories conveyed through the life mapping conversations is the ongoing, steady work with tourism, the community, national actors, funding instruments and political ideas of "good projects." In between frustrations and challenging surroundings, hopes and ideas, tourism actors run their businesses, slowly working sometimes back, sometimes forward in their work. In these maps and talks, tourism is a part of an everyday, of getting by, feeling left out, but also of being together. The narratives are rooted neither solely in despair nor in the certain belief in progress. Rather, they are concrete examples for response-ability in frustrating, collaborative, exciting, mundane situations. Methodologically, the life map approach shows that when looking and listening more closely, stories of tourism worlding emerge.

Through the comparison and contrast of a tourism landscape multiple (Mol, 2002), new ways of enacting, living with and imagining tourism beyond a mere economic activity emerge.

Who to be like? Situated comparison in Arctic tourism

Tourism research in the Arctic is gradually adjusting to research funding realities that provide novel opportunities to share knowledge and insights across distances and destinations, that have previously been addressed and understood singularly. This has offered new possibilities to build synergies, cross-case learning and capacity through research and for the benefit of often small destinations and tourism actors. As displayed, this can take place through comparison, exploring "who to be like" and how to develop accordingly in ways that expand beyond, and are more meaningful than, colonial or cookie-cutter models of the past.

This way of working comparatively in larger cross-cutting projects begs further tailoring and reflexivity to advance the development of a methodological and analytical toolbox for comparisons. Only in such a way will comparison be able to withstand reductionist survey designs and statistical analysis. This, we argue, will enable researchers to provide relevant and valuable input to theory as well as practice, hence enriching the broader field of Arctic tourism as well as the single destinations. So how and in what way does comparison become an advantage in imagining, planning and developing a sustainable Arctic future? This chapter sought to sketch out a few initial trajectories.

By questioning what and how to compare, it pointed to comparison as a heuristic tool for researchers, as first demonstrated, but also as the destination's own political and strategic tool of aligning with some, rather than other "Others." This strategic re-purposing of comparison also leads to reflecting on a third "ontological" mode of comparison, which allows actors to speculate and deliberate around new possible tourism future. These diverse understandings and applications of comparison demand us to reflect on the performativity of comparison as methodological and analytical tools as they foreground certain things while shadowing others. This demands us to navigate more carefully and sensitively in comparing, while also enabling us to discover nuances and overlooked perspectives, as in the consequences for East Greenland of the hegemonic narrative of "one Greenland" in recent nation-building attempts.

In the case of Greenland introduced in this chapter, comparison means asking whether and how Greenland as an emerging destination could or should be "like" a Nordic destination by emphasizing things such as safety and sustainability, or "like" an Indigenous or Inuit destination foregrounding a unique and authentic identity and material culture. Or should Greenland rather be marketed as an adventure destination competing on the global market or an Arctic or perhaps as a North-Atlantic destination, collaborating and competing with Iceland and Faroe Islands destinations? Regardless of what is selected by those marketing (and researching) the destination, making Greenland – and other Arctic destinations – comparable entails adapting and shaping places and their narratives.

The different modes of comparison in Arctic tourism matter in multiple ways and, as argued, there are many ways to think about and deploy comparison in Arctic tourism research. Whether as a methodology to explore sameness and difference across destinations, as an epistemology to learn how destinations or destination actors compare and make themselves comparable between themselves or as an ontology enabling actors to envision new destination realities. The multi-modality of comparison allows researchers, destinations and other tourism actors to reflect about and learn from other destinations and to speculate about tourism realities by also comparing tourism to other ways of worlding.

Moving forward, the development of comparative research methodologies and using comparison as a meeting ground for lived realities in and around tourism may offer ways to build knowledge and foster learning within and across Arctic destinations. For researchers, comparison may also serve as a way to see and make sense of tourism as something that is much more than just an industry (Higgins-Desbiolles, 2006; Ren and Chimirri, 2018). What connects these modes of comparison is how they are all situated within a place-based, Arctic setting and take their departure in Arctic realities and desirable futures. By doing so, situated comparison can offer locally relevant and meaningful avenues by which to develop communities and destinations for the future.

References

Chimirri, D., & Ren, C. (2022). Tourism worlding: Collective becoming in East Greenland. *Polar Record*, *58*, e33.

Exner-Pirot, H., Heininen, L., and Plouffe, J. (2017). Introduction. Change and Innovation in the Arctic. In L. Heininen, H. Exner-Pirot and J. Plouffe (Eds.), *Arctic Yearbook* 2017, 11–18. Northern Research Forum.

Franklin, A. (2003) *Tourism: An Introduction*. Sage.

Franklin, A. (2004). Tourism as an ordering: Towards a new ontology of tourism. *Tourist Studies*, *4*(3), 277–301.

Gad, U. P. (2021). Kan Grønland være andet end arktisk? Postkolonial sammenligningspolitik som forskningsdagsorden. *Økonomi & Politik*, *2021*(2), 99–114.

Granås, B. (2018). Destinizing Finnmark: Place making through dogsledding. *Annals of Tourism Research*, *72*, 48–57.

Higgins-Desbiolles, F. (2006). More than an "industry": The forgotten power of tourism as a social force. *Tourism Management*, *27*(6), 1192–1208.

Jóhannesson, G. Þ., Welling, J., Müller, D. K., Lundmark, L., Nilsson, R., de la Barre, S., Granås, B., Kvidal-Rovik, T., Rantala, O., Tervo-Kankare, K., and Maher, P. (2022). *Arctic Tourism in Times of Change: Uncertain Futures – From Overtourism to Re-starting Tourism*. Nordic Council of Ministers.

Knecht, S. (2013). Arctic regionalism in theory and practice: From cooperation to integration? *Arctic Yearbook, 2013*. https://arcticyearbook.com/images/yearbook/2013/Scholarly_Papers/8.KNECHT.pdf.

Law, J., and Urry, J. (2004). Enacting the social. *Economy and Society*, *33*(3), 390–410.

Maher, P. T., Stewart, E., and Lück, M. (Eds.) (2011). *Polar Tourism: Human, Environmental and Governance Dimensions*. Cognizant Communication Corporation.

Markussen, U. (2023) Bagsiden af nation-building: Om spændinger mellem lokal og national empowerment. *Social kritik* #169.

Markussen, U. & C. Ren (2024) A just destination? Exploring local hopes, fears, and power asymmetries in East Greenlandic (Tunu) tourism development. *Études Inuit Studies* (in print).

Mol, A. (1999). Ontological politics. A word and some questions. *The Sociological Review*, *47*(1_suppl), 74–89.

Mol, A. (2002). *The Body Multiple: Ontology in Medical Practice*. Duke University Press.

Müller, D. K., Carson, D. A., de la Barre, S., Granås, B., Jóhannesson, G. T., Øyen, G., Rantala, O., Saarinen, J., Salmela, T., Tervo-Kankare, K., and Welling, J. (2020). *Arctic Tourism in Times of Change: Dimensions of Urban Tourism*. Nordic Council of Ministers.

Müller D. K., Lundmark, L., and Lemelin, R. H. (Eds.) (2013). *New Issues in Polar Tourism: Communities, Environments, Politics*. Springer.

Pashkevich, A., Dawson, J., and Stewart, E. J. (2015). Governance of expedition cruise ship tourism in the Arctic: A comparison of the Canadian and Russian Arctic. *Tourism in Marine Environments, 10*(3–4), 225–40.

Rantala, O., de la Barre, S., Granås, B., Jóhannesson, G. Þ., Müller, D. K., Saarinen, J., Tervo-Kankare, K., Maher, P. T., and Niskala, M. (2019). *Arctic Tourism in Times of Change: Seasonality.* Nordic Council of Ministers.

Ren, C., and Abildgaard, M. S. (2021). Greenlandic independence and tourism futures: Exploring modern and ethnic logics. In D, Hall (Ed.), *Tourism, Climate Change and a Geopolitics of Arctic Development: The Critical Case of* Greenland, 178–86. CABI.

Ren, C. B., and Chimirri, D. (2018). *Arctic Tourism: More than an Industry?* The Arctic Institute. https://www.thearcticinstitute.org/arctic-tourism-industry/.

Ren, C., and Jóhannesson, G. T. (2018). Collaborative becoming: Exploring tourism knowledge collectives. In C. Ren, G. T. Jóhannesson and R. van der Duim (Eds.), *Co-Creating Tourism Research. Towards Collaborative Ways of Knowing,* 24–38. Routledge.

Ren, C., and Jóhannesson, G. T. (2023). To be or not to be like Iceland? (Ontological) Politics of comparison in Greenlandic tourism development. *Polar Record, 59*, e9.

Ryall, A., Schimanski, J., and Wærp, H.H, (Eds.) (2010). *Arctic Discourses.* Cambridge Scholars.

Rud, S. (2017). Toward a postcolonial Greenland: Culture, identity, and colonial legacy. In S. Rud (Ed.), *Colonialism in Greenland: Tradition, Governance and Legacy,* 119–44. Springer.

Stewart, E. J. (2009). *Comparing Resident Attitudes toward Tourism: Community-based Cases from Arctic Canada.* PhD-thesis. University of Calgary.

Tribe, J., and Airey, D. (2007). A review of tourism research. In J. Tribe and D. Airey (Eds.), *Developments in Tourism Research,* 3–14. Routledge.

Viken, A., and Granås, B. (Eds.) (2014). *Tourism Destination Development: Turns and Tactics.* Ashgate.

Viken, A., and Müller, D.K. (Eds.) (2017). *Tourism and Indigeneity in the Arctic.* Channel View.

Wright, R. J. (2017). *"Nå er vi blitt så trygg i oss selv at vi kan selge oss til turister" Samisk turisme mellom kommersielle interesser, lokal kunnskap og verdensskapende praksiser.* PhD-thesis. UiT.

9 Framing by opening up: Approaching matters of concern in nature-based tourism

Brynhild Granås, Mats J. Hoel and June Anthonsen Røsbø

Introduction

As inhabitants of northern Norway, we witness a growing use of northern landscapes for the production of commercial nature experiences. This is the region in Norway that recently has experienced the strongest growth in nature-based tourism (Stensland et al., 2018; NHO, 2018). Outdoor activities offered to paying customers are numerous and include hiking, climbing, snowmobiling, skiing, and much more. Like in the rest of the Nordic Arctic, this tourism is unevenly distributed in time and space (Jóhannesson et al., 2022, p.12). Accordingly, people may experience overcrowding in Lofoten, while the tourism growth is felt less in western Finnmark throughout all seasons. Moreover, and inspired by traditions, new technologies, and outdoor trends, tourists are offered access to ever more – and more diverse – nature experiences.

All these are changes that we ourselves experience when we go hiking, skiing, berry picking, and more. In the Nordic Arctic, outdoor recreation is referred to as *friluftsliv* (free/open air life) (Ween and Abram, 2012). In Norway, the concept indicates a national identity that assesses Norway as a nation of outdoor people (Breivik, 1978; Goksøyr, 1994; Gurholt, 2008). As commercial nature experiences are produced, they interweave with friluftsliv as well as convoluted traditional and new landscape practices that prevail in Norwegian landscapes. *Allemannsretten* (everyone's right), meaning people's right in the Nordic north to roam the outfields of land owned by others, is embedded in the Outdoor Recreation Act (*Friluftsloven*) of 1957. Everyone's right is the treasured cultural twin that facilitates Norwegian *friluftsliv* in accordance with the egalitarian democratic principles that this tradition entails (Gurholt, 2008). Notably, the modern roaming right from 1957 accommodates mobile lives and is neither for locals nor Norwegians only. More so, any visitor can use the right, and so can any guide or entrepreneur who would like to make a living by selling nature experiences in Norway. Thus, the rivers and mountains we ourselves cross in our outdoor lives and the infrastructure we make use of are the same as those of vacationists, nature guides, and paying customers. So are the floras, faunas, and people we encounter along the way.

When in the outdoors, who or what is touristic is not always easy to assess – when is a skier a tourist? Moreover, the tourist identity may lose some of its significance in nature encounters, like for reindeer who are disturbed by skiers, or villagers who are annoyed by hikers who cross their gardens or infields. Thus, the concept "tourism" seldom mirrors opaque on-ground realities. Neither does the concept "nature." More so, enactments of nature-based tourism are culturally and materially saturated at the same time. Different practices that come together in landscapes are full of all kinds of lives, histories, and meanings, and thus imply situations where the realms indicated by binary distinctions like nature – culture or local – tourist come together.

Altogether, nature-based tourism is imbued with ambiguities that tell of tourism as deeply intertwined in the development of northern places. It is commonly acknowledged that tourism affects places, and vice versa. The question of how the two entangle, however, denotes grey zones of world-making that, for good and for bad, condition the development of tourism businesses as well as communities. Our research on commercial nature guiding in Lofoten and western Finnmark tells of mixtures of footloose and place-committed small-scale entrepreneurs and guides that engage there. When they meet up in northern places, they are involved in practices that construct tourism economies and transform places from below. While doing so, they take part in and make use of the "material and cultural relationships" of globalization, and the "places and people, distant and nearby" to which they are connected (Clifford, 2013, p. 6). Thus, and as with the places where they operate, the products they sell become part of a wider geography and history than the here and now of a nature experience tell of (cf. Massey, 1994, 2005).

When considering the sustainability of nature-based tourism and place development in the Arctic, all the encounters, connections, and relations denoted above are significant. With the entwined relation between tourism and place as a point of departure, this chapter suggests that researchers attend to nature-based tourism as an open relational historical-geographical phenomenon. Methodologically, we argue for studying tourism practices up-close and in place, to tap into the relational dynamics of the commercial nature experiences that are enacted there, including relations to the different materialities and more than human living involved. A constituent aspect of the approach is historical-geographical and acknowledges commercial nature experiences as contingent on where and when they are enacted. Altogether, we are inspired by the idea of framing research by opening up instead of closing down, as outlined by Krzywoszynska (2023, p. 397) and Stirling (2008). The logics of the approach are in line with the idea of seeing nature-based tourism as a dynamic and porous formation (Franklin and Crang, 2001; Huijbens and Müller, 2022). Based on experiences from northern Norway, we specify and explore methodological implications of such logics, and demonstrate the matters of concern they may bring into focus in power-relevant research on Arctic tourism, such as relations of care for people, places, and ecologies.

We start the chapter by presenting our methodological argument in more detail. Then, and assisted by the periphery concept, we outline some of the historical-geographical relations that become significant in the nature-based tourism we study. Further, we present empirical examples from ongoing ethnographic studies in Lofoten and Western Finnmark respectively, to demonstrate the value of the approach we suggest. Finally, we discuss some of the implications that the open framing of nature-based tourism may have for research in the Arctic in the time to come.

Opening up and getting close to address matters of concern

Our way of reasoning relates to the recent critique from tourism scholars towards "the narrow focus on capitalist tourism systems" (Rantala et al., 2024, p. 63) and towards approaches that have made tourism "fetishized as a thing, a product, a behaviour" (Franklin and Crang, 2001, p. 6). Our experiences tell of enigmas found at the fringes of what is institutionally and policy-wise regarded as nature-based tourism, based on frames that acknowledge the close relation between tourism and place but nevertheless attend to tourism as a closed phenomenon. Such experiences encourage us to pursue ideas that help us unpack tourism's contingent relations to place processes and ecologies. Krzywoszynska's conceptualization of soils as relational "dynamic assemblages between different materials and organisms (including humans), which co-constitute one another" (Krzywoszynska, 2023, p. 397), inspires us to consider nature-based tourism along related lines and as an open relational phenomenon in place. Krzywoszynska's conceptualization opens up soil and thus helps her in her aim to illuminate "what matters' within soil assemblages (Krzywoszynska, 2023, p. 398) and "how to care for the needs of soil" (ibid, p. 397). Similarly, we open up nature-based tourism with the aim of understanding better what is at stake within relations where nature experiences are created. This way, and as Krzywoszynska puts it with reference to Latour (2004), we transform "matters of fact" within nature-based tourism into "matters of concern."

Further, and based on Anna L. Tsing's assemblage thinking (2015), we consider the creation of nature experiences as an outcome of relations that assemble in place. When experiences are produced within place assemblages, guides, paying customers, and other people involved are joined by more than humans, such as snow, plants, reindeer, cell phones, and more. We take interest in what is at stake – for whom and for what – within the relations of the assemblage where experiences are produced, instead of pursuing all those and that involved as the stakeholders of tourism (Mitchell et al,. 1997; Starik, 1995; Choi and Wang, 2009; Kaltenborn and Linell, 2019; Tallberg et al., 2022). Who or what is involved in the production of nature experiences is an empirical question, and so is the stakeholder-related question of who or what affects who or what. Accordingly, power relations, relations of control, and subject and object positions are shifting within processes where commercial nature experiences come to life.

When such experiences are practiced, the many involved connect to times and places that tell of ideas and meanings that become part of experiences while remaking places at the same time (Massey, 1994, 2005; Clifford, 2013). Nature-based tourism implies that different values that come with for example local traditions for nature use, new outdoor trends, a national outdoor recreation culture, or wilderness perceptions of landscapes, intersect in place (Massey, 2005), based on the humans and more than humans that are present there, and the times and places they relate the place and the nature experience to. Similarly, different nature cosmologies and ethical approaches to interactions with other livelihoods and lives are brought together. As an ecological, moral, and political historical configuration, places are where different lives, ways of life, and interests meet and are negotiated (Massey, 2005). One example would be when the female reindeer with calves encounter skiers who are moved by their presence and venture too close to take their picture. Another would be when farmers feel their livelihood is disrespected by summer hikers who cross their infields on their way into the mountains. Altogether, nature-based tourism is marked by constitutive encounters and productive frictions (Tsing, 2005) that may spur innovation, learning, and moral growth as well as situations of regret, conflict, and loss.

As Stirling (2008) as well as Krzywoszynska (2023) emphasize, a critical element in opening up concerns bringing new voices and marginalized perspectives in. This highlighting reflects Donna Haraway's argument that "It matters what stories tell stories; it matters whose stories tell stories" (Haraway, 2019, p. 570). Opening up is also a heuristic analytic move that involves 'exploring previously ignored attachments or conceptualizations' (Krzywoszynska, 2023, p. 398). Further, the open framing that comes with a relational emphasis acknowledges tourism as ontologically messy (Ren et al., 2021, p. 1), and requires researchers to "stay with the trouble" (Haraway, 2016; Rantala et al., 2023, p. 8). This includes enduring the uncomfortable feeling that may come with sticking to an anti-reductive approach that offers no comforting numbers. At the same time, the open framing is where science matters through the attendance given to matters of concern (Latour, 2004), and to matter as "simultaneously fluid and solid" (Haraway, 2019, p. 120).

Epistemologically, framing by opening up implies addressing the wider ranges of relations that can unveil matters of concern. To enable such observations, researchers must attend to encounters, attendances, and interactions, and the relations they tell of. This altogether calls for not limiting oneself methodologically (Vannini, 2015, pp. 318–319) and for embracing proximity (Rantala et al., 2023). When relations and concerns are identified in specific places, research findings can be of general interest and have local value. Still, the dynamics of a specific assemblage that produces nature experiences are ungeneralizable.

Rather, commercial nature experiences are historically, geographically, and materially contingent outcomes of encounters in place. Our attentiveness to where and when tourism is practiced is reflected in the chapter's attendance to the centre-periphery relation and to the juridical-cultural allemannsretten in research on tourism in northern Norway. This does not delimit the relevance of our argument to research in areas that are enacted as peripheries or areas where allemannsretten prevails. More so, we address the significance of history and geography in tourism development, as denoted by allemannsretten as well as by the relational geography within which the places we study are identified as peripheries.

With concerns for the climate- and nature crisis and with the future of Arctic places as ecological, moral, and political configurations at stake, framing nature-based tourism by opening up implies an epistemology of getting close as well as an axiology of addressing matters of concern in tourism development, as empirical examples will demonstrate. The examples are taken from ethnographic fieldworks where the researcher's corporeal presence in landscapes establishes a decisive proximity that comes with "staying geographically near" and affectively close (Rantala et al., 2023, p. 6). There, relations are noticed, and meanings, values, and concerns of those and that involved are sensed, in processes where tourism manifests in place and becomes part of historical-geographical transformations there.

Centre–periphery relations in nature-based tourism of the historical-geographical north

Northern Norway, which is located as far away from the capital of Norway as one gets, makes up around 35% of the nation's land but holds only a little over 9% of its population. With its "few people and much nature," northern Norway has developed within center–periphery relations all throughout modernity (Müller and Viken, 2017; Granås and Mathisen, 2022), meaning that the region has been denoted as the periphery of others, by others, within a geography of asymmetrical power relations. National and international interested parties have practiced northern natures as capitalist-economic resources within fisheries, fish farming, and extractive industries. Such relational geographical enactments continue in these times of climate crisis, as the region is exposed to industrial green transition in terms of wind power plants and other land-intensive forms of production. When considering the lack of control with the unpredictable tourism flows towards the north (cf. Massey, 1994, pp. 149–150), and bearing in mind that visitors and entrepreneurs located elsewhere value northern places as recreation areas, playgrounds, and sources of income (Viken 2023, p. 217), tourism adds further layers to the practicing of northern places as peripheries.

The low inhabitant numbers of northern Norway's cities and towns, and the distances between villages and settlements, make space for what in a European context are relatively extensive landscapes on and off the coast with little or no permanent settlements. On maps, in photos, and through art and media, representations of landscapes that seem more or less "untouched by humans" have spread universal wilderness perceptions (Tsing 2005, p. 100) of the area for centuries (Hastrup, 2009; Huijbens and Benediktsson, 2009). Today, tourism marketing frames northern landscapes along similar lines and as fit for the contemplative and playful engagements that nature-based tourism can offer. At the same time, such representations smooth the way for continued enactments of northern landscapes as suitable for extractive industries (Granås, 2018; Herva et al., 2020; Granås and Mathisen, 2022).

Landscape representations, which make up what Olwig (2019) calls "abstract landscapes." are nevertheless reductive and do not mirror the compound realities of the "practiced landscapes" (Olwig, 2019). Northern landscapes have been practiced by humans for thousands of years, since after the last glacial period. Premodern traditional outdoor practices still prevail in landscapes where inhabitants continue to make a living and a life through hunting, gathering, fishing, farming, reindeer herding, and the like. More so, many inhabitants, be they ethnically rooted in the Norwegian, Kven/Norwegian-Finnish, or indigenous Sami culture which have made up the multi-ethnic landscapes of the region for centuries, connect to the friluftsliv tradition and enjoy the outdoors for recreational purposes as part of their everyday lives. Among them are inhabitants who bring northern nature experiences to the marketplace.

While landscape imaginaries make northern Norway comprehensible and interesting for tourists, the region is made accessible in highly practical terms. For different historical reasons and with varying emphasis, the Norwegian state has pursued rural development ideas to ensure continued settlements in the north from early on. Within the neoliberal paradigm, rural development policies have nevertheless been weakened, and deregulations, as well as centralization processes, have entangled places in competitive networks of a global range (Harvey, 1989; Hall, 2001). During the last decades, the north has been marked by out migration, aging populations, and economic recession. Still, the transport- and welfare infrastructure of the Norwegian welfare state continue to provide tourists access to northern Norway. Adding to this, the moderate sub-Arctic climate makes stays here endurable for more people. Varied physical topographies along the extensive coastline accommodate diverse activities for customers in nature-based tourism with different preferences, skills, and desires. Conditioned by allemannsretten, the northern periphery is indeed up for grabs in tourism development.

Touristic enactments of northern places as peripheries unfold within asymmetrical relations and are related to colonialism in the ways they imply dynamics that "other" northerners in general and indigenous Sami people in particular. Othering processes continue to imprint on how inhabitants are understood by others and understand themselves (Mathisen, 2017), as a little less important and a little less civilized (Paulgaard, 2008), but also as fascinating and exotic (Kramvig, 2017; Herva et al., 2020).

Such understandings become part of host–guest relational dynamics. For good and for bad, they energize communities in their welcoming and appreciation of tourism (Müller and Jansson, 2007; Müller and Viken, 2017; Huijbens and Jóhannesson, 2019). Narratives of crises in terms of depopulation and recession have dominated development discourses in the area for decades. Thus, we witness how tourism entangles in place processes where inhabitants are experiencing that the future of place livelihoods is at stake. Tourism reminds of a development potential that brings hope and may propose a "softer" and "greener" alternative to extractive industries. Considering the climate crisis and biodiversity loss, marginalization, however, prepares inhabitants to embrace any hope that can strengthen the local economy (Granås and Mathisen, 2022). Altogether, the spaces for northern communities to prioritize and take responsibility for the nature crisis of our times are limited.

The delight of tourism for many northerners is the chances tourism offers for highly welcomed and encouraging attention and recognition. Nature-based tourism may inspire more inhabitants to acknowledge the qualities of their places and the possibilities they offer, not least for nature experiences. Still, the positivity discourse that follows tourism development makes it hard to relate to tourism in critical ways on behalf of one's own community and the ecologies that traditional livelihoods there rely on. This delimited space for critical discussions hampers the questioning of how nature-based tourism actually contributes to local employment and revenues. Altogether, the periphery status of northern places makes them vulnerable in the meeting with nature-based tourism. Thus, concerns for sustainability can be put on hold.

In the following, we provide examples from the ethnographic fieldworks of Mats' and June's ongoing PhD research in Lofoten and western Finnmark respectively. The examples demonstrate the value of the methodological working mode that, based on an open framing, goes up close to observe the relational practicing of nature-based tourism in places marked by the historical and geographical dynamics described above. The elaborations do not do justice to the depth and breadth of either of the studies. Similarly, they do not aim to provide a full overview of matters of concern in northern nature-based tourism today.

Exploring the value of framing openly and getting close to unveil matters of concern

Who produces commercial experiences where allemannsretten prevails?

In the middle of her fieldwork, a friend called June one day to let her know there was a "ski & sail" boat in the area. June drove straight to the harbour in the municipal centre of Øksfjord in western Finnmark to locate them. At this point, she found herself part of a "hunt" together with some of the nature guides in the area. The hunt involved figuring out what other guides were there, since it is difficult to keep an overview of who the commercial landscape users around are. People knew about June's hunt, and acquaintances had started calling her to help her out. When arriving at the harbour, she could not see any skiers or sailors. Instead, she met an old fisherman and acquaintance of hers. The man turned out to have a lot to divulge about the entrepreneurs and guides in ski & sail tourism in Western Finnmark. They had called him for advice on several occasions and he had established cooperation with some of them. These days, he was selling them stock fish. Ski & sail is a commercial concept where customers are accommodated on a boat that docks along the coast and guides guests on ski touring in alpine mountains. Thus, they integrate less into the land-based infrastructure of villages and towns. In western Finnmark, the challenge of keeping an overview of commercial operators concerns the ski & sail actors in particular.

June's corporeal presence and participation in the field illuminates a simple, but important question in tourism in Norwegian landscapes: With allemannsretten, nature-based tourism is notably unregulated. In accordance with the right, neither public authorities, DMOs, nor landowners have any formal authority to control who can sell nature experiences. Accordingly, any record-keeping on the matter is difficult. Even nature guides and other outdoor people who stroll an area regularly struggle to get a full overview, in a quest which is like adding puzzle-pieces to a puzzle with no frame. Of concern is the power geometry involved and the lack of control in the receiving end of nature-based tourism flows (Massey, 1994, pp. 149–150) that are spurred by allemannsretten and energized further by continuous wilderness depictions of northern landscapes.

Sensing concerns at the quay and in the mountain

It is possible to gather considerate information about who produces nature experiences by reading business registers and conducting different types of interviews (see e.g. Stensland et al., 2018). However, participant observation can provide substantive knowledge about how nature-based tourism is enacted. More specifically, a researcher that is present in the landscape can get to know not only who is selling nature experiences there, but who meets up when experiences are practiced there and how these encounters play out.

One example that can illustrate how closeness and presence can provide such knowledge, was when June went by motorboat to a small settlement in one of the fjords of western Finnmark in May one year, to go skiing there with friends. As they docked at the quay, they usually make use of, and when her friends left the boat, the owners came down to let them know that this was a private quay. As June came off the boat, the owners recognized her – hey, is it you? They told her that there had been so many sailboats there this winter, arriving at all hours. Some of the visitors had been crossing social boundaries and altogether made the public use of their quay problematic. They stood there talking for a while, before June led her group onboard again and decided to anchor the boat in the fjord, which is a less convenient way of accessing the landscape.

This incident reminds of how difficult it can be to identify commercial actors among the many landscape users of an area. Further, the situation at the quay enables a sense of relations at play in encounters where commercial nature experiences are practiced, and the frictions (cf. Tsing, 2005) they may imply where matters of intimacy, ownership, and control are at stake. The meeting with the quay owners was a constitutive encounter (Tsing, 2015, pp. 292–293) for June that provided new insight and made her understand better the substantive quality of further landscape encounters involved in the tourism-place nexus of her field. The methodological point is that June's presence and partaking implied learning, and that the knowledge produced was an outcome of her corporeal presence in a place assemblage (cf. Tsing, 2015). Her leaving the quay was an effect of staying affectively close (Rantala et al., 2023, p. 6).

During summer, Mats spent time around the famous climb and popular recreational area Svolværgeita in Lofoten. Safety concerns restrict guides from bringing more than two tourists climbing at a time. Given the season's economic importance, Mats was mindful to not ask to replace paying clients. Instead, he stayed at a considerate distance and monitored the climbing through his binoculars. Afterwards, his observations became a point of departure in a conversation with the guide, who explained how his company had installed the rope there and was maintaining the trail. The next day, the guide unexpectedly invited him to come along. Right before they were to start the climb, two foreign hikers passed them on the track below. As the hikers were about to continue up the mountain, the guide intervened and told them that their planned route was dangerous, and then redirected them to a safer point. He told Mats that he had contacted the authorities and requested them to remove this track from public maps. Despite the numerous rescues that he and his colleagues had conducted here as volunteers, the authorities had ignored him. Mats realized that the man was not only a guide, but a visitor manager and custodian of other hikers' and climbers' safety.

It was the intimacy of participation that made these observations possible and enabled Mats to sense the man's worries and frustrations. He noticed the engagements and the care of a guide that is committed within relations (Puig de la Bellacasa, 2017; Krzywoszynska, 2020) in an area and has to "stay with the trouble" (cf. Haraway, 2019) in the collective practicing of a landscape. Guides' potential involvement in informal management of landscapes is, however, ignored in public conversation and research on nature-based tourism, where concerns for the technicalities of guiding and ensuring safety dominate in Norway. In this way, Mats attends to matters of concern (Latour, 2004) in nature-based tourism by unveiling "previously ignored attachments" (Krzywoszynska, 2023, p. 398) of the phenomenon. Altogether, the situation from Svolværgeita tells of how the distinction between tourism and place may dissolve when guides practice a landscape.

"Light in the houses" of the tourism-place nexus

When Mats asked about his hopes for collaboration within his research, one of the ski guides in Lofoten told him that his main worry is not about the technical skills needed to move around safely – what frustrates him is not having the right tools to deal with sustainability. As part of landscapes where the concerns that come with tourism are obviously related to more than littering, the guide found the sustainability concept altogether fuzzy. More experiences from Lofoten tell of guides that worry about the lack of governance and local job creation in tourism. The underlying concern for sustainability connects to a growth in nature-based tourism that is unpredictable and out of control (cf. Massey, 1994, pp. 149–150).

The ethnographic insights above tell of matters at stake that responsible governmental institutions, such as for example municipalities, may not request knowledge about. Still, the knowledge of relational frictions that come with an open framing of nature-based tourism, speaks back to the concerns of guides. If municipalities are to pursue sustainable development of nature-based tourism, in-depth knowledge of the relational enactments of nature experiences is highly relevant. First, knowing who the commercial actors are concerns the important topic "lys i husan" (light in the houses), which is a commonly used phrase in the north. In this context, the phrase addresses the local revenues of nature-based tourism, and whether the phenomenon leads to more inhabited "lit" houses throughout the year. Further, knowledge about and cooperation with the commercial actors is decisive for municipalities that are to deal with the downsides of nature-based tourism, such as problems with littering, use of the outdoors for toilet purposes, degradation of vegetation, disturbing of local faunas, farming, and reindeer herding, etc. appear. Moreover, relations and matters of concern at play in commercial nature experiences tell of the pros and cons of tourism development for communities. Accordingly, such knowledge concerns sustainability in place development.

Altogether, the grey zones of world-making that condition the development of tourism businesses as well as places entail matters of concern for people and ecologies of relevance to different institutionally responsible parties. In northern places marked by recession, this may inspire localist ideas about the particular value of companies that are solidly place-bound and provide local jobs and thus "light in the houses." Further insights from western Finnmark as well as Lofoten however indicate that this picture is less black and white.

Concluding remarks

> But be careful... about the capitalist interests and the private interests. Don't let them wiggle their way into the framework. That's my one piece of advice from the US. (Nature guide, Lofoten)

Framing processes denote power struggles (Krzywoszynska, 2023, p. 398) in tourism. This is where researchers depart on different routes within tourism studies – what matters to us when we formulate research questions? Our framing by opening up, takes us to situations where we can sense varieties of concerns and mutual dependencies on-ground. Among them we find a guide who worries that mobile capitalism may "wiggle into the framework" in Lofoten landscapes. In landscape assemblages we observe face-to-face negotiations, based on physical presences and interdependencies, commitments, and care (Puig de la Bellacasa, 2017) that togetherness in place can imply. If uncommitted entrepreneurs, be they footloose, faceless, or opportunists in the waves of tourism growth should "reap the rewards" (cf. Tsing, 2005, p. 27) of northern landscapes, ways of life based on allemannsretten within and outside of the tourism economy would be at stake. So would the sustainability of tourism and place development.

So far, tourism in Norway has been weakly governed. The Official Norwegian Report (NOU, 2023:10) "To live and experience – destinations for a sustainable future," however, addresses the issue explicitly. In the wake of the report, political signals have suggested more regulations. Tourist taxation is a key element in the report (cf. Viken, 2023). The NOU, however, stresses the significance of preserving allemannsretten. So far, municipalities have hesitated to use the right that the Outdoor Recreation Act of 1957 provides them with to restrict allemannsretten. Recently, some have nevertheless used this opportunity, like in Lofoten, where tenting has been banned in several places. A signal in the NOU is that municipalities should take more responsibility for visitor management in the time to come. At the same time, DMOs position themselves as representatives in the flourishing field of visitor managers.

With visitor management, institutional expert regimes make demands on positions to manage landscapes from above. Meanwhile, guides continue to negotiate their presence within landscapes where experiences are produced, and vulnerable northern places are transformed. Among the guides are those who take responsibility in place development and in informal management of nature as well as visitors, while "staying with the trouble." It is this response-ability (Haraway, 2016) and trouble we suggest for institutional actors to acknowledge and for researchers to take interest in, through opening up nature-based tourism and engaging in explorations up-close. As Stirling (2008) emphasizes, "Instead of focusing on unitary prescriptive recommendations," opening up means posing "alternative questions, [that] focuses on neglected issues, includes marginalized perspectives, [...] considers ignored uncertainties, examines different possibilities, and highlights new options" (Stirling, 2008, pp. 279–280). This way, research can represent other connections and voices than the expert systems in landscape management and tourism development, through alternative and critical ways of nuancing tourism.

References

Breivik, G. (1978). To tradisjoner i norsk friluftsliv. In G. Breivik and H. Løvmo (Eds.), *Friluftsliv fra Fridtjof Nansen til våre* dager, 7–16. Universitetsforlaget.

Choi, J., and Wang, H. (2009). Stakeholder relations and the persistence of corporate financial performance. *Strategic Management Journal, 30*(8), 895–907.

Clifford, J. (2013). *Returns: Becoming Indigenous in the Twenty-first Century*. Harvard University Press.

Franklin, A. and Crang, M. (2001). The trouble with tourism and travel theory? *Tourist Studies, 1*(1), 5–22.

Goksøyr, M. (1994). Nasjonal identitetsbygging gjennom idrett og frilufts-liv. *Nytt Norsk Tidsskrift, 2*, 181–93.

Granås, B. (2018). Destinizing Finnmark: Place making through dogsledding. *Annals of Tourism Research, 72*, 48–57.

Granås, B., and Mathisen, L. (2022). Unfinished indigenous geographies: The endurances and becomings of a Sámi tourism venture. *Polar Record, 58*, e18.

Gurholt, K. P. (2008). Norwegian friluftsliv and ideals of becoming an "educated man". *Journal of Adventure Education and Outdoor Learning, 8*(1), 55–70.

Hall, T. (2001). *Urban Geography*. Routledge.

Haraway, D. (2016). *Staying with the Trouble: Making Kin in the Chthulucene*. Duke University Press.

Haraway, D. (2019). It matters what stories tell stories; It matters whose stories tell stories. *Auto/Biography Studies, 35*(3), 565–75.

Harvey, D. (1989). From managerialism to entrepreneurialism: The transformation of urban governance in late capitalism. *Geografiska Annaler B, 71*(1), 3–17.

Hastrup, K. (2009). Images of Thule: Maps and metaphors in Polar explorations. In S. Jakobsson (Ed.), *Images of the North: Histories, Identities*, Ideas, 103–16. Brill.

Herva, V.-P., Varnajot, A., and Pashkevich, A. (2020). Bad Santa: Cultural heritage, mystification of the Arctic, and tourism as an extractive industry, *The Polar Journal, 10*(2), 375–96.

Huijbens, E. and Benediktsson, K. (2009). Geared for the sublime: Mobile images of the north. In S. Jakobsson (Ed.), *Images of the North: Histories, Identities*, Ideas, 117–30. Brill.

Huijbens, E. H., and Jóhannesson, G. T. (2019). Tending to destinations: Conceptualising tourism's transformative capacities. *Tourist Studies, 19*(3), 279–94.

Huijbens, E. H., and Müller, D. K. (2022). The socio-spatial articulations of tourism studies in Nordic geography. In P. Jakobsen, E. Jönsson and H. G. Larsen (Eds.), *Socio-Spatial Theory in Nordic Geography: Intellectual Histories and Critical Interventions*, 169–90. Springer.

Jóhannesson, G. T., Welling, J., Müller, D. K., Lundmark, L., Nilsson, R. O., de la Barre, S., Granås, B., Kvidal-Røvik, T., Rantala, O., Tervo-Kankare, K., and Maher, P. (2022). *Arctic tourism in times of change. Uncertain Futures – From Overtourism to Re-starting Tourism*. Nordic Council of Ministers.

Kaltenborn, B. P., and Linnell, J. D. C. (2019). Who are legitimate stakeholders? National and local perceptions of environmental change in the Lofoten islands, Norway. *Polar Geography, 42*(4), 236–52.

Kramvig, B. (2017). Orientalism or cultural encounters? Tourism assemblages in cultures, capital, and identities. In A. Viken and D. K. Müller (Eds.), *Tourism and Indigeneity in the Arctic*, 169–87. Channel View.

Krzywoszynska, A. (2020). To know, to dwell, to care: Towards and actionable, place-based knowledge of soils. In J. F. Salazar, C. Granjou, M. Kearns, A. Krzywoszynska and M. Tironi (Eds.), *Thinking with Soils. Material Politics and Social Theory*, 89–106. Bloomsbury Publishing.

Krzywoszynska, A. (2023). Taking soil care seriously: A proposition. In N. Patzel, S. Grunwald, E. C. Brevik and C. Feller (Eds.), *Cultural Understanding of Soils: The Importance of Cultural Diversity and the Inner* World, 395–408. Springer.

Latour, B. (2004). Why has critique run out of steam? From matters of fact to matters of concern. *Critical Inquiry, 30*(2), 225–48.

Mathisen, S. R. (2017). Mellom borealisme og orientalisme. Fortellinger og forestill-inger om de andre i nordlysturismen. *Tidsskrift for kulturforskning, 16*(1), 55–70.

Massey, D. (1994). *Space, Place, and Gender*. University of Minnesota Press.

Massey, D. (2005). *For Space*. Sage.

Mitchell, R. K., Agle, B. R., and Wood, D. J. (1997). Toward a theory of stakeholder identification and salience: Defining the principle of who and what really counts. *Academy of Management Review, 22*(4), 853–86.

Müller, D. K., and Jansson, B. (2007). The difficult business of making pleasure periph-eries prosperous. Perspectives on space, place, and environment. In D. K. Müller and

B. Jansson (Eds.), *Tourism in Peripheries: Perspectives from the Far North and South*, 3–18. CABI.

Müller, D. K., and Viken, A. (2017). Indigenous tourism in the Arctic. In A. Viken and D. K. Müller (Eds.), *Tourism and Indigeneity in the Arctic*, 3–15. Channel View.

NHO reiseliv (2018). *Nordnorsk reiselivsstatistikk*. https://www.reiselivinord.no/2018/09/nordnorsk-reiselivsstatistikk-2018/.

NOU 2023:10 (2023). *To live and experience – destinations for a sustainable future.* https://www.regjeringen.no/no/dokumenter/nou-2023-10/id2968657/.

Olwig, K. (2019). *The Meanings of Landscape: Essays on Place, Space, Environment and Justice*. Routledge.

Paulgaard, G. (2008). Re-centring periphery: Negotiating identities in time and space. In B. Granås and J. O. Bærenholdt (Eds.), *Mobility and Place: Enacting Northern European Peripheries*, 49–59. Ashgate.

Puig de la Bellacasa, M. (2017). *Matters of Care: Speculative Ethics in More Than Human Worlds. Minneapolis.* University of Minnesota Press.

Rantala, O., Kinnunen, V., Höckert, E., Grimwood, B. S., Hurst, C. E., Jóhannesson, G. T., Salla, J., Ren, C., Stinson, M. J., Valtonen, A., and Vola, J. (2023). Staying proximate. In O. Rantala, V. Kinnunen, and E. Höckert (Eds.). (2024) *Researching with Proximity: Relational Methodologies for the Anthropocene*, 1–19. Springer.

Ren, C., van der Duim, R., and Jóhannesson, G. T. (2021). Messy realities and collaborative knowledge production in tourism. *Tourist Studies 21*(2), 143–55.

Starik, M. (1995). Should trees have managerial standing? Toward stakeholder status for non-human nature. *Journal of Business Ethics, 14*, 207–17.

Stensland, S., Fossgard, K., Hansen, B. B., Fredman, P., Morken, I.-B., Thyrrestrup, G., and Haukeland, J. V. (2018). *Naturbaserte reiselivsbedrifter i Norge: Statusoversikt, resultater og metode fra en nasjonal spørreundersøkelse.* MINA fagrapport 52. Ås: NMBU.

Stirling, A. (2008). "Opening up" and "closing down": Power, participation, and pluralism in the social appraisal of technology. *Science, Technology and Human Values, 33*, 262–94.

Tallberg, L., García-Rosell, J.-C., and Haanpää, M. (2022). Human–Animal Relations in Business and Society: Advancing the Feminist Interpretation of Stakeholder Theory. *Journal of Business Ethics, 180*(1), 1–16.

Tsing, A. L. (2005). *Frictions. An Ethnography of Global Connection.* Princeton University Press.

Tsing, A. L. (2015). *The Mushroom at the End of the World: On the Possibility of Life in Capitalist Ruin.* Princeton University Press.

Vannini, P. (2015). Non-representational ethnography: New ways of animating lifeworlds. *Cultural Geographies, 22*(2), 317–27.

Viken, A. (2023). Turisme, naturressurser og grunnrenteskatt. In R. E. Nilsen, O. Brox, E. Eythorsson and S. Jentoft (Eds.), *Allmenningsressurser i nord. Fellesskap og grunnrente*, 215–40. Orkana Akademiske.

Ween, G., and Abram, S. (2012). The Norwegian Trekking Association: Trekking as constituting the nation. *Landscape Research, 37*(2), 155–71.

10 Nature-based tourism as part of Arctic land use and just transition

Seija Tuulentie

Introduction

When a total of 15 young people from Greenland, Iceland, Norway, Sweden, and Finland met in a workshop in late summer 2023 discussing the future of the Arctic region, tourism emerged as a central part of the future threat scenario. Their justification for talking about tourism instead of mining, for example, was that they saw that tourism is usually marketed as a benefactor for remote regions. However, the downsides of tourism were rarely mentioned. The downsides of tourism raised by this group of young people were that 'must-see' places and especially wilderness areas become overcrowded, cruise tourism is not socially sustainable, nature suffers and there is no money to build the necessary infrastructure. This youth workshop was part of the Future Workshops series of a Horizon2020 project ArcticHubs (No 869580) in August 2023 and took place in Inari, Finland. The project focuses on exploring the consequences of increasing global competition for Arctic natural resources, looking in particular at livelihoods such as mining, fish farming, forestry and tourism.

Given the rapid growth of tourism in the Arctic (Maher, 2017), and its uneven distribution across regions and countries (Maher et al., 2022), it is no surprise that young people are concerned. This uneven growth has led to overcrowding in some places at some times (Lundmark et al., 2020; Ólafsdóttir et al., 2020), and the image of overtourism has been supported by media portrayals (Sæþórsdóttir et al., 2020). Runge et al. (2020), in their spatial study of the footprint of Arctic tourism based on social media data, found that growth has indeed been rapid in some places, while much of the Arctic remains unaffected by tourism. However, the boom is continuing, and new parts are opening up to tourism as accessibility continues to improve (Sisneros-Kidd et al., 2019).

Land use management is becoming an increasingly important issue in many parts of the Arctic, as landscapes that were traditionally based on primary production, such as herding, agriculture and forestry, are increasingly subject to other demands (Daugstad, 2008). In addition to the growth of tourism and recreation, the demand for minerals and renewable energy needed for the green transition has targeted northern regions due to existing resources and sparsely populated areas. Conflicts with activities that require large areas and pristine nature, such as reindeer husbandry, tourism or nature conservation, are expected to increase (Latola et al., 2016; Pettersson et al., 2017). In addition, not all types of tourism activities are compatible with the same natural areas.

In general, nature-based tourism practised in Arctic landscapes is seen as soft and sustainable compared to natural resource use such as mining and forestry. Nature-based tourism is also seen as economically beneficial in terms of rural development (e.g. Hall et al., 2009; Müller, 2015; Ólafsdóttir et al., 2020; Jóhannesson et al., 2022) and as part of a local and decentralised way of life (Suopajärvi et al., 2017). However, similar to extractive industries, Arctic tourism has been perceived as subject to debates about sustainability, conservation, land use and indigenous rights (Herva et al. 2020), and the need to pay attention to the environmental dimensions of tourism growth has been noted (e.g. Hall and Saarinen, 2010).

In this chapter, I discuss future research needs related to the ever-increasing land use modes in the green transition operating environment. Decisions about how land is used and for what purposes raise issues of equity, and conflicts between different actors are difficult to avoid. It would therefore be important to examine the fairness of actions and decisions and to recognise the conflict potential of choices. I discuss, first, the importance of a justice perspective for tourism land use, second, how land and natural resource use issues have been understood in Arctic tourism studies, and third, the need to take justice issues seriously and to consider fairness from a broader perspective.

The question of justice in tourism landscapes

As part of the need to reconcile different land uses, nature-based tourism is a multifaceted issue. In a survey of land use and environmental conflicts in Finland, tourism was seen as having the most conflictual relationship with mining, wind power and forestry (Pettersson et al., 2017). In Arctic tourism research, issues related to wind power and mining have emerged especially in the last two decades, while the relationship between tourism and nature conservation and forestry has been discussed and studied for a long time. Landscape and the natural environment are important resources for tourism, but nature-based tourism is not just about tourists visiting nature. The natural environment as a basis for tourism poses many challenges for communities and natural resource management (Fredman and Tyrväinen, 2010). From outside the region, large wilderness areas in the north are often seen as empty spaces for recreational and tourist use, marketed, for example, as Europe's last wilderness. Although the concept of wilderness often evokes meanings and images of wild, remote and untouched natural areas, many of these areas are the products of human activities, reflecting past relationships with the environment and current preferences and values (Sæþórsdóttir et al., 2011).

In the context of land use and related green transition projects, justice is increasingly recognised as a key issue. Here, justice is understood based on the framework outlined by McCauley and Heffron (2018) and Droubi et al. (2022), which distinguishes between:

(a)   distributive justice (who benefits and who suffers),
(b)   procedural justice (focus on legal process),
(c)   recognition justice (are all different groups recognised?),
(d)   cosmopolitan justice (have impacts beyond national borders been considered?), and
(e)   restorative justice (issue of compensation).

When considering tourism land use issues in the Arctic, distributive justice is related to land ownership and use rights, procedural justice is related to the right to have a say in decision-making, and recognition has been discussed in relation to the traditional rights of local actors and indigenous peoples. The importance of thinking beyond national boundaries, i.e. cosmopolitan justice, is particularly evident in remote wilderness areas where borders are difficult to discern. Restorative justice comes into play when there is a need to compensate for losses, for example by providing areas for tourism activities when traditionally used areas are taken for other purposes.

However, there has been little research on a just tourism transition. In their discussion of the transition of tourism to a zero-carbon economy, Rastegar and Ruhanen (2023) note that as the transition to just tourism is mainly driven by global initiatives, there is a fear of top-down, non-participatory approaches that ignore local knowledge and values. The concept of 'green colonialism' (Normann, 2021; Ohlsson and Wood-Donnelly, 2023) has been raised in relation to land use in Arctic regions, particularly from the perspective of indigenous peoples. The concept essentially implies a contradiction between the green transition and traditional land use systems. The discussion of green colonialism is particularly relevant to wind energy and mining but will also need to be addressed in the future from the perspective of land use for tourism.

The discussion on just transition offers a new space for developing an interdisciplinary transition-sensitive approach to exploring and promoting not only distributional (share of benefits and harms) and procedural (fairness of processes and engagement of actors) but also recognition-based justice considering which sections of society are ignored or misrepresented (Jenkins et al., 2016; McCauley and Heffron, 2018).

Fundamentally, the issue of tourism land use in Arctic areas is about justice in relation to local land use traditions and the possibility of practising different types of use in the same areas, i.e. multifunctionality, a concept particularly favoured in forestry circles. Multifunctionality – or multiple use or integrated land use – aims at the simultaneous presence of a heterogeneous range of land use values and functions beyond primary production (Solbär et al., 2019; Huuskonen et al., 2021), but this kind of multifunctionality has been shown not to be possible in all cases.

Justice issues in nature-based tourism land use

Protected areas as arenas for recreation and tourism

Protected areas, especially national parks, with their 'pristine' nature have long been important resources for recreation and tourism (Puhakka and Saarinen, 2013; Maher et al., 2014). However, they have restrictions on commercial use (Byström and Müller, 2014) and there are many tourism activities that cannot be carried out in protected areas.

National parks, with their dual mandate to protect nature and provide recreational opportunities for people, are seen as a guarantee of the nature values sought by tourists (Wall Reinius and Fredman, 2007). They have also long been a focus of interest for nature-based tourism research. In addition to visitor issues (e.g. Butler and Boyd, 2000; McCool et al., 2005; Maher, 2010), the environmental impacts of activities such as horse riding, skiing and hiking (Törn et al., 2009) and tensions between different users (e.g. Rosen, 1993; Carothers et al., 2001; Pröbstl-Haider et al., 2018) have been addressed. However, national park and protected area issues have not only been of interest in nature-based tourism research in the past. With the growth of new modes of movement in wilderness and landscape, these issues are becoming more acute.

While Michael (2000) analysed hiking boots as a technology that mediates between the human body and nature – and damages nature – there is still a lack of similar analysis of other technologies used to enter the wilderness. In particular, electric mountain bikes and fat bikes allow access to previously inaccessible parts of the wilderness. Rosen (1993) has noted that the dominant discourse about mountain biking from the outset has been one of seeking wilderness areas untainted by modernisation. Most activities require trails, making them an important land use issue.

Another, and particularly Arctic, issue concerning tensions in tourism activities relates to animal safaris. In northern Europe they, along with some other growing activities, are revealing the grey area of public access rights, the so-called everyone's rights, and testing the guidelines for the use of protected areas. Husky safaris are very popular in northern Scandinavia, but they cause tensions in reindeer husbandry areas and raise discussions about traditions and identities. In the Finnish Sami region of Inari, the debate has centred on the fact that almost anyone can set up a husky farm wherever they like without asking their neighbours. This has caused disturbances and problems for nearby reindeer herders, who can only complain afterwards (interviews in Inari, 2023/ArcticHubs project).

The issue of justice that has been raised in relation to protected areas has mainly been the issue of local rights (Puhakka et al., 2009), which relates to many dimensions of justice, from distributive to procedural and recognition justice. Less discussed in the Arctic is more than human or multi-species justice in relation to recognition justice. The topic is emerging (e.g. Hurst, 2023; Rantala and Höckert, 2023; Rantala et al., 2024), but needs more attention, especially in relation to the use of protected areas.

Widespread production forests

Important characteristics of production forests from a tourism and recreation perspective are that they cover large areas, can be used for multiple purposes, and are owned locally or at least nationally (Mason, 2013; Svensson et al., 2020). Due to the long tradition of forestry, its relationship with nature-based tourism has also received a lot of attention in Arctic production forest areas, especially in Finland and Sweden. From a justice perspective, the most important issues are the distribution of benefits and harms. In the Nordic countries, the question of public access rights (allemannsretten in Norway, allemansrätten in Sweden, and jokaisenoikeus in Finland) is becoming a central justice issue as user groups and types of use increase.

Although nature-based tourism often takes place in national parks and other protected areas, it does not necessarily require protected areas (Lundmark and Müller, 2010), so forestry areas are also important for tourism activities. For example, motorised activities are rarely allowed in protected areas, and other activities such as mountain biking and husky safaris are either prohibited in protected areas or require long routes through production forests.

Forest clear-cuts as part of artefacts of civilisation are perceived to be 'polluting' the visual and auditory landscapes (Margaryan, 2018). Studies of tourists' landscape preferences have shown that beautiful scenery is the most important motive for choosing a destination and participating in outdoor recreation. Tyrväinen et al. (2017) highlight the importance of seasons on perceived landscape quality in commercial forests: seasonal differences are greatest in clear-cut areas, as snow cover mitigates the effects of forestry operations, while even-aged, middle-aged and mature forest stands are suitable for tourism in both summer and winter.

In an important tourism region of Muonio in Finland, a dispute over the planned loggings of some old-growth forests took place in 2006. The parties to the dispute were the Finnish state forestry company Metsähallitus and a local coalition, the key group of which consisted of tourism entrepreneurs, reindeer herders, representatives of a game association, the municipality, and a local nature conservation NGO (Sarkki, 2008). The Muonio case is interesting from a distributive justice perspective, as the benefits of tourism were perceived to be much greater than the benefits of forestry, and the new role of nature-based tourism was tested. The outcome of the dispute was that the forest area was leased to tourism entrepreneurs – a solution that pleased the local coalition more than Metsähallitus (Sarkki, 2008).

One of the measures to solve the problem of distribution of benefits between nature-based tourism and forestry has been to develop a system for private forest owners to trade forest landscapes and recreational values by compensating forest owners for economic losses. However, such a mechanism has not yet been put into practice, and results from north-eastern Finland show that despite the general willingness of landowners to participate, their expectations of the level of compensation vary widely (Tyrväinen et al., 2021).

Towards green transition: Dilemma of wind power

The use of land for renewable energy construction and mining in the context of the green transition has recently been discussed in the field of tourism. When comparing land use modes in a Finnish study, tourism was perceived to be particularly contradictory to wind power construction (Pettersson et al., 2017). However, the relationship between tourism and wind energy is complicated. In remote northern regions, where pristine landscapes are important for nature-based tourism, wind farms have been perceived as detracting from the tourist experience, while at the same time green energy is also welcomed by tourists. In Iceland, studies on preconceived attitudes towards wind farm construction (Ólafsdóttir et al., 2019; Sæþórsdóttir et al., 2021) show that the main issues for tourism service providers are the proximity of wind turbines and their impact on the most scenic mountain views. In Finnish Lapland, a DMO representative from one of the largest tourist resorts says that since windmills are associated with sustainable production of renewable energy, tourists understand and appreciate this, and therefore the tourism industry has nothing against wind turbines (Sorvali et al., 2023).

However, an interesting tourism-wind power case in terms of procedural justice is a plan to build a large wind farm in Kuusamo, north-east Finland. The plan was rejected by the Supreme Administrative Court on the basis of the Reindeer Herding Act. Both the local reindeer herders' cooperative and the tourism association appealed to the court, but only the reindeer herders' appeal was considered. The tourism association in the neighbouring municipality complained about the wind farm's proximity to the national park in its area and its disturbing presence in the tourist landscape. The complaint was not considered because the tourism association was not considered a relevant party, as it was in a different municipality and the wind farm would be five kilometres from the national park (Nousiainen et al., 2024). The issue of procedural justice is concerned with who is involved in and able to influence ongoing processes, whereas the issue of distributive justice is concerned with who experiences loss and harm. Here, the legal process does not support the losses that tourism is perceived to be experiencing in the neighbourhood. In the case of an earlier dispute between wind power and tourism in Finnish Lapland, the wilderness image needed for nature-based tourism was considered so important by the municipality that the wind farm was rejected (Hast, 2013).

These justice issues raise the question of ownership of the landscape. Wind farms benefit the community and landowners economically but may conflict with other interests in landscape use (Nousiainen et al. 2024). The issue of indigenous peoples' rights and justice in the green transition is related to both traditional livelihoods, such as reindeer herding, and tourism. In Finland, Metsähallitus, which manages state-owned land, has decided that no wind farms will be planned in the Sami homeland until 2027 (Metsähallitus, 2022). State-owned land covers over 90 per cent of the land in the Sami region of Finland. While in Iceland and Finland tourism has been a hot topic in relation to wind energy planning, in Norway indigenous issues have been more prominent than tourism (e.g. Cambou, 2024), but often these issues are intertwined.

Mining-tourism nexus

In the green transition, mining issues go hand in hand with wind energy discussions. The development and growth of mining is one of the key drivers of economic development in the Arctic (Haley et al., 2011; Tolvanen et al., 2019) and in green transition, especially at the EU level (Smol et al., 2020). The general limitations of mining in the Arctic are related to the fragile environment, remote locations and limited labour supply (Haley et al., 2011). This has implications for Arctic tourism in two ways: competition for labour and landscape change. In research, mining has been seen as conflicting with tourism (Kosenius and Horne, 2016; Brown et al., 2017; Similä and Jokinen, 2018; Tolvanen et al., 2019). Although old mining communities and even some operating mines seem to be compatible with tourism or even tourist attractions (Naum, 2019; Herva et al., 2020; Byström, 2022), conflicts are particularly likely to arise when a new mine is opened near tourist areas, as mining activities can dramatically change the landscape that is essential for tourism (Similä and Jokinen, 2018). In a Finnish study, mining and tourism, including second homes, were considered to be one of the most conflictual land uses (Pettersson et al., 2017). However, the research literature on this mining–tourism relationship in the Arctic is scarce – recently the issue has received attention mainly in northern Finland (Similä and Jokinen, 2018; Kangas et al., 2022). This may be due to the strong development of mineral exploration and mining plans, as well as the importance of tourism in northern Finland.

The relationship between mining and tourism is considered to be asymmetrical, as a mine only benefits from the neighbouring tourist destination, while the nature-based tourism business may suffer significantly from the proximity of the mine (Similä and Jokinen, 2018). Thus, like the location issues of wind farms, the fundamental question of tourism and mining coexistence is related to location: if the mine is planned too close to an existing tourist destination, problems will arise. An example of an existing mine in an important tourist area in Finnish Lapland is Suurikuusikko, near the Levi tourist resort in Kittilä, where tourism and mining are seen as synergistic: the gold mine is far enough away from the resort and the employment opportunities in both the mine and the tourism industry fit well together (Mononen et al., 2023). In addition, the image of gold is more positive than that of some other minerals (Herva et al., 2020).

In contrast to the Levi case, the proposed mines in Hannukainen, near the tourist resort of Ylläs, and Kuusamo, near the tourist resort of Ruka, have provoked opposition from tourism service providers, local residents and visitors. In Kuusamo, the strong wilderness image is seen as threatened if the mine comes, but there are also major concerns about the impact on waterways in national parks that are important for tourism (Lyytimäki and Peltonen, 2016). In the case of Ylläs, the viability of the community was seen as threatened because almost half of the population derives its income from tourism and the proposed mine would be close to areas of tourism activity (Suopajärvi et al. 2017). However, as Komu (2019, 2020) shows, the local people's own understanding of the situation between reindeer herding, nature-based tourism and mining is not exclusively defined by conflict, and she emphasises that the situation should be understood in terms of coexistence rather than a conflict/consent binary. In line with Komu's resistance to binary thinking, studies on mining and tourism note that nature-based tourism or ecotourism is not necessarily more beneficial to nature than mining (Franklin, 2012). A crucial question for the future of the mining–tourism nexus is, like the wind power dilemma, related to procedural and recognitional justice: how does the acceptance of mining develop in areas important for tourism, as rare earth metals become more and more important for the EU's self-sufficiency and for the green transition in general? Whose voice is heard and how?

Conclusion

Looking at these examples of land use issues in tourism, more explicit attention should be given to the justice perspectives. At present research, these issues are often secondary. In addition, tourism is often taken for granted as a benefit for remote Arctic regions, while the recognition of all relevant groups and land use modes might remain vague. Multi-species issues are beginning to receive more attention but could be placed higher on the research agenda. In particular, the consequences of the green transition needed to mitigate climate change should receive more attention from the perspective of land use in remote wilderness areas. Trying to understand different viewpoints and concepts of justice is a good starting point for research on land use tensions, especially as it is likely that in the future it will be necessary to focus on finding strategies to build resilient rural areas through the coexistence of various green transition livelihoods (Moyle et al. 2018).

The studies on wind power and mining have shown that siting is crucial in relation to nature-based tourism areas. There is a clear need for more and better negotiation and management measures. The importance of local and indigenous knowledge cannot be overemphasised. There is a need for research into the use of different types of knowledge and for spatial analysis. In many northern areas it would be possible to find places where there is no tension between extractive land uses and tourism, but there are other limiting factors. For mining, it is the location of the ore, while for wind power it is not just the wind but other issues such as indigenous rights, transmission lines and military permission. In forestry, it is easier to manage operations so that they do not disturb tourist areas. In addition, forest management requirements for climate change and biodiversity are consistent with recreation and tourism needs.

It is almost a cliché to stress the need for more research on public participation. However, despite the extensive academic literature on the subject, practice is not well developed. In practice, there are authorities and planners who see it as too time-consuming and costly and do not really see the value of spending time at the beginning of land use planning processes. Another problem for tourism is that land use is rarely part of large projects that require environmental impact assessment, such as mining and wind power projects. From a justice perspective, land use issues related to tourism in the Arctic are strongly intertwined with indigenous and local rights. While activities such as mining and energy production have been labelled 'green colonialism' in discussions with indigenous peoples and other local people in Arctic regions, tourism has not been. In this sense, despite some tensions between tourism activities and non-extractive land uses, well-managed nature-based tourism can be seen as having synergies with traditional land uses.

The increase in visitor numbers is not necessarily a sign of a problem but high visitor numbers do put additional pressure on destinations that lack robust land use management plans. This in turn can lead to tensions between local people and visitors, as well as a degraded visitor experience. While such cascading effects will vary in time and space depending on local conditions, there is clear evidence of the importance of integrating local knowledge into both planning and management processes at the earliest possible stage. This will not only help to reduce potential conflicts or unexpected tensions but will also help to ensure a sustainable tourism product.

From a justice perspective, in addition to procedural justice, which is an obvious prerequisite, and distributive justice, which is more easily included in the agenda, it is also necessary to consider recognition justice, but other dimensions of justice, such as ecological justice, are also becoming more important as it is likely that the future of Arctic land use will be characterised by an increase in all kinds of activities. Therefore, the need to look beyond current tensions and think about alternatives and desired futures is becoming increasingly important.

References

Brown, G., Kangas, K., Juutinen, A., and Tolvanen, A. (2017). Identifying environmental and natural resource management conflict potential using participatory mapping. *Society and Natural Resources, 30*, 1458–75.

Butler, R., and Boyd, S. W. (2000). *Tourism and National Parks*. Wiley.

Byström, J. (2022) Mining tourism in abandoned and existing mines in the Swedish Far North. *Polar Record, 58*, e40.

Byström, J., and Müller, D. K. (2014). Tourism labor market impacts of National Parks: The case of Swedish Lapland. *Zeitschrift für Wirtschaftsgeographie, 58*(1), 115–26.

Cambou, D. (2024). The significance of the Fosen decision for protecting the cultural rights of the Sámi Indigenous people in the green transition. In D. Cambou and Ø. Ravna (Eds.), *The Significance of Sámi Rights*, 52–71. Routledge.

Carothers, P., Vaske, J. J, and Donnelly, M. P. (2001). Social values versus interpersonal conflict among hikers and mountain bikers. *Leisure Sciences, 23*(1), 47–61.

Daugstad, K. (2008). Negotiating landscape in rural tourism. *Annals of Tourism Research, 35*(2), 402–26.

Droubi, S., Heffron, R. J., & McCauley, D. (2022). A critical review of energy democracy: A failure to deliver justice? *Energy Research & Social Science, 86*, 102444.

Franklin, A. (2012). Viewing nature politically. In A. Holden and D. Fennell (Eds.), *The Routledge Handbook of Tourism and the* Environment, 75–83. Routledge.

Fredman, P., and Tyrväinen, L. (2010). Frontiers in nature-based tourism. *Scandinavian Journal of Hospitality and Tourism, 10*(3), 177–89.

Haley, S., Klick, M., Szymoniak, N., and Crow, A. (2011). Observing trends and assessing data for Arctic mining. *Polar Geography, 34*(1–2), 37–61.

Hall, C. M., Müller, D. K., and Saarinen, J. (2009). *Nordic Tourism: Issues and Cases.* Channel View.

Hall, C.M. and Saarinen, J. (2010) Polar tourism: Definitions and dimensions, *Scandinavian Journal of Hospitality and Tourism, 10*(4), 448–67.

Hast, S. (2013). Taistelu tuulimyllyjä vastaan. Tieto ja oikeuttaminen kahden Länsi-Lapin luonnonvarakiistan hallinnassa [The battle against windmills. Information and justification in the management of two natural resource disputes in Western Lapland]. *Sosiologia, 4*, 342–57.

Herva, V.-P., Varnajot, A. and Pashkevich, A. (2020). Bad Santa: Cultural heritage, mystification of the Arctic, and tourism as an extractive industry. *The Polar Journal, 10*(2), 375–96.

Hurst, C. (2023). Becoming-with More-than-human Protected Areas. UWSpace. http://hdl.handle.net/10012/20120.

Huuskonen, S., Domisch, T., Finér, L., Hantula, J., Hynynen, J., Matala, J., Miina, J., Neuvonen, S., Nevalainen, S., Niemistö, P., Nikula, A., Piri, T., Siitonen, J., Smolander, A., Tonteri, T., Uotila, K., and Viiri, H. (2021). What is the potential for replacing monocultures with mixed species stands to enhance ecosystem services in boreal forests in Fennoscandia? *Forest Ecology and Management, 479*, 118558.

Jenkins K., McCauley D.A., Heffron R., Stephan H., and Rehner R. (2016). Energy justice: A conceptual review. *Energy Research & Social Science, 11*, 174–82.

Jóhannesson, G. T., Welling, J., Müller, D. K., Lundmark, L., Nilsson, R. O., de la Barre, S., Granås, B., Kvidal-Røvik, T., Rantala, O., Tervo-Kankare, O., and Maher, P. (2022). *Arctic Tourism in Times of Change: Uncertain Futures – From Overtourism to Restarting Tourism*. Nordic Council of Ministers.

Kangas, K., Brown, G., Kivinen, M., Tolvanen, A., Tuulentie, S., Karhu, J., Markovaara-Koivisto, M., Eilu, P., Tarvainen, O., Similä, J., and Juutinen, A. (2022). Land use synergies and conflicts identification in the framework of compatibility analyses and spatial assessment of ecological, socio-cultural and economic values. *Journal of Environmental Management, 316*, 115–74.

Komu, T. (2019). Dreams of treasures and dreams of wilderness – engaging with the beyond-the-rational in extractive industries in northern Fennoscandia, *The Polar Journal, 9*(1), 113–32.

Komu, T. (2020). *Pursuing the Good Life in the North: Examining the Coexistence of Reindeer Herding, Extractive Industries and Nature-based Tourism in Northern Fennoscandia*. University of Oulu.

Kosenius, A.K., and Horne, P. (2016). Welfare effects of mining externalities: A combined travel cost and contingent behaviour study. *Journal of Environmental Economics and Policy, 5*, 265–82.

Latola, K., Sarkki, S., Stępień, A., and Jokinen, M. (2016). Activities affecting land use in the European Arctic. In A. Stepien, T. Koivurova and P. Kankaanpää (Eds.), *The Changing Arctic and the European Union*, 186–212. Brill.

Lundmark, L., and Müller, D. K. (2010) The supply of nature-based tourism activities in Sweden. *Tourism, 58*(4), 379–93.

Lundmark, L., Müller, D. K., and Bohn, D. (2020). Arctification and the paradox of overtourism in sparsely populated areas. In L. Lundmark, D. B. Carson, and M. Eimermann (Eds.), *Dipping in to the North: Living, Working and Traveling in Sparsely Populated Areas*, 349–71. Palgrave Macmillan.

Lyytimäki J., and Peltonen L. (2016). Mining through controversies: Public perceptions and the legitimacy of a planned gold mine near a tourist destination. *Land Use Policy, 54*, 479–86.

Maher, P. T. (2010). Cruise tourist experiences and management implications for Auyuittuq, Sirmilik and Quttinirpaaq National Parks, Nunavut, Canada. In C. M. Hall and J. Saarinen (Eds.), *Tourism and Change in Polar Regions: Climate, Environment and Experience*, 119–35. Routledge.

Maher, P. T. (2017). Tourism futures in the Arctic. In K. Latola and H. Sahvela (Eds.), *The Interconnected Arctic*, 312–20. Springer.

Maher, P. T., Gelter, H., Hillmer-Pegram, K., Hovgaard, G., Hull, J., Jóhannesson, G. T., Karlsdóttir, A., Rantala, O., and Pashkevich, A. (2014). Arctic tourism: Realities and possibilities. *Arctic Yearbook*, 2014, 290–306.

Maher, P. T., Jóhannesson, G. T., Kvidal-Røvik, T., Müller, D. K., and Rantala, O. (2022). Touring in the Arctic: Shades of grey towards a sustainable future. In D.

C. Natcher and T. Koivurova (Eds.), *Renewable Economies in the Arctic*, 81–98. Routledge.

Margaryan, L. (2018). Nature as a commercial setting: The case of nature-based tourism providers in Sweden. *Current Issues in Tourism, 21*(16), 1893–911.

Mason, P. (2013). Zoning, land-use planning and tourism. In A. Holden and D. Fennell (Eds.), *The Routledge Handbook of Tourism and the Environment*, 266–75. Routledge.

McCauley, D., and Heffron, R. (2018). Just transition: Integrating climate, energy and environmental justice. *Energy Policy, 119*, 1–7.

McCool, S. F., Lachapelle, P. R., Gertsch, F., Gosselin, H., and Sahanatien, V. (2005). Managing recreational experiences in Arctic national parks: A process for identifying indicators. In A. Watson, L. Dean and J. Sproull (Eds.), *Science and Stewardship to Protect and Sustain Wilderness Values*. WILD Foundation.

Metsähallitus (2022) *Saamelaisten kotiseutualueen luonnonvarasuunnitelma 2022–2027*. [Natural resources plan for the Sámi home region 2022–2027].

Michael, M. (2000). These boots are made for walking…: Mundane technology, the body and human–environment relations. *Body & Society, 6*(3–4), 107–26.

Mononen, T., Sihvonen, J., Sairinen, R., and Tiainen, H. (2023). Local governance of the mining industry – five Finnish examples. *Resources Policy, 82*, 103478.

Moyle, B. D., Moyle, C. L. J., and Bec, A. (2018). The coexistence of tourism and mining: A strategic framework for cross-sectoral interaction. *Current Issues in Tourism, 21*(17), 1966–1987.

Müller, D. K. (2015). Issues in Arctic tourism. In B. Evengård, J. Nymand Larsen and Ø. Paasche (Eds.), *The New Arctic*, 147–58. Springer.

Naum, M. (2019). Enchantment of the underground. Touring mines in early modern Sweden, *Journal of Tourism History, 11*(1), 1–21.

Normann, S. (2021). Green colonialism in the Nordic context: Exploring Southern Saami representations of wind energy development. *Journal of Community Psychology, 49*(1), 77–94.

Nousiainen, M., Rantala, O., and Tuulentie, S. (2024). Rush hour in a national park: Mobile encounters in a peripheral tourism landscape. In B. Thorsteinsson, K. A. Lund, G. T. Jóhannesson and G. R. Jóhannesdottir (Eds), *Mobilities on the Margins: Creative Processes of Place-Making*, 225–43. Springer.

Ohlsson, J., and Wood-Donnelly, C. (2023). Conclusion: Making connections between justice and studies of the Arctic. In C. Wood-Donnelly and J. Ohlsson (Eds.), *Arctic Justice: Environment, Society and Governance*, 183–89). Bristol University Press.

Ólafsdóttir, R., Sæþórsdóttir, A. D., Noordhuizen, J., and Nijkrake, W. (2019). Planning sustainable leisure landscapes in Arctic rural communities. In A. Törn-Laapio (Ed.), *Special Issues in Responsible Tourism*, 44–9. JAMK.

Ólafsdóttir, R., Tuulentie, S., Hovgaard, G., Zinglersen, K. B., Svartá, M., Poulsen, H. H., and Søndergaard, M. (2020). The contradictory role of tourism in the northern peripheries: Overcrowding, overtourism and the importance of tourism for rural development. In J. McDonagh and S. Tuulentie (Eds.), *Sharing Knowledge for Land Use Management: Decision-Making and Expertise in Europe's Northern Periphery*, 86–99. Edward Elgar Publishing.

Pettersson, S. K., Hallikainen, V., Naskali, A., Rovanperä, S., and Tuulentie, S. (2017). Ympäristökonfliktit Suomessa: Mistä on kiistelty ja miksi? [English abstract: Environmental conflicts in Finland: What issues have been disputed over and why?]. *Terra, 129*(2), 87–107.

Pröbstl-Haider, U., Lund-Durlacher, D., Antonschmidt, H., and Hödl, C. (2018). Mountain bike tourism in Austria and the Alpine region – towards a sustainable model for multi-stakeholder product development. *Journal of Sustainable Tourism*, 26(4), 567–82.

Puhakka, R., and Saarinen, J. (2013) New role of tourism in national park planning in Finland. *The Journal of Environment & Development*, 22(4), 411–34.

Puhakka, R., Sarkki, S., Cottrell, S. P., and Siikamäki, P. (2009) Local discourses and international initiatives: Sociocultural sustainability of tourism in Oulanka National Park, Finland. *Journal of Sustainable Tourism*, 17(5), 529–49.

Rantala, O., and Höckert, E. (2023). Multispecies Stories from the Margins. In B. Thorsteinsson, K. A. Lund, G. T. Jóhannesson and G. R. Jóhannesdóttir (Eds.), *Mobilities on the Margins: Creative Processes of Place-Making*, 61–79. Springer.

Rantala, O., Kinnunen, V., and Höckert, E. (Eds.) (2024). *Researching with Proximity: Relational Methodologies for the Anthropocene*. Palgrave Macmillan.

Rastegar, R., & Ruhanen, L. (2023). Climate change and tourism transition: From cosmopolitan to local justice. *Annals of Tourism Research*, 100, 103565.

Rosen, P. (1993). The social construction of mountain bikes: Technology and postmodernity in the cycle industry. *Social Studies of Science*, 23(3), 479–513.

Runge, C. A., Daigle, R. M., and Hausner, V. H. (2020). Quantifying tourism booms and the increasing footprint in the Arctic with social media data. *PLoS ONE*, 15(1), e0227189.

Sæþórsdóttir, A. D., Hall, C. M., and Saarinen, J. (2011). Making wilderness: Tourism and the history of the wilderness idea in Iceland. *Polar Geography*, 34(4), 249–73.

Sæþórsdóttir, A. D., Hall, C. M., and Wendt, M. (2020). Overtourism in Iceland: Fantasy or Reality? *Sustainability*, 12(18).

Sæþórsdóttir, A. D., Wendt, M., and Tverijonaite, E. (2021). Wealth of wind and visitors: Tourist industry attitudes towards wind energy development in Iceland. *Land*, 10(7), 693.

Sarkki, S. (2008) Forest dispute and change in Muonio, Northern Finland. *Journal of Northern Studies*, 2, 7–27.

Similä, J., and Jokinen, M. (2018). Governing conflicts between mining and tourism in the Arctic. *Arctic Review on Law and Politics*, 9, 148–73.

Sisneros-Kidd, A. M., Monz, C., Hausner, V., Schmidt, J., and Clark, D. (2019). Nature-based tourism, resource dependence, and resilience of Arctic communities: Framing complex issues in a changing environment. *Journal of Sustainable Tourism*, 27(8), 1259–76.

Smol, M., Marcinek, P., Duda, J., and Szołdrowska, D. (2020). Importance of sustainable mineral resource management in implementing the circular economy (CE) model and the European Green Deal strategy. *Resources*. 9(5), 55.

Solbär, L., Marcianó, P., and Pettersson, M. (2019). Land-use planning and designated national interests in Sweden: Arctic perspectives on landscape multifunctionality. *Journal of Environmental Planning and Management*, 62(12), 2145–65.

Sorvali, J., Lyytimäki, J., Lähteenmäki-Uutela, A., Huttunen, S., Inkilä, E., Weckroth, M., and Tuulentie, S. (2023). Reiluus puntarissa: Kuusamon tuulivoima- ja kaivossuunnitelmat alueellisina kestävyyskiistoina oikeudessa, mediassa ja mielipiteissä [Fairness to be valuated: Kuusamo's wind power and mining plans as regional sustainability disputes]. *Alue ja Ympäristö*, 52(2), 67–88.

Suopajärvi, L., Ejdemo, T., Klyuchnikova, E., Korchak, E., Nygaard, V., and Poelzer, G. A. (2017). Social impacts of the "glocal" mining business: Case studies from Northern Europe. *Mineral Economics*, 30, 31–9.

Svensson, J., Neumann, W., Bjärstig, T., Zachrisson, A., and Thellbro, C. (2020). Landscape approaches to sustainability: Aspects of conflict, integration, and synergy in national public land-use interests. *Sustainability, 12*(12), 5113.

Tolvanen, A., Eilu, P., Juutinen, A., Kangas, K., Kivinen, M., Markovaara-Koivisto, M., Naskali, A., Salokannel, V. Tuulentie, S., and Similä, J. (2019). Mining in the Arctic environment: A review from ecological, socioeconomic and legal perspectives. *Journal of Environmental Management, 233,* 832–44.

Törn, A., Tolvanen, A., Norokorpi, Y., Tervo, R., and Siikamäki, P. (2009). Comparing the impacts of hiking, skiing and horse riding on trail and vegetation in different types of forest. *Journal of Environmental Management, 90*(3), 1427–34.

Tyrväinen, L., Mäntymaa, E., Juutinen, A., Kurttila, M., and Ovaskainen, V. (2021). Private landowners' preferences for trading forest landscape and recreational values: A choice experiment application in Kuusamo, Finland. *Land Use Policy, 107,* 104478.

Tyrväinen, L., Silvennoinen, H., and Hallikainen, V. (2017). Effect of the season and forest management on the visual quality of the nature-based tourism environment: A case from Finnish Lapland. *Scandinavian Journal of Forest Research, 32*(4), 349–59.

Tyrväinen, L., Uusitalo, M., Silvennoinen, H., and Hasu, E. (2014). Towards sustainable growth in nature-based tourism destinations: Clients' views of land use options in Finnish Lapland. *Landscape and Urban Planning, 122,* 1–15.

Wall Reinius, S., and Fredman, P. (2007). Protected areas as attractions. *Annals of Tourism Research, 34*(4), 839–54.

11   Who owns the Arctic tourism industry? Economic-geographical perspectives

Dieter K. Müller

Introduction

Since the publication of Hall and Johnston's seminal book "Polar Tourism: Tourism in the Arctic and Antarctic Regions" in 1995, tourism in the Arctic has gained substantial research interest. While Hall and Johnston could likely not foresee this, the Arctic has turned into a hotspot in other aspects than just tourism. It is the combined impacts of climate change, renewed interest in northern resources including tourism, and geopolitical struggle that have triggered public and academic attention to the region.

In this context, tourism is often seen as a tool for regional development with the potential to meliorate structural conditions related to population and labor markets (Grenier and Müller, 2011). Still, this attention is not entirely mirrored in the scientific literature. While the cruise ship industry has drawn quite some attention (e.g. Lück et al., 2010), one can argue that more needs to be done to fully understand the economic-geographical dimensions of Arctic tourism. Acknowledging that tourism development should entail positive local and regional impacts, employment, spending, and ownership patterns become core aspects to be scrutinized.

This chapter takes its departure from this notion. Already Butler's (1980) Tourism Area Life Cycle (TALC) model acknowledges the fact that the development of tourism areas is signified by a changing ownership of the industry. While initial services are provided by local companies, a growing destination attracts investment from outside, thereby altering the modus operandi of businesses, their local embeddedness, and the economic relations of the destination. Still, this notion has seldom been developed any further. Exceptions involve, for example, family businesses (Getz and Carlsen, 2005), indigenous tourism (Hillmer-Pegram, 2016; Müller and Hoppstadius, 2017), and other small- and medium-sized enterprises, highlighting issues such as place attachment (Hallak et al., 2013) and economic performance (Yeh, 2019). Furthermore, these studies often originate from development studies and the Global South (e.g. Hampton and Jeyacheya, 2015), while Arctic areas are largely neglected.

Against this backdrop, the purposes of this chapter are to discuss the need to analyze the geography of industry ownership within an Arctic tourism context, and to outline a research agenda meliorating this noted shortcoming.

The problem of developing tourism for local and regional development

In his original contribution to the TALC, Butler (1980) simply notes that an area that manages to attract growing tourist numbers also attracts the attention of larger companies such as hotel chains. Investments in hotels and other tourism services at booming destinations promise a return on investment, and thus may be seen as good opportunities within a capitalist accumulation logic.

The Arctic and other northern places have thus even historically been integrated into global capitalist systems of resource exploitation. An explanation for this, the staple thesis, is usually derived from the development of the Canadian North, where natural resources such as timber, furs, and minerals were identified as tradable resources and consecutively harvested for export markets (Innis, 1933). The resulting so-called staple economy typically did not lead to a positive societal and cultural development of the north, but rather created an export-based growth in service of southern centres. At the same time, northern places remained stuck in a staple trap, dependent on single industries and with limited capacity to successfully adapt to economic restructuring and resource cycles (Clapp, 1998). Hence, even when staple export has been a successful recipe for national economies to get established on a global market, regional economies may have been left behind since economic diversification has taken place elsewhere. The degree to which the development of regional economies is based on the export of staples formatively influences these economies' economic, social, and political development (Halseth and Ryser, 2019).

Several researchers have addressed the role of tourism within such a context. Tourism has been considered a diversification strategy for local and regional economies, and thus a way to break a path of dependency on staple exports (Baum, 1999; Hall, 2007; Brouder, 2012). However, tourism has not always been a self-evident alternative. Müller (2013) showed that decline in employment within northern staple economies in Sweden tends to be accompanied by an increase in tourism and vice versa. Hence, historically, tourism has often been seen as a remedy in times of crisis but has been disregarded during booms of traditional industries (Jóhannesson, 2016). However, seasonality and overall low wage levels make tourism employment a poor alternative, forcing tourism to compete for labour with other low-income sectors of the regional economies (Müller, 2022). Furthermore, factors such as the setup of competencies among the workforce, societal institutions, and cultural traditions make the persistence of staple industries appealing and create path dependence (Gunton, 2003). Even tourism itself has been considered a potential staple industry (Schmallegger and Carson, 2010). A resort-based development favouring tourism over other economic activities creates a lock-in situation and hinders diversification into other sectors, for example to safeguard environmental and aesthetic qualities of the destination landscape. In the Arctic, such a development can be seen today at remote skiing destinations (Kulusjärvi, 2016).

Hence, while Schmallegger and Carson (2010) point out that staple-based development may indeed have advantages for communities, utilizing tourism for broader societal development is not an easy undertaking. Economic diversification in peripheral regions requires major changes to even underlying structures and procedures, including capacity-building and the creation of new alliances not least between the public and private sectors (Müller and Jansson, 2007; Carson and Carson, 2011).

It is also important to recognize that even though destinations may be within the same Arctic region, destination communities do not need to resemble each other, and nor are they homogenous units. Their location in relation to transport systems and major demand markets, as well as the availability of touristic assets, influence the extent to which they attract the interest of investors (Hall and Boyd, 2005). At the same time, economic and cultural development paths constrain how government, community, and businesses seize future opportunities.

Hence, the evolution of tourism in place usually entails that the local business community ultimately consists of different stakeholders with varying local anchoring. Depending on their embeddedness, companies will engage in common strategies and activities (Kulusjärvi, 2016; Müller, 2019). Still, there is a risk that growth-oriented agendas of large stakeholders will formatively influence local development and trigger power asymmetries in destination communities (Kulusjärvi, 2020; Lundén et al., 2023). Even from a public policy perspective, distances within the Arctic region and diverging ideas about development favor top-down approaches over alternative development (Petridou et al., 2019). The role of public support for tourism thus also varies. While Jenkins and Hall (1998) argue that tourism is a government response to rural restructuring, Almstedt et al. (2016) show that direct government investment in tourism remains relatively limited. And indeed, even public investment and support strategies differ among countries, favoring either resort-oriented or community-oriented development (Bohn et al., 2023).

Industry ownership and tourism impact

While Butler's (1980) TALC predicted that successful tourism development would entail a shift from local ownership of the industry to investments by global hotel chains and transport companies, Murphy's (1985) community approach opened avenues for alternative lines. Additionally inspired by sustainable development discourses, variations on this approach have been promoted to achieve a greater embeddedness of tourism in the local community, including positive local economic impacts. Most recently, regenerative tourism resembles the idea that tourism should contribute positively to destination communities and their environment instead of only consuming resources (Dredge, 2022; Bellato et al., 2023). Such a notion places the idea of local benefit from tourism at the core of the debate.

Positive impacts or benefits can be gained from tourism in various ways; this is typically structured as impacts on the environment, the economy, and the social and cultural dimensions of community (Hall and Lew, 2009; Stoffelen and Ioannides, 2022). Moreover, benefits can be gained on different levels. Accordingly, while individuals, communities, regions, and states can all see positive impacts from tourism, there is no guarantee that perceptions of positive impacts are aligned among these levels. Hence, while tourism may be very good for the national economy, a local community may still benefit merely marginally. Another example involves tourism development being appreciated in the local community while other economic activities such as mining are valued more highly in southern capitals.

These geographical orderings of tourism impacts underline the political dimensions of tourism as well. Ultimately, the notion of tourism development being the result of not only economic but also political processes has been the basis for a political economy of tourism (Mosedale, 2010a, 2016). While empirical assessments of tourism's economic contributions to development dominated early approaches, Bianchi (2018) claims that more theoretical reasoning is also needed, considering not least recent developments in platform economies and other new practices of tourism production. Meanwhile, he admits that the current understanding of the capitalist production of tourism is still imperfect, and this certainly applies to the Arctic region, where tourism has seldom been addressed from a political economy perspective. Brouder (2019) adds that this should be done from a geographical perspective as well, acknowledging the spatial dimensions of economic relations that are expressed in core–periphery relationships. Hence, understanding tourism development in the Arctic region is always impregnated with political-economic dimensions and an obvious question to ask is for whom tourism development is positive, particularly considering the conditions of the periphery with limited access to capital, political, and economic decision-making power as well as information flows (Botterill et al., 2000; Hall and Boyd, 2005).

To answer the question above, a short excursion into the basics of economic impact assessment is necessary. Economic impacts from tourism can be direct, indirect, and induced, and emanate from the spendings of tourists as well as companies and their employees (e.g. Saarinen, 2003). From a local economic perspective, a circulation of capital within the local arena is desirable as it shares the economic benefits beyond the tourism company. Direct impacts involve the direct spending of the tourist companies in the chosen geographical unit, for example on salaries and supplies. Indirect impacts are triggered by business-to-business transactions that are enabled by the initial spendings of the tourism companies. Finally, induced impacts result from the spendings of the employees of the directly and indirectly affected companies.

Hence, the local economic impact of tourism is dependent primarily on the share of tourist spendings that remains in the local economy. When revenues leave the local economy, as is the case for companies with owners based outside the local community, economic impacts are likely to occur elsewhere, while social, cultural, and environmental costs usually remain within the local arena. However, it is not only the presence of revenues remaining in the local community that affects the overall economic impact; the share of salary that stays local is also influential. Lundmark (2006) shows that in a situation in which labor cannot be recruited locally, tax incomes will mainly occur elsewhere. Seasonal labor and fly-in/fly-out arrangements are thus seldom economically beneficial to the local community, and there may also be challenges in relation to social and cultural development (Tuulentie and Heimtun, 2014). In peripheries, even economic linkages between different sectors are weaker, partly because supplies of goods and services are not always available in place;

thus, even the indirect and induced local impacts of tourism may be limited (Botterill et al., 2000).

Thus, far from all economic impacts are local; and indeed, tourism growth does not necessarily lead to positive local economic impacts either. With such an insight in mind, it is important to assess the structural preconditions set through policy within the political system. In a neoliberal setting, trust in market forces dominates and state involvement may be limited to guaranteeing a smooth operation of capitalist production processes (Mosedale, 2016; Wearing et al., 2019). Providing favourable tax schemes and regulations supporting tourism mobility are examples of such policy regimes. However, neoliberalism does not mean that government is absent. Instead, the provision of infrastructure and subsidies for transportation may be well in line with a neoliberal agenda, expecting the market to be best suited to deal with the challenges of peripheral places. Attracting private capital into peripheries and optimizing its performance are therefore seen as ways of providing a good solution for dealing with issues of employment and as an effective use of the periphery's resources. This usually triggers large-scale solutions based on economies of scale, and the market presence of large international companies such as the Holland–America Line in Alaska, Hurtigruten in Svalbard, or TUI in Rovaniemi is a clear indication of the economic profitability of operating in the Arctic, though it remains unclear whether their presence is due to public engagement. At the same time, regional and local tourism companies contribute to the overall product within many peripheral locations. Indeed, in some locations, these companies seem to dominate, possibly showing the marginal role of peripheral places in relation to global tourism; more profit can be gained elsewhere.

A different approach to understanding the structural preconditions set by the political system is based on assumptions derived from regulation theory. In accordance with this theory, government intervenes in market mechanisms in order to correct unwanted consequences or failure to achieve the desired outcome (Halseth and Ryser, 2019). Regulations, in the form of institutions, rules, or agreements, are launched to modify the processes of economic accumulation to stabilize the societal outcomes (Mosedale, 2010b). In such policy environment, tourism is a regulated mode of production and capital accumulation whereby company gains are balanced against the potential societal costs of this accumulation.

In this context, it is not only specific regulation of the tourism industry that should be considered. Infrastructure and various kinds of services that enable tourism development are also important elements of the Arctic tourism system. Moreover, hygienic standards and permit systems for entering national parks are regulations that are widely employed. Hence, as mentioned earlier, it is the degree of trust that market forces will solve societal challenges and the related reaction of regulating the market that discerns different systems. Furthermore, cultural and symbolic dimensions of economic accumulation have been regarded as influential in determining which regimes are established (Mosedale, 2010b). Hence, it is not only the factual economic balance that is decisive for the system in place.

Finally, tourism development in the Arctic also needs to be seen in the light of geopolitical change in the region. It has been shown that the Arctic states' national Arctic strategies do often not highlight tourism (Müller, 2021). The Nordic states are an exception to this, however, seeing tourism as a tool for regional development. Timothy (2010) and Erickson (2021) also argue that Arctic national parks and tourism in North America can be seen as a way to demonstrate presence, securing national sovereignty. Hence, it is no surprise that Chinese interests in establishing tourism operations in the Arctic create concern regarding their motivations and the consequences this could have for national sovereignty (Huijbens and Alessio, 2015). Still, Chinese tourism has also been seen as an opportunity in a China-centered global economy, with interests in not only tourism but also mining and transportation (Jørgensen and Bertelsen, 2020). In any case, this illustrates the increasingly global dimensions of Arctic tourism, and the interests that are motivated by economic considerations and by geopolitical ambitions beyond the immediate boundaries of tourism.

Suggestions for future research

Against the background discussed above, the political-economic geographies of Arctic tourism are more relevant now than ever. Particularly the following aspects, revolving around the core question – who owns Arctic tourism – should be addressed.

Mapping tourism ownership has the potential to reveal variations within the Arctic region, and a temporal dimension allows for assessing the evolution of Arctic economic geographies. In this context, the ownership of Arctic tourism should also be related to ownership patterns in other economic sectors in order to single out the tourism-specific element within the overall tendencies. This could potentially also disclose whether tourism is an industry to be developed in its own right, or as an industry supporting other sectors of the economy.

Furthermore, analysis of ownership should also be done, acknowledging the economic linkages between the Arctic periphery and southern core areas but also the vertical and horizontal integration of the tourism industry.

A knowledge of ownership patterns would also allow for an assessment of the performance and impact of tourism operations. Do places with external owners perform differently than locally owned businesses? And, more importantly, how do companies with different ownership types relate to the local community, and vice versa? Hence, this is about embeddedness in the local community. The marginality of many Arctic places makes them dependent on the import of goods and services, and thus the potential local impacts seem to be limited compared to places in more densely populated areas. This also applies in relation to the seasonality of tourism and tourism employment, often comprising substantial shares of incoming workers.

As tourism development is also an outcome of political decisions on various geographical scales, the impacts of these decisions on the economy should be scrutinized as well. Is tourism the end of policy efforts, or is it a tool for achieving other local or regional development goals? Considering the state of the planet, it is also important to look at how environmental dimensions are acknowledged in policymaking and industry practices.

The globalization of Arctic tourism also calls for an assessment of such a change. How does international ownership influence the political economy of Arctic tourism? What does it mean when international companies seize an opportunity to benefit from the economic potential of Arctic tourism operations, and how is such activity assessed by national and regional governments?

While the above questions and challenges are certainly not comprehensive, they may offer some direction for future research. Obviously, a complex setting also requires a variety of methodological approaches and methods. Today, there is a dominance of approaches highlighting the personal experiences of tourists and inhabitants of the Arctic, while structural dimensions are more seldom addressed. This has also led to a lack of quantitative information on various aspects of Arctic tourism. A research agenda should account for this, particularly when political-economic dimensions are in focus. Furthermore, comparative research would allow for distinguishing the impact of regulations on different scales and for identifying factual commonalities. This calls for joint efforts and international collaboration in line with previous projects undertaken by the UArctic Thematic Network on Northern Tourism (Rantala et al., 2019; Müller et al., 2020; Jóhannesson et al., 2022; Maher et al., 2022).

Conclusion

Despite the great expectations related to tourism development, scientific concern has often been expressed regarding the consumption and immediate production of Arctic tourism, as well as its relation to climate change. At the same time, geopolitical change and a shifting position of Arctic regions in the global economy make it almost mandatory to assess the political and economic reasons for tourism development on various geographical scales, as well as the consequences for the local and regional economies and communities. Understanding the political economy of tourism development is hence an important step in moving beyond the practice of assessing the tourism industry as an isolated entity; it has the potential to contribute to a broader understanding of processes of regional and local development in the Arctic as well as the role of tourism.

References

Almstedt, Å., Lundmark, L., and Pettersson, Ö. (2016). Public spending on rural tourism in Sweden. *Fennia*, *194*(1), 18–31.

Baum, T. (1999). The decline of the traditional North Atlantic fisheries and tourism's response: The cases of Iceland and Newfoundland. *Current Issues in Tourism*, *2*(1), 47–67.

Bellato, L., Frantzeskaki, N., and Nygaard, C. A. (2023). Regenerative tourism: A conceptual framework leveraging theory and practice. *Tourism Geographies*, *25*(4), 1026–46.

Bianchi, R. (2018). The political economy of tourism development: A critical review. *Annals of Tourism Research*, *70*, 88–102.

Bohn, D., Carson, D. A., Demiroglu, O. C., and Lundmark, L. (2023). Public funding and destination evolution in sparsely populated Arctic regions. *Tourism Geographies*, *25*(8), 1833–85.

Botterill, D., Owen, R. E., Emanuel, L., Foster, N., Gale, T., Nelson, C., and Selby, M. (2000). Perceptions from the periphery: The experience of Wales. In F. Brown and D. Hall (Eds.), *Tourism in Peripheral Areas: Case Studies*, 7–38. Clevedon: Channel View.

Brouder, P. (2012). Creative outposts: Tourism's place in rural innovation. *Tourism Planning and Development*, *9*(4), 383–96.

Brouder, P. (2019). Towards a geographical political economy of tourism. In D. K. Müller (Ed.), *A Research Agenda for Tourism Geographies*, 71–8. Edward Elgar.

Butler, R. W. (1980). The concept of a tourist area cycle of evolution: Implications for management of resources. *Canadian Geographer*, *24*(1), 5–12.

Carson, D. A., and Carson, D. B. (2011). Why tourism may not be everybody's business: The challenge of tradition in resource peripheries. *The Rangeland Journal*, *33*(4), 373–83.

Clapp, R. A. (1998). The resource cycle in forestry and fishing. *Canadian Geographer,* 42(2), 129–44.

Dredge, D. (2022). Regenerative tourism: Transforming mindsets, systems and practices. *Journal of Tourism Futures,* 8(3), 269–81.

Erickson, B. (2021). The Neoliberal Tourist: Affect, Policy and Economy in the Canadian North. *ACME: An International Journal for Critical Geographies,* 20(1), 58–80.

Getz, D., and Carlsen, J. (2005). Family business in tourism: State of the art. *Annals of Tourism Research,* 32(1), 237–58.

Grenier A. A., and Müller, D. K. (Eds.) (2011). *Polar Tourism: A Tool for Regional Development.* Montreal: Presses de l'Université du Québec.

Gunton, T. (2003). Natural resources and regional development: An assessment of dependency and comparative advantage paradigms. *Economic Geography,* 79(1), 67–94.

Hall, C. M. (2007). North–south perspectives on tourism, regional development and peripheral areas. In D. K. Müller and B. Jansson (Eds.), *Tourism in Peripheries: Perspectives from the Far North and South,* 19–37. Wallingford UK: CABI.

Hall, C. M., and Boyd, S. (2005). Nature-based tourism in peripheral areas: Introduction. In C. M. Hall and S. Boyd (Eds.), *Nature-based Tourism in Peripheral Areas: Development or Disaster,* 3–17. Clevedon: Channel View.

Hall, C. M., and Johnston, M. E. (Eds.) (1995). *Polar Tourism: Tourism in the Arctic and Antarctic Regions.* Chichester: Wiley.

Hall, C. M., and Lew, A. A. (2009). *Understanding and Managing Tourism Impacts: An Integrated Approach.* London: Routledge.

Hallak, R., Brown, G., and Lindsay, N. J. (2013). Examining tourism SME owners' place attachment, support for community and business performance: The role of the enlightened self-interest model. *Journal of Sustainable Tourism,* 21(5), 658–78.

Halseth, G., and Ryser, L. (2019). *Towards a Political Economy of Resource-dependent Regions.* London: Routledge.

Hampton, M. P., and Jeyacheya, J. (2015). Power, ownership and tourism in small islands: Evidence from Indonesia. *World Development,* 70, 481–95.

Hillmer-Pegram, K. (2016). Integrating Indigenous values with capitalism through tourism: Alaskan experiences and outstanding issues. *Journal of Sustainable Tourism,* 24(8–9), 1194–210.

Huijbens, E. H., and Alessio, D. (2015). Arctic 'concessions' and icebreaker diplomacy? Chinese tourism development in Iceland. *Current Issues in Tourism,* 18(5), 433–49.

Innis, H. (1933). *Problems of Staple Production in Canada.* Toronto: Ryerson Press.

Jenkins, J. M., and Hall, C. M. (1998). The restructuring of rural economies: Rural tourism and recreation as a government response. In R. Butler, C. M. Hall, and J. Jenkins (Eds.), *Tourism and Recreation in Rural Areas,* 43–68. Chichester: Wiley.

Jóhannesson, G. T. (2016). A fish called tourism: Emergent realities of tourism policy in Iceland. In G. T. Jóhannesson, C. Ren, and R. van der Duim (Eds.), *Tourism Encounters and Controversies,* 181–200. Routledge.

Jóhannesson, G. T., Welling, J., Müller, D. K., Lundmark, L., Nilsson, R. O., de la Barre, S., Granås, B., Kvidal-Røvik, T., Rantala, O., Tervo-Kankare, K., and Maher, P. (2022). *Arctic Tourism in Times of Change – Uncertain Futures: From Overtourism to Re-starting Tourism.* TemaNord 2022:516. Copenhagen: Nordic Council of Ministers.

Jørgensen, M. T., and Bertelsen, R. G. (2020). Chinese tourism in the Nordic Arctic – Opportunities beyond the economic. *Scandinavian Journal of Hospitality and Tourism*, 20(2), 166–77.

Kulusjärvi, O. (2016). Resort-oriented tourism development and local tourism networks – a case study from Northern Finland. *Fennia*, *194*(1), 3–17.

Kulusjärvi, O. (2020). Towards just production of tourism space via dialogical everyday politics in destination communities. *Environment and Planning C: Politics and Space*, *38*(4), 751–67.

Lück, M., Maher, P. T., and Stewart, E. J. (Eds.) (2010). *Cruise Tourism in Polar Regions: Promoting Environmental and Social Sustainability?* London: Earthscan.

Lundén, A., Varnajot, A., Kulusjärvi, O., and Partanen, M. (2023). Globalised imaginaries, arctification and resistance in Arctic tourism: An arctification perspective on tourism actors' views on seasonality and growth in Ylläs tourism destination. *The Polar Journal*. Doi: 10.1080/2154896X.2023.2241248.

Lundmark, L. (2006). Mobility, migration and seasonal tourism employment: Evidence from Swedish mountain municipalities. *Scandinavian Journal of Hospitality and Tourism*, 6(3), 197–213.

Maher, P. T., Jóhannesson, G. Þ., Kvidal Røvik, T., Müller, D. K. and Rantala, O. (2022). Touring in the Arctic: Shades of gray towards a sustainable future. In D. C. Natcher and T. Koivurova (Eds.), *Renewable Economies in the Arctic*, 81–98. London: Routledge.

Mosedale, J. (Ed.) (2010a). *Political Economy and Tourism: A Critical Perspective*. London: Routledge.

Mosedale, J. (2010b). Re-introducing tourism to political economy. In J. Mosedale (Ed.), *Political Economy and Tourism: A Critical Perspective*, 1–13. London: Routledge.

Mosedale, J. (Ed.) (2016). *Neoliberalism and the Political Economy of Tourism*. London: Routledge.

Müller, D. K. (2013). Hibernating economic decline? Tourism and labor market change in Europe's northern periphery. In G. Visser and S. Ferreira (Eds.), *Tourism and Crisis*, 113–28. London: Routledge.

Müller, D. K. (2019). An Evolutionary Economic Geography perspective on tourism development in the periphery: The case of Tärnaby/Hemavan in the Swedish mountains. In R. L. Koster and D. A. Carson (Eds.), *The Exotic, the Fringe and the Boring Bits In Between: New Perspectives on Rural Tourism Geographies*, 137–57. Cham: Springer.

Müller, D. K. (2021). Tourism in national Arctic strategies: A perspective on the tourism-geopolitics nexus. In M. Mostafanezhad, M. Córdoba Azcárate, and R. Norum (Eds.), *The Geopolitics of Tourism: Assemblages of Power, Mobility and the State*, 91–111. Tucson: University of Arizona Press.

Müller D. K. (2022). National parks, protected areas and tourism labor markets in Arctic Sweden. In A. L. Svalastog, D. K. Müller and I. Jenkins (Eds.), *Tourism as a Resource-based Industry: Based on the Work of Sondre* Svalastog, 76–88. Wallingford: CABI.

Müller, D. K. and Hoppstadius, F. (2017). Sami tourism at the crossroads: Globalization as a challenge for business, environment and culture in Swedish Sápmi. In A. Viken and D. K. Müller (Eds.), *Tourism and Indigeneity in the Arctic*, 71–86. Bristol: Channel View.

Müller, D. K., and Jansson, B. (2007). The difficult business of making pleasure peripheries prosperous: Perspectives on space, place and environment. In D. K. Müller and

B. Jansson (Eds.), *Tourism in Peripheries: Perspectives from the Far North and South*, 3–18). Wallingford: CABI.

Müller, D. K., Carson, D. A., de la Barre, S., Granås, B., Jóhannesson, G. T., Øyen, G., Rantala, O., Saarinen, J., Salmela, T., Tervo-Kankare, K., and Welling, J. (2020). *Arctic Tourism in Times of Change: Dimensions of Urban Tourism*. TemaNord 2020:529. Copenhagen: Nordic Council of Ministers.

Murphy, P. (1985). *Tourism: A Community Approach*. London: Thomson International.

Petridou, E., Olausson, P. M., and Ioannides, D. (2019). Nascent island tourism policy development in Greenland: A network perspective. *Island Studies Journal, 14*(2), 227–44.

Rantala, O., de la Barre, S., Granås, B., Jóhannesson, G. Þ., Müller, D. K., Saarinen, J., Tervo-Kankare, K., Maher, P. T. and Niskala M. (2019). *Arctic Tourism in Times of Change: Seasonality*. TemaNord 2019:528. Copenhagen: Nordic Council of Ministers.

Saarinen, J. (2003). The regional economics of tourism in Northern Finland: The socio-economic implications of recent tourism development and future possibilities for regional development. *Scandinavian Journal of Hospitality and Tourism, 3*(2), 91–113.

Schmallegger, D., and Carson, D. (2010). Is tourism just another staple? A new perspective on tourism in remote regions. *Current Issues in Tourism, 13*(3), 201–21.

Stoffelen, A., and Ioannides, D. (Eds.) (2022). *Handbook of Tourism Impacts: Social and Environmental Perspectives*. Edward Elgar Publishing.

Timothy, D. J. (2010). Contested place and the legitimization of sovereignty through tourism in polar regions. In C. M. Hall and J. Saarinen (Eds.), *Tourism and Change in Polar Regions*, 306–18. London: Routledge.

Tuulentie, S., and Heimtun, B. (2014). New rural residents or working tourists? Place attachment of mobile tourism workers in Finnish Lapland and Northern Norway. *Scandinavian Journal of Hospitality and Tourism, 14*(4), 367–84.

Wearing, S., McDonald, M., Taylor, G., and Ronen, T. (2019). Neoliberalism and global tourism. In D. J. Timothy (Ed.), *Handbook of Globalisation and Tourism*, 27–43. Edward Elgar Publishing.

Yeh, C. M. (2019). Ownership structure and firm performance of listed tourism firms. *International Journal of Tourism Research, 21*(2), 165–79.

12 Post-Arctic tourism and the need to rethink the aesthetics of Arctic tourism in the context of climate change

Alix Varnajot

Introduction

In the autumn of 2018, Finnish Lapland saw relatively milder temperatures and a significant lack of snow. Combined with the long winter nights typical of these latitudes, the region appeared particularly gloomy and dark, far from expected representations replete with white vistas. While late winters are not unusual in Finnish Lapland, many tourists left disappointed and dispirited because their experiences did not match their expectations of Lapland and its – supposedly – promised snow. This episode led British tabloids to rename 'Lapland' as 'Crapland', generating bad publicity for the region (Varnajot, 2020). Although this Crapland incident might seem like an epiphenomenon, it can also be interpreted as a foretaste of what the future of Arctic tourism may look like from a mid-term perspective. As such, it raises interesting questions regarding tourists' representations and expectations of the Arctic in a rapidly changing region. It also prompts considerations about current adaptation strategies, which are essential not only to prevent similar episodes, but more importantly, to build efficient resilient capacities for local Arctic communities that are often dependent on tourism (Kaján, 2014). In tourism, adaptation generally refers to 'actions aiming to reduce the negative effects (and to benefit from the positive effects) of climate change' (Tervo-Kankare et al., 2018, p. 203). However, it is worth noting that defining adaptation can be a challenging task, as Kaján et al. (2015) pointed out, given the diverse interpretations that tourism actors may attach to the concept.

This chapter delves into the future of Arctic tourism in the European Arctic, and particularly focuses on adaptation strategies to climate change. It is argued that adaptation strategies currently in use by tourism stakeholders further increase the dependence of Arctic tourism on snow and ice. Furthermore, in light of climate change projections and estimated impacts on the cryosphere, these strategies are likely to become increasingly unsustainable and anachronistic, calling for urgent rethinking of adaptation strategies. Therefore, using the Post-Arctic tourism paradigm recently developed by Varnajot and Saarinen (2021, 2022), this chapter contends that current tourism adaptation strategies to climate change might be referred to as maladaptation (see Scott et al., 2024). Maladaptation to climate change generally refers to strategies that create lock-ins of vulnerability and produce increased exposure and risks that are difficult and expensive to change (IPCC, 2022). In addition, building on the recommendations from Rantala et al. (2019), it proposes to rethink the aesthetics of Arctic tourism. The next section introduces the Post-Arctic tourism paradigm, also providing definitions and contextualization of Arctic tourism in the European Arctic geographical context. Then, the focus shifts to climate change adaptation strategies in Arctic tourism, highlighting their main limitations in the Post-Arctic paradigm. The section also advocates rethinking the aesthetics of Arctic tourism as a smarter and more efficient strategy for local Arctic communities to become more resilient in the ongoing climate crisis.

Definition and contextualization of Post-Arctic tourism

The idea of Post-Arctic tourism was coined by Varnajot and Saarinen (2021). Grounded in post-apocalyptic narratives and in the Anthropocene, the authors proposed a vision of Arctic tourism in an ice- and snowless Arctic. According to the authors, a post-apocalyptic and dystopian future, labelled Post-Arctic tourism, may take place if the tourism industry remains 'dependent on a sole idea of Arctic tourism' (Varnajot and Saarinen, 2022, p. 366). Generally, the Anthropocene refers to a new epoch wherein the 'human imprint on the global environment has now become so large and active that it rivals some of the great forces of Nature in its impact on the functioning of the Earth system' (Steffen et al., 2011, p. 842). The Anthropocene is also commonly associated with post-apocalyptic narratives (see Huijbens, 2021; Swyngedouw, 2019). Although the term Apocalypse is religiously charged, in our contemporary times, what we generally consider to be apocalypses 'encompasses a broad range of beliefs, and social processes centred on cultural disjunctures concerned with "the end of the world" and thereafter' (Hall, 2009, p. 2). In this context, Post-Arctic tourism is not only concerned with the collapse of the Arctic tourism industry as we know it today but also with following – post-apocalyptic – futures.

These apocalypses or disjunctures may be economic or health crises, or environmental or man-made catastrophes, also known as disasters. The United

Nations Office for Disaster Risk Reduction (UNDRR, n.d.) considers two types of disasters: sudden-onset and slow-onset disasters. While sudden-onset disasters are triggered by a hazardous event that emerges quickly or unexpectedly (e.g., earthquakes, flash floods, chemical explosions, etc.), slow-onset disasters emerge steadily over time and space (UNDRR, n.d.). They are gradual, accretive, and incremental (Nixon, 2011), and have sometimes been referred to as slow catastrophes (see Shepherd, 2019). Examples of slow-onset disasters include droughts, desertification, sea-level rise, or the global melting cryosphere, among others. Post-apocalyptic narratives are therefore set in a temporal perspective 'where a new situation, world or system takes place after a disruptive event that is significant enough to alter the conditions of the "pre-event" situation' (Varnajot and Saarinen, 2022, p. 359). Nevertheless, the receding of the cryosphere does not take place at the same pace everywhere in the Arctic (see IPCC, 2019) and as such, slow-onset apocalyptic events can also be viewed as transition periods from the pre- to the post-event situation. In this scenario, some Arctic destinations may face challenges from the increasing seasonal variability and absence of lack of snow and ice (see the Crapland incident) while some others may still temporarily thrive, and this dynamic can create problematic situations from a competition perspective (Varnajot and Saarinen, 2022). Therefore, it becomes critical to gain a deeper understanding of the melting cryosphere as a slow-onset disaster and its various impacts on local communities. This is vital for destinations, municipalities and the various stakeholders involved in the tourism industry to effectively navigate the ongoing transition to a Post-Arctic tourism future.

In addition, from a conceptual perspective, Post-Arctic tourism is also concerned with last-chance tourism (LCT). LCT refers to the desire for tourists to witness vanishing landscapes, seascapes, or iconic animal species before they are gone for good or irrevocably changed (Lemelin et al., 2010). Although LCT speaks to apocalyptic narratives of ruination and to an imagined state of loss, those threatened Arctic elements are still there (and may not all disappear in the future). As such, Post-Arctic tourism 'gradually emerges along LCT but only becomes a concrete reality after LCT opportunities are gone' (Varnajot and Saarinen, 2022, p. 360).

Against this backdrop, the pre-event situation refers to Arctic tourism as we know it today. In line with this, since the overall argument of this chapter is rooted in the interpretation of Arctic tourism, it is critical to delve into its conceptualization, construction, and dimensions, however briefly. Then, there is first, a need to differentiate 'Arctic tourism' from 'tourism in the Arctic'. Indeed, 'tourism in the Arctic' is rather straightforward and is grounded in a geographical approach. It refers to all tourism activities taking place within the border of the Arctic, raising the long-discussed challenge of geographically delimiting the Arctic. Nevertheless, despite the various boundaries adopted by different academic disciplines to delineate the Arctic (Grenier, 2007), the astronomical Arctic Circle appears to be the most widely accepted (Viken, 2013). The Arctic Circle is also prevalent within the tourism industry, as pointed out by Varnajot (2019), where it often serves as an opportunity for economic development, featuring crossing ceremonies for example.

Arctic tourism, however, is more intricate to define. Some authors like Saarinen and Varnajot (2019) or Viken (2013) have raised the unique, special, and almost oneiric nature of the Arctic in tourism, which adds to the challenge of establishing a clear conceptualization. Maher (2007) even claimed that providing a sound definition for Arctic tourism is virtually impossible. In spite of these considerations, Grenier (2011) proposed a sociological approach, where Arctic tourism is defined in terms of specific extreme and unusual experiences, opposed to the idea of normality. Thus, following Grenier's view-point, for Arctic experiences to be *extra*-ordinary, Arctic tourism needs to be defined by and produced for outsiders (Saarinen and Varnajot, 2019). As such, Arctic tourism can also be understood as the production and reproduction of outsiders' extreme, unusual, and extraordinary representations of the Arctic. As exemplified by the 2018 Crapland incident, these representations involve stereotypical imaginaries of snowy, cold, and white landscapes (Rantala et al., 2019; Herva et al., 2020; Nilsson and Demiroglu, 2023), and this social phenomenon has been termed Arctification (see Müller and Viken, 2017). Although Arctification is not a recent phenomenon, it has recently been increasingly explored by Nordic scholars (see Rantala et al., 2019; Carson, 2020; Bohn and Varnajot, 2021; Marjavaara et al., 2022; Varnajot and Saarinen, 2022; Bohn et al., 2023).

Arctification refers to the production of 'particular representations of the North among consumers as well as the industry and political stakeholders' (Carson, 2020, p. 6), using meanings, symbols or names related to the Arctic (see Marjavaara et al., 2022). By creating an overrepresentation of these winter-based meanings and symbols in Arctic imaginaries, Arctification leads to the overlooking of other seasons. Visit Kemi (n.d.), for example, proudly promotes a recently built ice gallery (Figure 12.1). Their website reads: 'now you have a chance to experience snow & ice even in the summertime'. Besides this intensification of winter-based representations, Arctification also leads to a standardization of Arctic tourism products and experiences. Indeed, Saarinen and Varnajot (2019) conducted a simple descriptive analysis of tourism products offered under the name of 'Arctic' across several popular Arctic destinations (Rovaniemi, Reykjavik, Longyearbyen, Tromsø, Sisimiut,

Iqaluit, Whitehorse, Fairbanks, and Yakutsk). Although these destinations are culturally, historically, and geographically distinct, Saarinen and Varnajot (2019) identified a strong core of common tourism activities offered in all of them. These activities are reindeer- and dogsledding, viewing northern lights, snowmobiling, and ice-fishing, and are therefore mostly nature- and winter-based. Additionally, Arctification can also be observed through the tourism accommodation sector, with for example, snow and ice castles/hotels or glass igloos, and these have become popular attractions particularly in the Nordic countries (Varnajot and Lundén, in press). While glass igloos draw from the Inuit culture, ice castles and hotels originate from a Swedish initiative and have more recently spread to other Arctic, Nordic, and more generally, to cold and alpine destinations (e.g., Québec City, Canada, Val Thorens, in the French Alps). The Icehotel of Jukkasjärvi was indeed the first of its kind to have been developed as a tourist attraction where 'the unique elements of the Arctic winter were regarded as an asset' (Hall et al., 2009, p. 241). As such, Arctic tourism is produced regardless of the local cultural and geographical context, reflecting the broader standardization, homogenization, and globalization of destinations and tourism products (Simpson, 2016; Eriksen, 2021).

Arctification appears to be the main driving force of Arctic tourism. Nevertheless, the melting of the cryosphere as a slow-onset disaster involves projections of a general reduction in Arctic snow cover – the very resource of Arctic tourism – duration for all regions of the Arctic, particularly in northern Europe (IPCC, 2019). Also, increasing weather variability in the winter is projected to increase rain-on-snow events, which is problematic for tourism, especially for activities such as dogsledding, snowmobiling, and more generally for pedestrian transport (Serreze et al., 2021). In line with this, Post-Arctic tourism gradually emerges as the cryosphere recedes (Varnajot and Saarinen, 2022).

Source: Varnajot, 2023.

Figure 12.1   The ice gallery, in Kemi, Finland, is a hangar wherein freezing temperatures are maintained all year round

Tourism adaptation strategies to climate change

Current adaptation strategies

The influence of Arctification does not stop at the modes of production of Arctic tourism. Because Arctification shapes and manipulates representations of the Arctic in tourism (and beyond), it also impacts decision-making processes related to climate change adaptation strategies. Indeed, the tourism industry tends to adapt to international tourists' representations and expectations of the Arctic rather than to the actual challenges brought by the climate crisis. In line with this, these strategies generally focus on the lack of snow, particularly in the early winter season (November–December). However, these strategies lead to increasing dependence on snow and ice and reinforce the biased and stereotypical representations of the Arctic in tourism. Considering climate change projections, this dependence is likely to become anachronistic in the long-term perspective, and therefore unsustainable. This resonates with

Kaján and Saarinen's (2013) review of tourism adaptation and climate change, in which they highlighted that most studies focusing on the topic have demonstrated a limited level of action from tourism stakeholders, despite growing climate change awareness (see also Tervo-Kankare, 2019). In fact, increasing knowledge and awareness about climate change impacts on the tourism industry generally does not translate to effective proactive actions from tourism actors (see Becken, 2005; Hambira et al., 2013; Tervo-Kankare, 2019; Varnajot and Lundén, in press).

It is, however, important to note that 'adaptation to climate change in tourism is not restricted to adjusting to changes in the long-term mean climate variables, as also variability, which includes the weather extremes, is changing' (Tervo-Kankare et al., 2018, p. 206). Indeed, the increasing weather variability is challenging day-to-day tourism operations. Short-term weather variability, for example, generates extra costs for companies. Kaján et al. (2015) showed that in Finnish Lapland the increasing weather variability, particularly in the early winter season, leads to extra costs related to energy consumption, workforce due to wrong timing of recruitment, and maintenance work. In addition, delayed openings of the season due to late snowfalls (see IPCC, 2019) generally impact overall turnovers (Kaján et al., 2015). It is therefore critical to not overlook short-term adaptation strategies (Smit et al., 2000; Becken, 2013). Short-term adaptation is also important since authors like Denstadli et al. (2011) and Førland et al. (2013) have shown that weather variables (temperatures, precipitation, cloudiness, etc.) can have significant influence on tourists' preferences for a destination, and then further impact destinations' attractiveness. In line with this, current adaptation strategies are locked in short-term goals, aiming at maintaining the attractiveness of the Arctic as it has been produced in the past three decades – from the outsiders' perspective. As a result, a significant effort is put into maintaining the 'cryospheric gaze', to use Varnajot's (2020, p. 67) words. These efforts commonly involve snow farming, snowmaking, and increasingly so, the construction of 'domes' (with indoor artificial snow production), all aiming to secure the presence of snow on the ground. Nevertheless, adaptation strategies generally aim to transform operations within an industry, a unit, or a system considering expected changes (see Pielke, 1998; Kelly and Adger, 2000; Tervo-Kankare et al., 2018), but not to maintain past or current practices. More so, in a Post-Arctic tourism context and considering climate change projections in the European Arctic, 'maintaining the attractive image of a snow-covered wonderland may become impossible' (Tervo-Kankare et al., 2013, p. 292).

Briefly, snow farming (or snow storing) refers to 'the conservation of snow during the warm season of the year' (Grünewald et al., 2018, p. 385). At the end of the spring, piles of snow are made on slopes, covered by sawdust and/or geo-textiles, and are then spread over in the early autumn. Snowmaking, however, is the production of artificial snow and has been widely used by the ski industry for several decades. Nevertheless, snowmaking is only possible when temperatures remain low enough and when there are available water resources nearby (Gerbaux et al., 2020; François et al., 2023; Knowles et al., 2023). In contrast, domes with indoor snow production and controlled temperatures, allow activities engaging with snow and ice all year round. These domes range from common and small hangars (see Figure 12.1) to extravagant projects such as the Republic of Santa Claus, planned on the outskirts of Rovaniemi (see Varnajot, 2020; Lundén, 2022). Another dome – a planetarium – was also recently built in the Kakslauttanen tourism resort (nearby Saariselkä), allowing tourists to see northern lights, even if weather conditions are not favourable (Melamies, 2022). By controlling natural elements like snow or northern lights (or by providing an illusion of control), these strategies and infrastructures are designed to reduce the scarcity of sought-after 'arctified' elements.

Nevertheless, these strategies used to maintain the cryospheric gaze in a warming Arctic come with sustainability limitations, depending on local climate change impacts, policy decisions regarding destinations' energy mixes, and tourism markets. For example, François et al. (2023) showed that in some instances, water demand and electricity carbon footprint associated with snowmaking might decrease in the early winter season (November), simply because temperatures would be too high for snow cannons to work. However, from a global and annual perspective, water demand for snowmaking is projected to increase from +8% to +25% in a +2°C warming scenario, and from +14% to +42% in a +4°C warming scenario (François et al., 2023). Similarly, the global electricity demand for snowmaking is projected to increase on average by 18% in a +2°C scenario and by 24% in a +4°C scenario (François et al., 2023). Besides these challenges from the environmental perspective, maintaining a cryospheric gaze in a Post-Arctic tourism also raises issues for social sustainability and ethics. Indeed, in times of energy crises, reflected by rising prices, electricity shortages, and calls for energy sufficiency for the population (like in Finland in the 2022–2023 winter), the industry and decision-makers will increasingly face challenges to justify these strategies. Generally, in a Post-Arctic tourism future, Arctification and the associated efforts to maintain the cryospheric gaze are expected to become socially, economically, and environmentally anachronistic. Therefore, strategies adopted with the sole goal of pleasing outsiders' experiences can be understood as climate change maladaptation, to use the words of Knowles et al. (2023) and Scott et al. (2024).

De-Arctification strategies for a charming Post-Arctic tourism

Studies on climate change adaptation in tourism have mainly focused on reactive and practical adaptation strategies (e.g., snowmaking and storing) (Kaján et al., 2015; Tervo-Kankare et al., 2018). However, more recently, authors like Lundén et al. (2023), Rantala et al. (2019) or Varnajot (in press) have suggested the need to shift focus on anticipatory strategies, such as changing the narratives and imaginaries associated with the Arctic, and therefore limiting the influence of Arctification (Rantala et al., 2019). In this respect, building on Rantala et al.'s (2019) recommendations, Cooper et al. (2020) have suggested de-Arctification strategies to mitigate the negative impacts of Arctification and an associated post-apocalyptic Arctic in tourism. In a nutshell, Rantala et al. (2019, p. 14) recommended to 'develop high-season tourism based on local tourism perspective' with 'a variety of Arctic meanings and experiences'. In other words, to emancipate Arctic tourism from Arctification. This, in turn, should contribute to '[avoiding] stereotypical production and marketing of winter tourism' (Rantala et al., 2019, p. 14).

In line with this, Lundén et al. (2023) developed the idea of endogenous de-Arctification, in which adaptation strategies to climate change value contextual and seasonal diversities, beyond cryospheric-based representations and activities. This, for example, implies the need to develop tourism products outside the core nature-based activities identified by Saarinen and Varnajot (2019), and that are 'environmentally less stressful and based on local rhythms of the year, with activities rooted in diverse and dynamic local customs, histories, and cultures' (Lundén et al. 2023, p. 17). To do so, it is also critical to change the narratives and aesthetics associated with the Arctic in tourism. Consequently, Varnajot (in press) proposed geopoetics as a more relevant climate change adaptation strategy for Arctic tourism. As recommended by the IPCC (2022), with flexible, inclusive, and long-term planning and implementation, such de-Arctification strategies can attenuate, counteract, and balance the negative consequences of maladaptation.

As argued by Magrane (2015, p. 87), geopoetics describes how 'we live on and with the Earth', thus highlighting the connections between geography and creative narratives. In the context of tourism, geopoetics can take multiple forms, through for example, the use of promotional materials, social media, travel magazines, blogs, and even guided tours (Varnajot, in press). According to Magrane (2021, p. 11) geopoetics can trigger 'a critical awareness of the social and cultural constructions of […] place, space, landscape, nature, and scale; a reflexive consideration of how places are represented and, in turn made; [and] an engagement with speculative futures'. Therefore, the use of geopoetics appears to be a relevant tool for changing the aesthetics and narratives of the Arctic in outsiders' representations, and thus follows the recommendations of Rantala et al. (2019) (see Cresswell, 2022), and also making Arctic tourism more resilient in a Post-Arctic tourism future. Lastly, geopoetics can further be used to mitigate anxiety-driven ruination and post-apocalyptic narratives associated with slow-onset disasters and LCT, which could potentially, lead to the 'possibilities of a charming' Post-Arctic future, to use Buck's (2015, p. 369) words.

Conclusion

It is important to remind the reader that Post-Arctic tourism does not mean the end of tourism in the Arctic. People will keep visiting friends and relatives; they will keep hiking in national parks during the summer, spending time in their second home or attending festivals and sporting events. Nevertheless, Arctic tourism, driven and produced by the process of Arctification will face significant environmental, economic, and social challenges that become particularly evident in a Post-Arctic future. These challenges are further emphasized by current climate change (mal)adaptation strategies that are focussed on maintaining Arctification, its associated cryospheric gaze, products, and experiences in tourism. This chapter invites researchers, municipalities, entrepreneurs, and tourism actors in general to reinvent their Arctic narratives. A proposed approach is the use of geopoetics, calling to experiment with language and creative writing (Cresswell, 2021). Given the close intricacies between language and place (see Tuan, 1991), combining geopoetics and tourism narratives offers a fresh and innovative perspective on the future of Arctic tourism, and can help us think differently about the slow-onset Arctic apocalypse that is upon us.

References

Becken, S. (2005). Harmonising climate change adaptation and mitigation: The case of tourist resorts in Fiji. *Global Environmental Change, 15*, 381–93.
Becken, S. (2013). Measuring the effects of weather on tourism: A destination- and activity-based analysis. *Journal of Travel Research, 52*(2), 156–67.
Bohn, D., and Varnajot, A. (2021). A geopolitical outlook on Arctification in Northern Europe: Insights from tourism, regional branding and higher education institutions. In L. Heininen, H. Exner-Pirot, and J. Barnes (Eds.), *Arctic Yearbook 2021: Defining and Mapping Sovereignties, Policies and Perceptions*, 279–92. Arctic Portal.

Bohn, D., Carson, D. A., Demiroglu, O. C., and Lundmark, L. (2023). Public funding and destination evolution in sparsely populated Arctic regions. *Tourism Geographies,* *25*(8), 1833–55.

Buck, H. J. (2015). On the possibilities of a charming Anthropocene. *Annals of the Association of American Geographers, 105*(2), 369–77.

Carson, D. (2020). Urban tourism in the Arctic: A framework for comparison. In D. K. Müller, D. A. Carson, S. de la Barre, B. Granås, G. Þ. Jóhannesson, G. Øyen, O. Rantala, J. Saarinen, T. Salmela, K. Tervo-Kankare and J. Welling (Eds.), *Arctic Tourism in Times of Changes: Dimensions of Urban Tourism,* 6–17. Nordic Council of Ministers.

Cooper, E. A., Spinei, M., and Varnajot, A. (2020). Countering "arctification": Dawson city's "sourtoe cocktail". *Journal of Tourism Futures, 6*(1), 70–82.

Cresswell, T. (2021) Beyond geopoetics: For hybrid texts. *Dialogues in Human Geography, 11*(1), 36–9.

Cresswell, T. (2022) Writing (new) worlds: Poetry and place in a time of emergency. *Geografiska Annaler B, 104*(4), 374–89.

Denstadli, J. M., Jacobsen, J. K. S., and Lohmann, M. (2011). Tourist perceptions of summer weather in Scandinavia. *Annals of Tourism Research, 38*(3), 920–40.

Eriksen, T. H. (2021). The loss of diversity in the Anthropocene biological and cultural dimensions. *Frontiers in Political Science, 3,* 743610.

Førland, E. J., Jacobsen, J. K. S., Denstadli, J. M., Lohmann, M., Hanssen-Bauer, I., Hygen, H. O., and Tømmervik, H. (2013). Cool weather tourism under global warming: Comparing Arctic summer tourists' weather preferences with regional climate statistics and projections. *Tourism Management, 36,* 567–79.

François, H., Samacoïts, R., Bird, D. N., Köberl, J., Prettenthaler, F., and Morin, S. (2023). Climate change exacerbates snow-water-energy challenges for European ski tourism. *Nature Climate Change, 13*(9), 935–42.

Gerbaux, M., Spandre, P., François, H., George, E., and Morin, S. (2020). Snow reliability and water availability for snowmaking in the ski resorts of the Isère Departement (French Alps), under current and future climate conditions. *Journal of Alpine Research, 108,* 1.

Grenier, A. A. (2007). The diversity of polar tourism: Some challenges facing the industry in Rovaniemi, Finland. *Polar Geography, 30*(1–2), 55–72.

Grenier, A. A. (2011). Conceptualization of Polar tourism: Mapping an experience in the far reaches if the imaginary. In A. A. Grenier and D. K. Müller (Eds.), *Polar Tourism: A Tool for Regional Development,* 61–86. Presses Universitaires du Québec.

Grünewald, T., Wolfsperger, F., and Lehning, M. (2018). Snow farming: Conserving snow over the summer season. *The Cryosphere, 12*(1), 385–400.

Hall, C. M., Müller, D. K., and Saarinen, J. (2009). *Nordic Tourism: Issues and Cases.* Channel View.

Hall, J. R. (2009). *Apocalypse: From Antiquity to the Empire of Modernity.* Polity Press.

Hambira, W. L., Saarinen, J., Manwa, H., and Atlhopheng, J. R. (2013). Climate change adaptation practices in nature-based tourism in Maun in the Okavango Delta area, Botswana: How prepared are the tourism businesses? *Tourism Review International, 17*(1), 19–29.

Herva, V.-P., Varnajot, A., and Pashkevich, A. (2020). Bad Santa: Cultural heritage, mystification of the Arctic, and tourism as an extractive industry. *The Polar Journal, 10*(2), 375–96.

Huijbens, E. H. (2021). The emerging earths of climatic emergencies: On the island geography of life in modernity's ruins. *Geografiska Annaler B, 103*(2), 88–102.

IPCC (2019). *The Ocean and Cryosphere in a Changing Climate*. Cambridge University Press.

IPCC (2022). *Climate Change 2022: Impacts, Adaptation and Vulnerability*. Cambridge University Press.

Kaján, E. (2014). Arctic tourism and sustainable adaptation: Community perspectives to vulnerability and climate change. *Scandinavian Journal of Hospitality and Tourism, 14*(1), 60–79.

Kaján, E., and Saarinen, J. (2013) Tourism, climate change and adaptation: A review. *Current Issues in Tourism, 16*, 167–95.

Kaján, E., Tervo-Kankare, K., and Saarinen, J. (2015). Cost of adaptation to climate change in tourism: Methodological challenges and trends for future studies in adaptation. *Scandinavian Journal of Hospitality and Tourism, 15*(3), 311–17.

Kelly, P. M., and Adger, W. N. (2000). Theory and practice in assessing vulnerability to climate change and facilitating adaptation. *Climatic Change, 47*(4), 325–52.

Knowles, N., Scott, D., and Steiger, R. (2023). Sustainability of snowmaking as climate change (mal)adaptation: An assessment of water, energy, and emissions in Canada's ski industry. *Current Issues in Tourism*. DOI: 10.1080/13683500.2023.2214358.

Lemelin, H., Dawson, J., Stewart, E. J., Maher, P., and Lueck, M. (2010). Last-chance tourism: The boom, doom, and gloom of visiting vanishing destinations. *Current Issues in Tourism, 13*(5), 477–93.

Lundén, A. (2022). The biopolitics of Arctic tourism development and sustainability. *Via. Tourism Review*, 2022, 21.

Lundén, A., Varnajot, A., Kulusjärvi, O., and Partanen, M. (2023). Globalised imaginaries, Arctification and resistance in Arctic tourism – an Arctification perspective on tourism actors' views on seasonality and growth in Ylläs tourism destination. *The Polar Journal, 13*(2), 312–35.

Magrane, E. (2015). Situating geopoetics. *GeoHumanities, 1*(1), 86–102.

Magrane, E. (2021). Climate geopoetics (the earth is a composted poem). *Dialogues in Human Geography, 11*(1), 8–22.

Maher, P. T. (2007). Arctic tourism: A complex system of visitors, communities, and environments. *Polar Geography, 30*(1–2), 1–5.

Marjavaara, R., Nilsson, R. O., and Müller, D. K. (2022). The Arctification of northern tourism: A longitudinal geographical analysis of firm names in Sweden. *Polar Geography, 45*(2), 119–36.

Melamies, E. (2022, March 17). Kakslauttasen matkailukeitaaseen nousi planetaario, joka näyttää revontulet joka säällä. *Lapin Kansa*. https://www.lapinkansa.fi/kakslauttasen-matkailukeitaaseen-nousi-planetaario/4443231.

Müller, D. K., and Viken, A. (2017). Toward a de-essentializing of indigenous tourism? In A. Viken, and D. K. Müller (Eds.), *Tourism and Indigeneity in the Arctic*, 290–306. Channel View.

Nilsson, R. O., and Demiroglu, O. C. (2023). Impacts of climate change on dogsledding recreation and tourism in Arctic Sweden. *International Journal of Biometeorology*. DOI: 10.1007/s00484-023-02542-z.

Nixon, R. (2011). *Slow Violence and the Environmentalism of the Poor*. Harvard University Press.

Pielke, R. A. (1998). Rethinking the role of adaptation in climate policy. *Global Environmental Change, 8*(2), 159–70.

Rantala, O., de la Barre, S., Granås, B., Jóhannesson, G. Þ., Müller, D. K., Saarinen, J., Tervo-Kankare, K., Maher, P. T., and Niskala, M. (2019). *Arctic Tourism in Times of Change: Seasonality*. Nordic Council of Ministers.

Saarinen, J., and Varnajot, A. (2019). The Arctic in tourism: Complementing and contesting perspectives on tourism in the Arctic. *Polar Geography*, *42*(2), 109–24.

Scott, D., Knowles, N., and Steiger, R. (2024). Is snowmaking climate change maladaptation? *Journal of Sustainable Tourism*, *32*(2), 282–303.

Serreze, M. C., Gustafson, J., Barrett, A. P., Druckenmiller, M. L., Fox, S., Voveris, J., Stroeve, J., Sheffield, B., Forbes, B. C., Rasmus, S., Laptander, R., Brook, M., Brubaker, M., Temte, J., McCrystall, M. R., and Bartsch, A. (2021). Arctic rain on snow events: Bridging observations to understand environmental and livelihood impacts. *Environmental Research Letters*, *16*(10), 105009.

Shepherd, N. (2019). Making sense of "day zero": Slow catastrophes, anthropocene futures, and the story of Cape Town's water crisis. *Water*, *11*(9), 1744.

Simpson, T. (2016). Tourist utopias: Biopolitics and the genealogy of the post-world tourist city. *Current Issues in Tourism*, *19*(1), 27–59.

Smit, B., Burton, I., Klein, R. J., and Wandel, J. (2000). An anatomy of adaptation to climate change and variability. *Climatic Change*, *45*(1), 223–51.

Steffen, W., Grinevald, J., Crutzen, P., and McNeill, J. (2011). The Anthropocene: Conceptual and historical perspectives. *Philosophical Transactions of the Royal Society A: Mathematical, Physical and Engineering Sciences*, *369*(1938), 842–67.

Swyngedouw, E. (2019). The Anthropo(obs)cene. In T. Jazeel, A. Kent, K. McKittrick, N. Theodore, S. Chari, P. Chatterton, V. Gidwani, N. Heynen, W. Larner, J. Peck, J. Pickerill, M. Werner and M. W. Wright (Eds.), *Keywords in Radical Geography: Antipode at 50*, 253–58. Wiley.

Tervo-Kankare, K. (2019). Entrepreneurship in nature-based tourism under a changing climate. *Current Issues in Tourism*, *22*(11), 1380–92.

Tervo-Kankare, K., Hall, C. M., and Saarinen, J. (2013). Christmas tourists' perceptions to climate change in Rovaniemi, Finland. *Tourism Geographies*, *15*(2), 292–317.

Tervo-Kankare, K., Kaján, E., and Saarinen, J. (2018). Costs and benefits of environmental change: Tourism industry's responses in Arctic Finland. *Tourism Geographies*, *20*(2), 202–23.

Tuan, Y.-F. (1991). Language and the making of place: A narrative-descriptive approach. *Annals of the Association of American Geographers*, *81*(4), 684–96.

United Nations Office for Disaster Risk Reduction (n.d.). *Disaster*. https://www.undrr.org/terminology/disaster.

Varnajot, A. (2019). "Walk the line": An ethnographic study of the ritual of crossing the Arctic Circle – Case Rovaniemi. *Tourist Studies*, *19*(4), 434–52.

Varnajot, A. (2020). *Rethinking Arctic Tourism: Tourists' Practices and Perceptions of the Arctic in Rovaniemi*. PhD-thesis. University of Oulu.

Varnajot, A. (in press). Enlightening dark tourism horizons in a post-apocalyptic Arctic: A geopoetics approach. In P. Stone and D. M. Wright (Eds.), *The Future of Dark Tourism: Enlightening New Horizons*. Channel View Publications.

Varnajot, A., and Saarinen, J. (2021). 'After glaciers?' Towards post-Arctic tourism. *Annals of Tourism Research*, *91*, 103205.

Varnajot, A., and Saarinen, J. (2022). Emerging post-Arctic tourism in the age of Anthropocene: Case Finnish Lapland. *Scandinavian Journal of Hospitality and Tourism*, *22*(4–5), 357–71.

Varnajot, A. and Lundén, A. (in press). The short-term future of Arctic tourism: The complexity of seasonal uncertainties for nature-based tourism. In F. Kock, A. Lindgreen and S. Markovic (Eds.), *Research Handbook on Tourism, Complexity and Uncertainty*. Edward Elgar Publishing.

Viken, A. (2013). What is Arctic tourism, and who should define it? In D. K. Müller, L. Lundmark, and R. H. Lemelin (Eds.), *New Issues in Polar Tourism: Communities, Environment, Politics*, 37–50. Springer.

Visit Kemi (n.d.). *SnowExperience365*. https://visitkemi.fi/kohde/snowexperience365/?lang=en.

13 Convivial Arctic futures: Understanding the role of tourism in times of ecological crisis

Edward H. Huijbens

Introduction

> Doing science with awe and humility is a powerful act of reciprocity with the more-than-human world (Kimmerer, 2013, p. 252)

The opening quote is from the book *Braiding Sweetgrass*, dealing with how we make knowledge and what plants can teach us there about. The author, a US ecologist of indigenous background, encourages the reader to exercise gratitude through reciprocity for all that the Earth gives and the privilege to breathe (see also Pratt, 2022). For a research agenda for Arctic tourism I propose taking this hopeful encouragement from Kimmerer (2013) to heart. Thereby I suggest a research agenda exploring how convivial Arctic futures might be understood when incorporating the very spaces and places of the region as reciprocal agents in its constitution as these undergo transformations through tourism and the current ecological crisis unfolding with a rapidly changing climate.

The Arctic is framed, along with the Antarctic, as representing the only remaining great wildernesses on the planet, augmented by its remoteness and anonymity (Stewart et al., 2005, 2017; Hall and Saarinen, 2010). In addition to these, the Arctic's particular indigenous communities, biogeographic characteristics, extreme climatic conditions, widespread perceptions of being a relatively inhospitable environment (for humans), and high levels of marine biodiversity and productivity, have been shown to be readily identified and widely popularised attractions in the region. Tourists are attracted by the pristine character of the Arctic, its sparsely or non-populated wilderness, and unique historical and cultural assets. The emerging 'Arctification' of northern tourism in a global industry context and policy discourse confirms this (Müller et al., 2020, p. 5). These 'Arctified' exotic images form the staple for marketing and branding and thereby represent key resources for the promotion of tourism. Indeed, almost every policy document for regional development in the Arctic territories has identified tourism development as an opportunity (Müller et al., 2020, p. 4; see also: Jóhannesson, 2016). But as tourism is being evoked as an alternative livelihood and one of new hope, it is mainly represented as the lowest-hanging fruit for economic diversification without any substantial engagement with its implicit potential for cultural exchange, impacts on community, and social values or natural ecosystems (Huijbens, 2022). The Arctified framing animating this evocation of tourism is moreover faced with a challenge long since recognised by Aldo Leopold:

> But all conservation of wildness is self-defeating, for to cherish we must see and fondle, and when enough have seen and fondled, there is no wildness left to cherish. (Leopold, 1949, p. 76)

This chapter provides an understanding of the role of tourism in times of ecological crisis in the Arctic in the context of this untenability of conservation and the contradictions Arctic tourism throws up. Moreover, the chapter proposes methods on how to grapple with the region and its inhabitants through the emergent convivial tourism encounter of and in the Arctic.

A convivial tourism encounter is one premised on a human-centred, yet pluralistic, vital and enriching apprehension of places and spaces. To come to terms with the role of tourism therein, the chapter will start by laying the conceptual foundations of conviviality and reason its value when it comes to addressing challenges of climate change and the troublesome Arctified framing. Then the chapter will turn to the tourism encounter to explicate how visitors encountering others, landscapes and more-than/non-human life in the Arctic can be understood and explored. The research agenda thereby proposed is one of conviviality wherein what we attend and attach to matters, and the stories we tell thereof even more so.

From the frontier and other stories

Lewis and Maslin (2018) claim that the root cause of how humanity has come to multifaceted ecological crises driven by climate change lies in the ever intensifying, albeit uneven, globalised flows of capital. These flows are premised on overcoming frontiers of capital accumulation through appropriating natures and cultures and have been active at least since the time of colonial conquest but accelerated to the extreme in the post-war years (McNeill and

Engelke, 2016). As the Arctic is brought ever more into the sway of these accelerated globalised flows of capital it takes on the guise of such a frontier to be overcome, one of the last on the planet. Beyond this frontier is the icy wilderness and 'last chance to see' polar bears and glaciers. As subject to appropriation the Arctic thereby not only represents '... quite profoundly a human creation-indeed, [but also] the creation of very particular human cultures at very particular moments in human history' as William Cronon (1995, p. 69, see also Leopold, 1949, p. 105) famously pointed out in terms of the notion of wilderness. Thereby it is interesting to research the particular ways nature is seen through the prism of techno-industrial capitalist society steeped in the 'myth of progress' and the imperatives of capital for centuries (Latour, 2016; Mann and Wainwright, 2018). In this context it is urgent to understand what tourism research can contribute to the dynamic and global Arctic.

The point so eloquently argued by Cronon (1995) is that our knowledge and apprehension of nature and the environment is always limited, and always serves a particular purpose however informed. At present, our awareness of the interwovenness of techno-industrial capitalism and ecological crises is thereby not only a recognition of an 'autoimmune capitalism that seems determined to extract the last moment of circulation for itself, even at the expense of its host lifeworld' (Mirzoeff, 2014, p. 215), but also a recognition of a particular cultural disposition that needs to be reckoned with when confronting places of our making. In the web of techno-industrial capitalism, production that is merely figured on a quarterly basis, science which will not negotiate its own limits and knowledge applied only to instant use, a peculiar image of the Arctic appears. This is an image that becomes utilitarian, but not only objectively so. The very ways in which sense is made of the Arctic landscape and the affordances it provides get animated through the myths sustained by the engine of accumulation. This is the current 'trouble with wilderness' Cronon (1995) pointed out; it has become a given and staple of capital accumulation. As 'capitalism seamlessly occupies the horizons of the thinkable' (Fisher, 2009, p. 8), the Arctic frontier quietly expresses and reproduces the very values we seek to reject by promoting it.

The subject and reference of our actions and understanding of the environment are thus shaped by a man-made planet in search of profit. This is a planet rendered in the guise of capital frontiers to be overcome. But this planet is an Earth which is infinitely larger than we are, yet we are at one with it, it is in everything and something we will never wholly grasp or overcome. The Earth always eludes us and the only way to deal with that is to adopt conscious responsibility and care for our actions. Knowing that our aims and objectives 'enact the social' (Law and Urry, 2004), we need to also be clear how we thereby enact nature and our environment. Thereby it is imperative to ask what, along with who, is to be shown and given voice and how (Bennett, 2010), but to me most important is the 'where' of that enactment (Huijbens, 2021).

Evoking the 'where' calls for a radical realignment of knowledge production and science in action, whereby any diminutive apprehensions of nature or objective measures of places need to be countered (Hartman, 2016). Nature, as subject to capital extractivism is profoundly diminished and reduced as the Icelandic philosopher Páll Skúlason (2014, p. 95) would say:

> Once we stop admitting and respecting nature as an unfathomable creative force and only ascribe it meaning as a resource and raw material, it will lose its independence, stops being an alien, detached, threatening reality which envelops us, and becomes a mere subject of our imagination which will employ any means to weave it into its own web of technology and production.

Arctic tourism research can be a vehicle for making sense of this 'unfathomable creative force', thereby countering the predominantly utilitarian perspectives of the Arctic as a frontier of capital accumulation. The challenges of ecological crises fuelled by global climate change and brought about by the power of our technology and consumptive choices force us to face all that which eludes us. The Earth as a (w)hole has by now become the subject of our daily lives (see Gren and Huijbens, 2019). The implicit crisis of culture offers new opportunities for interpreting and engaging with nature and the environment. To achieve this, researchers can follow the lead of Glenn Albrecht (2019) in coming to terms with 'Earth Emotions' and developing a new vocabulary for our relationships with the Arctic. More profoundly, such an emotional reckoning on a 'defiant Earth' can be underpinned by what Hamilton (2020) calls a fifth ontology for the Anthropocene, one that is

> ...[an] expression of the emotional orientation, or attunement, of the Anthropocene, one that responds to and is true to the actual circumstances of the new epoch ... built on the crushing responsibility that goes with the power of our technology can save us (pp. 117–118).

This is an attunement and emotional orientation that cannot only follow the paths of science, extended to the planetary as they may be, but we also need to live through new information, pay attention to different things and communicate differently (Boetzkes, 2015). Most profoundly we need to

> ...engage properly with the becoming of a thing, we should strive to count and include all the concerns attached to it, all those who care for it. (Bellacasa, 2017, p. 44)

It matters thereby which story is told of our dealings with the environment and what meaning such stories have at each moment and each place. Enacting the Arctic, rather than an adjective to be appropriated, becomes a mode of being in a continuously changing relationship with the world. This is thus a speculative, experimental mode of inquiry coming to terms with our present times of rapid environmental transformation, pivoting around 'Researching with Proximity' as opposed to just being there (Rantala et al., 2024). As the earlier cited Skúlason (2014) highlights, wilderness is a much greater source of value than we realise. So, the Arctic can indeed be a source of value much beyond what we reckon. At the same time travel and tourism are at present the biggest venue for interrogating what we value at each time and how we understand ourselves (Hermann, Weeden and Peters, 2019). So, it matters what stories we tell and the concepts we use (Zylinska, 2014) in making sense of tourism. Cranberries and blueberries do expand tourism knowledge and moral imaginations, as Grimwood and Höckert (2023) neatly illustrate. These berries are thereby torn from the predefined and deadening pathways of techno-industrial capital and adopt life valuing at its core (Merola, 2014). Through travel and the encounter, we can thus enact the responsibility Kimmerer (2013) calls for and focus on reciprocity, reverence, care, conviviality and the art of paying attention to the places we encounter at each time and what animates them.

Earthly conviviality

As outlined above, the imperatives of climate change and multifaceted ecological crisis, Kimmerer's call (2013) and Hamilton's (2020) fifth ontology; all demand a shift in perspective which can be applied when researching tourism in the Arctic. Here I want to underpin such a shift with notions of conviviality and as with all good stories, some scene setting is needed.

Pjotr Kropotkin's (1939[1902]) work over a hundred years ago presented his ideals of a classless society and a withered State apparatus through established institutions of mutual aid. His ideas formed a counterpoint to the popular reception of the recently published seminal work of Charles Darwin on the evolution of humans in *The Descent of Man*. Going against the prevailing interpretation of the time,[1] that progressive evolution could only unfold through competition – rationalised with a Hobbesian view of the human, Kropotkin (1939[1902]) claimed that this was a misreading of Darwin. He claimed

---

[1] Which he found petty, unintelligent and narrow minded (see p. 18).

Darwin's use of competition was metaphorical, 'or as a way-of-speaking' rather than describing real scenarios of competition between species as their means of existence. Thinking competition-directed evolutionary progress was not only wholly unproven, but 'lacked confirmation from direct observation', Kropotkin suggests Darwin was conveying that species compete by way of developing competences to adapt (1939 [1902], p.14). Thereby what Kropotkin argues is that what concomitantly occurs with the occasional energy-exhausting fight for survival, and of far greater evolutionary importance, is mutual cooperation and aid (see also Albrecht, 2019, p. 4, citing Kropotkin as inspiration).[2] What propels mutual aid is:

> ...a feeling infinitely wider than love or personal sympathy – an instinct that has been slowly developed among animals and men in the course of an extremely long evolution, and which has taught animals and men alike the force they can borrow from the practice of mutual aid and support and the joys they can find in social life. (Kropotkin, 1939, p. 16)

Kropotkin, along with Reclus, were the bulwarks of anarchist geographies in the early 20th century and contributed to the lively debate Darwin's seminal work had fomented at the time (Ferretti, 2019). This debate holds relevance and resonance to date as Carl Sagan (1996) similarly explains in one of his last books that:

> ...modern Darwinism makes it abundantly clear that many less ruthless traits, some not always admired by robber barons and Führers – altruism, general intelligence, compassion – may be the key to survival. (Sagan, p. 260)

So as indeed Kropotkin postulated, evolution is driven by both cooperation and competition, and science is only just beginning to shed new light on the cooperative foundations for life that are provided by an understanding of the actions of symbiosis and symbiogenesis (see also Albrecht, 2019, p. 98 and Sheldrake, 2021, p. 162). As compassion and cooperation go a long way in explaining human development, another factor plays a crucial role. As Bregman (2020, p. 69, 214) underlines, humans are 'ultrasocial learning machines. We are born to learn, to bond and to play.' This creates a distinct evolutionary advantage (see also Wilson et al., 2023) one of paramount importance to humans who by all accounts lack physical prowess to outmanoeuvre most animals that could pose a threat.

---

2   Glenn Albrecht (2019), sees Kropotkin as 'an important thinker who saw much more than greed and selfishness in animal and human nature' (p. 110).

As an anti-positivist and a profoundly process-oriented philosophy, Kropotkin's doctrine of 'Mutual Aid' and its variations in modern day Darwinism and humanism harken to a vitalism imbuing people and matter with a creative spirit, countering inertia and 'blind' mechanisms (Sandberg, 2023). In this sense, the notion of mutual aid not only challenges the competitive ethos espoused by capitalism, but more profoundly builds on a process-oriented philosophy which is vitalist in the sense of it being focussed on expression, emotion, embodiment and the sensuous, whilst at the same time more spatial, nuanced and ecological, recognising as Graeber and Wengrow (2021) did how:

> We are projects of collective self-creation. ... [where] we treat people from the beginning, as imaginative, intelligent, playful creatures who deserve to be understood as such (p. 9)

The embodied ecological spatial register of this sentiment is neatly illustrated by Neimanis (2017) in the context of water:

> Water infiltrates and inhabits the vapour we breathe, the land we work, the animal, vegetable, meteorological and other earth others with whom we share this planet. As embodied beings, we are, primarily, bodies of water in a watery world. (p. 65)

> Water both connects us and makes us different. As water we are connected, we are different. (p. 99)

Our bodies thus always exceed what they 'are', across time, space, and species and a recognition thereof and caring therefore can animate the 'humankind' (Bregman, 2020) which in turn underpins notions of conviviality. Animating this caring can be achieved through grounded and contextual small group dynamics and expressed in what we do with our bodies making for the situations – the where – in which we find ourselves.

> Ethics in this sense is completely situational. It's completely pragmatic. And it happens between people, in the social gaps. There is no intrinsic good or evil (Massumi, 2015, p. 11, see also p. 43)

Effects get amplified through our complex web of relations to the global scale and it quite literally matters what we choose to attend to. Focusing squarely on the contextual and situational makes complexity the point of departure, and complexity sits at the core of any healthy ecology. This is the micro-political and politics of affect Massumi (2015) advocates. These affects of the everyday and the choices we attend to get translated into stories and symbolic thought which Wilson et al. (2023) state, along with prosociality and social control, accounts for the fact that we as a species have thrived in the context of highly co-operative groups whence our complex societal systems of the present have emerged.

The research agenda I therefore want to explore is how stories of creative encounters with the other and the more-than/non-human matter in making for spaces of compassion and collaboration I term 'convivial'. With a focus on stories, I want to maintain a human-focussed perspective in the mesh of more-than/non-human relational entanglements we find ourselves in (see Huijbens, 2023). These stories of conviviality are deliberately set to counter the predominant individualism and rampant competitive capitalist ethos which has permeated notions of self in the Global North in particular. As Ekberg et al. (2023) state:

> ... the timing of our climate emergency is particularly bad considering how the Global North nations particularly have been transformed from welfare states to market governance. (pp. 60–61)

With market governance eroding prosociality and social control it becomes particularly hard to tackle a macro-scale problem like climate change and its multifaceted ecological crises. But mobilising stories of conviviality grounded in the very places we encounter contributes new imaginaries which can feed future transformations.

> So, unlike the spectacular and visible forms through which consumerism is maintained, the emergence of alternative aesthetics might arguably come through changes and transformation in rather unspectacular and mundane everyday activities. (Schrage, 2023, p. 116)

Celebrating our world as patchy and diverse and seeing multiple solutions to problems inspired by detailing the varied place-specific tourism encounters in the Arctic is thus the core of a convivial research agenda.

The Arctic encounter

In the face of the reductive mechanistic thinking of humans as rational, selfish, and short-termist, coupled through the Industrial Revolution with productivity and capital, a modicum of opposition did always exist in vitalist ideas expressed for example in Rousseau's (1712–1778) romanticism and later variations as the environmental destruction of the industrial revolution became more and more evident. The emerging poetic love of the land has its manifestations in Henri D. Thoreau's (1817–1862) *Walden*, arguably an inspiration for a particular notion of 'fortress' conservation, wherein an idealised pristine nature was to be conserved from the polluting effects of human presence. Aldo Leopold was an influential thinker of the modern environmental movement drawing inspiration from these vitalist strains. In his *Sand County Almanac* (Leopold, 1949) he apprehends life unfolding from the ease of his chair at a cottage near the Baraboo Hills in Wisconsin. Frustrated by the quest for material possessions and the 'great acceleration' he sees emerging at the time, Leopold focussed on the emergent properties of life unfolding around him to the annual rhythms of the seasons. He states:

> Like people, my animals frequently disclose by their actions what they decline to divulge in words. It is difficult to predict when and how one of these disclosures will come to light. (p. 58)

For Leopold, these are disclosures of hidden meanings, 'long known among mountains, but seldom perceived among men' (p. 99). Leopold recognised that a sense of wilderness affords these potential disclosures, but '[i]t is last call, even in the Far North' (p. 147) for this appreciation. Leopold was an elitist scholar and easily interpreted as a fortress conservation idealist. If, however, Cronon's (1995) nuance is added it becomes clear that there is no wilderness in the sense of the untouched, only in terms of the far away. In terms of tourism, what thus emerges is a Simmelian formulation of strangehood in terms of the Arctic. It becomes thus about what 'is near and far at the same time' and thereby in relation to the stranger is:

> ...close to us, insofar as we feel between him and ourselves common features of a national, social, occupational, or generally human, nature. He is far from us, insofar as these common features extend beyond him or us, and connect us only because they connect a great many people. (In Wolff, 1950, p. 404)

With our mind's eye we encounter places and spaces of our making. This is the encounter Gibson (2012) argues is at the heart of tourism, defining and distinguishing tourism from other industries, such as mining, fishing and forestry which enact a purely extractive ethos framing the Arctic. In the same way querying people around their perceptions of future tourism development within the frame of techno-industrial progress, the only visions we get are those of a man-made wilderness Arctic for spectacularised consumption. As such our activities become naturalised as part of the wilderness experience and maintenance. Wilderness 'out there' does not exist and that should be obvious in times of climate change, but at the same time prompts us to recognise and value it as a source of limitless valuing. This apprehension of the Arctic stands in stark opposition to the extractivist ethos and reducing people to detached 'minds in a vat' somehow hovering above the land. The land becomes alive as expressed in the 20th century through Henri Bergson's (1859–1941) *élan vital* which post-structural theorists picked up on with ideas of becoming and life affirmation (see Deleuze, 2001). To these scholars and thinkers and numerous others, there was something distinctly more to being human than what could be measured and counted, or scientifically analysed as clockwork.

The exchanges that take place when visitors, often from far away, encounter a particular place or community have generally been theorised and analysed from the tourism industry perspective, e.g. in terms of entrepreneurship, innovation, product development or more broadly in terms of its economic impact or regional development (Viken and Granås, 2016). Also, considerable efforts have been devoted to understanding tourism encounters from a sensuous embodied perspective (see e.g. Little and Leyson, 2003; Crouch, 2010) and a number of tourism scholars have concentrated on exploring the complex social relationships loosely inscribed under the umbrella term of the 'tourism encounter' with nature and natural environments (Abram and Lien, 2011; Pearce et al., 2017). Zooming in on this last instance, Smith, Speiran and Graham (2021) argue in the context of megaliths as tourist attractions; 'certain rocks, stones and their settings are active participants in creating unique atmospheres, events, and experiences that become intimately woven into shared life-histories' (p. 338). In the Arctic context, the Intra-living in the Anthropocene (ILA) research group of the University of Lapland is devoted to exploring the where through proximity, enacting caring and feminist political ecology to re-think multi-species relations. These relations, both to the abiotic and biotic realm can surprise, overwhelm or confound expectations as things encountered orient worlds and constitutive of our thinking (Smith et al., 2021, p. 246, citing Clark, 1997).

The research agenda here proposed builds explicitly on valuing proximity (Rantala et al., 2024) and rendering the encounter even less prescriptive and more emergent from the terms of that which we see as encountered. What matters thus profoundly is context to live with – convivially. The 'where' matters in the encounter and how things are encountered there and then can be expressed to make sense to us; from the pre-individual singularity it expresses, towards informing our decisions. The present and place, the here and now, are situated presences, reliant on the encounter to make meaning matter. This is an emergent space, and thereby emergent is society, nature and culture and it matters what we do, from the smallest to the biggest. This calls for a maintenance of a horizontal relationship with our surroundings and affectual politics. Our geo-graphical more-than/non-human being is about this encounter. The place where all things and the Earth of which we are made unravel and unfold. It is the singularity, apprehensible in each encounter, with a history and power geometry that can be unravelled, but more over allowing for a gaggle of voices and opportunities to emerge.

To come to terms with this gaggle of voices, stories help reorient our values and what we hold dear. A story offers a conceptual grasp of complexity and the capacity to build emotional interest in it. Similarly, Abram (1996, p. 120) maintains that 'stories, like rhymed poems or songs, readily incorporate themselves into our felt experience'. But these are stories that can only be 'judged according to whether it makes sense' as in enlivening the senses for earthly attachments (ibid, p. 265). To take a tourism example; the megaliths of Smith, Speiran and Graham (2021) or the blueberries of Grimwood and Höckert (2023) can thereby 'serve as an object that links temporality, site and materiality, offering a location around which affective experience, sensory belonging, stories and memories accumulate' (Edensor, 2022, p. 115). Taking cue from Abram (1996) stories to me have a more profound role than expanding our consciousness in the here and now as we encounter particular stoniness or berriness. Stories are carriers of our capacity for symbolic thought, which accounts for our exceptional capacity for cultural evolution into the future and here the Arctic plays a role as a readily recognisable source for these valuings and stories in its wilderness framing.

Towards research

This chapter outlined the conceptual premises of research which can contribute to Arctic conviviality and how to understand the role of tourism therein. The chapter started by laying the conceptual foundations of conviviality and reason its value when it comes to addressing challenges of climate change fuelled ecological crisis and uncertain futures. Then the chapter turned to the tourism encounter to explicate how visitors encountering others, landscapes and biotic and abiotic more-than-human Arctic can be understood and explored. The research agenda thereby proposed is one of conviviality wherein what we attend and attach to matters, and the stories thereof even more so.

In tourism, the Arctic is popularly conceived as a relatively untouched, icy wilderness and home to hunter-gatherer nomads. At the same time the Arctic is the site of a thriving tourism industry and other means of resource exploitation. At our current juncture of climate change and rapidly expanding forces of capital accumulation we need to strive for a more holistic and renewed ethical relationships with the world. At the outset of the chapter Kimmerer (2013) was cited calling for awe and humility. The Arctic is to me a great source of such stances, but in order to achieve these the asymmetric relations established through capital accumulation, ontological divides of us and nature and historical legacies of exploitation and cultural decimation must be discussed, problematised and subsequently addressed as a means to enhance transformative processes of the Arctic encounter. All in all, drawing on Leopold's (1949) 'healthy contempt for the plethora of material blessings', understanding people is key to protecting the Arctic and the place for that understanding is at the encounter where people make sense of their visit, there and then.

So, when it comes to understanding current Arctic tourism it is not enough to simply research how to manage and regulate the growth of different types of tourism in different places. It is imperative that we realise the role of the very environment which is orienting our values. Thereby Arctic tourism research which holistically embraces the perception of the environment beyond utilitarian views translated into 'arctified' commodities and marketing strategies for tourism is emerging. The Arctic needs to be understood as a limitless source of valuing and how this can be apprehended in tourism practices, performances and operations. In other words, researchers adopting the thinking that more than our own frame of reference and mind's eye can make sense and be valued will contribute to a stronger future-oriented tourism research. The environment and the material matters. And indeed, we are at one with our environment and matter as should be abundantly clear in the Anthropocene.

The research agenda that I hereby propose is one that values place and the encounter in its emergent properties, explicitly countering its extractive capitalist framing. This research calls for methods involving speculative, creative and aesthetic endeavours to come to terms with existing means of appropriation. Researching with proximity (Rantala et al., 2024) could here unfold through 'speculative maps', which can be drawn involving patiently following things in their movements as they negotiate their current conditions. Making for such speculations involves thick descriptions and placing oneself proximate, and then at the heart of the encounter using '...the tool of walking, taking a journey as a way of grasping the world (sometimes quite literally, and physical contact with the ground as a characteristic of living beings' (Aït-Touati et al., 2022, p. 80). Tourism research on a quest to develop narratives and such 'maps of life' requires us to turn the globe inside out and reveal the thickness of the mesh of life within each plot of land or parcel of space. Important challenges for tourism research in the Arctic are thus to engage with transgressive practices from a relational perspective. This perspective calls for acknowledging the plurality of ways of knowing and perceiving reality and the different ways of structuring the Arctic that result from it. These can counter the deadening frontier of capital accumulation from within. Engaging with people, visitors and locals alike, needs to reflect their varied meanings, ways of relating and simultaneously the ways in which debates, political antagonism, struggle, reflexive engagement, disruptive action and purposeful collaboration-confrontation occur. Ideally, such research brings academia, local communities, public and private sectors, government agencies and others together to foster disruptive practices and support actions towards ecologically sustainable and socially just socio-ecological Arctic tourism.

References

Abram, D. (1996). *Spell of the Sensuous: Perception and Language in a More-than-Human World*. Vintage Books.

Abram, S., and Lien, M. E. (2011). Performing nature at World's Ends. *Ethnos: Journal of Anthropology, 76*(1), 3–18.

Albrecht, G. (2019). *Earth Emotions. New Words for a New World*. Cornell University Press.

Aït-Touati, F., Arènes, A., and Grégoire, A. (2022). *Terra Forma: A Book of Speculative Maps*. MIT Press.

Bellacasa, Puig de la, M. (2017). *Matters of Care: Speculative Ethics in More Than Human Worlds*. University of Minnesota Press.

Bennett, J. (2010). *Vibrant Matter: A Political Ecology of Things*. Duke University Press.

Boetzkes, A. (2015). Ecologicity, vision, and the neurological system. In H. Davies and E. Turpin (Eds.), *Art in the Anthropocene: Encounters Among Aesthetics, Politics, Environments and* Epistemologies, 271–92. Open Humanities Press.

Bregman, R. (2020). *Humankind: A Hopeful History*. Bloomsbury.

Clark, A. (1997). *Being There: Putting Brain, Body and World together again*. MIT Press.

Cronon, W. (1995). The trouble with wilderness: Or getting back to the wrong nature. In W. Cronon (Ed.), *Uncommon Ground: Towards Reinventing Nature*, 69–90. Norton.

Crouch, D. (2010). *Flirting with Space: Journeys and Creativity*. Ashgate.

Deleuze, G. (2001). *Pure Immanence: Essays on A Life*. Zone Books.

Edensor, T. (2022). *Landscape, Materiality and Heritage: An Object Biography*. Springer.

Ekberg, K., Forchtner, B., Hultman, M., & Jylhä, K. M. (2023). *Climate Obstruction: How Denial, Delay and Inaction are Heating the Planet*. Routledge.

Ferretti, F. (2019). *Anarchy and Geography: Reclus and Kropotkin in the UK*. Routledge.

Fisher, M. (2009). *Capitalist Realism: Is there no Alternative?* O Books.

Gibson, C. (2012). Geographies of tourism: Space, ethics and encounter. In J. Wilson (Ed.), *The Routledge Handbook of Tourism Geographies*, 55–60. Routledge.

Graeber, D., and Wengrow, D. (2021). *The Dawn of Everything: A New History of Humanity*. Allen Lane.

Gren, M., and Huijbens, E. H. (2019). Tourism geography in and of the Anthropocene. In D. K. Müller (Ed.), *A Research Agenda for Tourism Geographies*, 117–27. Edward Elgar Publishing.

Grimwood, B. S. R., and Höckert, E. (2023). Cultivating relations with plant stories. *Annals of Tourism Research, 103*, 103661.

Hall, C. M., and Saarinen, J. (2010). *Tourism and Change in Polar Regions: Climate, Environments and Experiences*. Routledge.

Hamilton, C. (2020). Towards a fifth ontology for the Anthropocene. *Angelaki*, 25(4), 110–19.

Hartman, S. (2016). Climate change, public engagement & integrated environmental humanities. In S. Siperstein, S. Hall and S. LeMenager (Eds.), *Teaching Climate Change in the Humanities*, 67–75. Routledge.

Hermann, I. Weeden, C., and Peters, K. M. B. (2019). Connecting the dots: Ethics, global citizenship and tourism. *Hospitality and Society*, 9(1), 3–8.

Huijbens, E. H. (2021). *Developing Earthly Attachments in the Anthropocene*. Routledge.

Huijbens, E. H. (2022). The Arctic as the last frontier: Tourism. In M. Finger and G. Rekvig (Eds.), *Global Arctic*, 129–46). Springer.

Huijbens, E. H. (2023). The spaces and places of the tourism encounter: On re-centring the human in a more-than/non-human world. *Humanities*, 12(4), 55.

Jóhannesson G. T. (2016). A fish called tourism: Emergent realities of tourism policy in Iceland. In R. van der Duim, C. Ren and G. T. Jóhannesson (Eds.), *Tourism Encounters and Controversies: Ontological Politics of Tourism Development*, 181–200. Ashgate.

Kimmerer, R.-W. (2013). *Braiding Sweetgrass. Indigenous Wisdom, Scientific Knowledge, and the Teaching of Plants*. Milkweed Editions.

Kropotkin, P. (1939[1902]). *Mutual Aid: A Factor of Evolution*. Pelican Books.

Latour, B. (2016). Onus Orbis Terrarum: About a possible shift in the definition of sovereignty. *Millennium: Journal of International Studies*, 44(3), 305–20.

Law, J., and Urry, J. (2004). Enacting the social. *Economy and Society*, 33(3), 390–410.

Leopold, A. (1949). *A Sand County Almanac: And Sketches Here and There*. Penguin Classics.

Lewis, S. L., and Maslin, M. (2018). *The Human Planet. How We Created the Anthropocene*. Yale University Press.

Little, J., and Leyson, M. (2003). Embodied rural geographies: Developing research agendas. *Progress in Human Geography*, 27(3), 257–72.

Mann, G., and Wainwright, J. (2018). *Climate Leviathan*. Verso.

Massumi, B. (2015). *Politics of Affect*. Polity.

McNeill, J. R., and Engelke, P. (2016). *The Great Acceleration. An Environmental History of the Anthropocene since 1945*. Harvard University Press.

Merola, N. M. (2014). Materializing a geotraumatic and melancholy anthropocene. *Minnesota Review*, 83, 122–32.

Mirzoeff, N. (2014). Visualizing the Anthropocene. *Public Culture*, 26(2), 213–32.

Müller, D. K., Carson, D. A., de la Barre, S., Granås, B., Jóhannesson, G. T., Øyen, G., Rantala, O., Saarinen, J., Salmela, T., Tervo-Kankare, K., and Welling, J. (2020). *Arctic Tourism in Times of Change: Dimensions of Urban Tourism*. Nordic Council of Ministers.

Neimanis, A. (2017). *Bodies of Water: Posthuman Feminist Phenomenology*. Bloomsbury Academic.

Pearce, J., Strickland-Munro, J., and Moore, S. A. (2017). What fosters awe-inspiring experiences in nature-based tourism destinations? *Journal of Sustainable Tourism*, 25(3), 362–78.

Pratt, M. L. (2022). *Planetary Longings*. Duke University Press.

Rantala, O., Kinnunen, V., and Höckert, E. (Eds.) (2024). *Researching with Proximity: Relational Methodologies for the Anthropocene*. Palgrave MacMillan.

Sagan, C. (1996). *The Demon-Haunted World: Science as a Candle in the Dark.* Ballantine Books.

Sandberg, O. M. (2023). 'Everything changes in nature': Kropotkin's process philosophy. *Anarchist Studies, 31*(2), 16–33.

Schrage, J. (2023). The good, the bad and the beautiful? The role of aesthetics in low-carbon consumption. In H. Haarstad, J. Grandin, K. Kjærås and E. Johnson (Eds.), *Haste: The Slow Politics of Climate Urgency,* 107–16. UCL Press.

Sheldrake, M. (2021). *Entangled Life: How Fungi Make Our Worlds, Change Our Minds & Shape Our Futures.* Random House.

Skúlason, P. (2014[1997]). Að nýta og að njóta. In P. Skúlason (Ed.), *Náttúrupælingar Háskólaútgáfan,* 89–97. Reykjavík.

Smith, M. Speiran, S., and Graham, P. (2021). Megaliths, material engagement, and the atmospherics of neo-lithic ethics: Presage for the end(s) of tourism. *Journal of Sustainable Tourism, 29*(2–3), 337–52.

Stewart, E. J., Draper, D., and Johnston, M.E. (2005). A review of tourism research in the polar regions. *Arctic, 58,* 383–94.

Stewart, E. J., Liggett, D., and Dawson, J. (2017). The evolution of polar tourism scholarship: Research themes, networks and agendas. *Polar Geography, 40*(1), 59–84.

Viken, A., and Granås, B. (2016). *Tourism Destination Development: Turns and Tactics.* Routledge.

Wilson, D. S., Madhavanc, G., Gelfand, M. J., Hayes, S. C., Atkins, P. W. B., and Colwell, R. R. (2023). Multilevel cultural evolution: From new theory to practical applications. *PNAS, 120*(16), e2218222120.

Wolff, K. (1950). *The Sociology of Georg Simmel.* Free Press.

Zylinska, J. (2014). *Minimal Ethics for the Anthropocene.* Open University Press.

14 Arctic tourism in the 21st century

Dieter K. Müller and Outi Rantala

Concluding thoughts on the volume

While the topic was largely ignored until the 1990s, academic interest in Arctic tourism has developed rapidly ever since. This has gone hand in hand with increased tourism to the Arctic and the subarctic regions, which made an academic approach to the multiple challenges presented by this development mandatory. In this volume, experts addressed some of the topics that have arisen on the academic agenda and elaborated on potential future pathways for research. However, this has not been an exhaustive review, and different research agendas may be proposed and followed. Hence, in this concluding chapter some overall developments that may affect the future of Arctic tourism are briefly introduced and further aligned with the research agendas presented in the chapters of this book.

The overarching challenge of climate change

Imaginaries of the Arctic are largely based on the presence of the cryosphere. Hence, ice and snow are important ingredients for tourist imaginaries, and experiencing them seems to be a major motivation for many tourists. The ongoing climate change challenges this recipe for success. Some authors note the phenomenon of last-chance tourism due to a warming Arctic, which lures tourists to see the Arctic in its white mantle and with its wildlife while these aspects are still available (Lemelin et al., 2010). From a short-term perspective, this may indeed trigger a tourism boom and an adaptation of the industry. This Arctification of tourism has entailed that businesses have adapted and rebranded their offers to fit the current demand for experiences in ice and snow (Marjavaara et al., 2022). However, from a longer-term perspective, increased travel to the Arctic region may – because of the greenhouse gas emissions of tourism – in fact contribute to the discontinuation of its own attraction (e.g. Tervo-Kankare et al., 2020; Demiroglu, this volume), particularly since a comparably high increase in temperatures has been reported for the Arctic (Previdi et al., 2021).

This situation has triggered Varnajot (this volume) and others to wonder about the future of Arctic tourism (Cooper et al., 2020; Varnajot and Saarinen, 2021, 2022; Lundén et al., 2023). Considering a vanishing cryosphere, they have called for a de-arctification of northern tourism and for new ideas for how to cope with a changing resource base. Some examples of adaptation can already be observed today. Icehotel 365 in Jukkasjärvi, Sweden, offers visitors an ice hotel experience throughout the year, even during the warm Arctic summer, and various polar exhibitions have brought Arctic wildlife indoors (Lundmark et al., 2020; Müller et al., 2020). In the long run, this creation of artificial environments causes the Arctic experience to be detached from the region and can indeed be made available everywhere, as is already done today with indoor ski slopes and ice bars around the world.

In such a situation, one may of course wonder whether a trip to the Arctic region is still attractive – possibly as an expression of dark tourism, to see the leftovers of a climate and a landscape that once upon a time were there? Or will the future climate be attractive to tourists from even warmer regions who seek relaxation in a now temperate climate zone? In contrast, some commentators warn of the impacts of a changing Gulf Stream on the climate not least in the European Arctic (Palter, 2015). A warming ocean may indeed lead to changing flows of warm air, delimiting the warming effect of anthropogenic emissions within the Arctic region, eventually causing a cooling of the Arctic. While this will not happen in the short run, uncertainty regarding the impacts of climate change is still significant. Hence, how the climate will change remains to be seen; but certainly, climate change entails that tourism in the Arctic is undergoing change and will continue to do so for the foreseeable time to come.

Political and economic uncertainties

The change, however, is not only due to the changing climate. Obviously, the past decade has been moulded by several global trends and phenomena that certainly affected tourism in ways that were not foreseen. The globalization and growth of tourism entailed an integration of the polar areas in global tourism itineraries, meaning not only improved accessibility but also a growth in numbers (for figures see Müller, 2015; Varnajot, 2020). Challenges related to this became obvious, for example in Iceland, where tourism numbers reached problematic peaks that brought pressure on infrastructure as well as communities. More local agglomerations of tourists also occurred elsewhere, resembling many of the characteristics known from overtourism at more southern destinations (Lundmark et al., 2020; Jóhannesson et al., 2022). Tourism in the Arctic is also increasingly coming to be an urban phenomenon, despite the region's wilderness image and its related product portfolio (Müller et al., 2020). The COVID-19 pandemic placed a sudden pause on these developments, but recent tourism figures suggest that this was only a temporary halt. Today, tourism development in the Arctic region appears to be continuing upward from its pre-pandemic levels. As several of the contributions to this volume suggest, such a development is not seen only in positive terms. In light of climate change, with significant repercussions in high-latitude environments, pertinent questions concerning the future of Arctic tourism need to be asked.

One issue that requires attention is the geopolitical development within the Arctic region. Since the 1980s the region has experienced a geopolitical thaw, triggered not least by then Soviet Premier Gorbachev and his policy of Glasnost. The development of political institutions such as the Arctic Council, applauding circumpolar research collaboration, also created hope for tourism development even in the Russian North (Nord, 2016). Almost all member countries identified tourism as a tool for development (Müller, 2021), although some commentators also saw it as a way of manifesting national sovereignty in an increasingly international region (Timothy, 2010). In any case, the geopolitical change contributed to making the region an attractive – and not yet regulated – space for tourism development, attracting international companies to operate even in Arctic waters (Lasserre and Têtu, 2015; Pashkevich et al., 2015). This potential for tourism development even included the Russian share of the Arctic, though serious challenges and constraints were recognized (Pashkevich and Stjernström, 2014; Timoshenko, 2020).

The most recent Russian invasion of Ukraine dramatically changed this situation, putting a halt to at least international tourism to the Russian north. Even on Svalbard, Russian sites like Barentsburg and Pyramiden have lost their tourism markets (Figure 14.1). The political tension has demanded a greater military presence in the northern region. A militarization of the Arctic may imply investments in infrastructure as well; thus, ironically, this could lead to improved accessibility to the North and a greater capacity in a post-war future to host tourists in a region that has largely remained outside the globalized tourism industry.

For the time being, the stressed geopolitical situation, also fuelled by growing Chinese interest in the Arctic region (Huijbens and Alessio, 2015; Bennett and

Source: Müller, 2023.

Figure 14.1   Pyramiden, Svalbard, from a distance

Iaquinto, 2023), implies mistrust and uncertainty regarding future development. Tourism has, for example, been seen as a potential arena to be included
in communication and propaganda strategies, as in China and Russia, making
tourism an instrument of soft power in geopolitical interactions (Bennett
and Iaquinto, 2023; Laine, 2017; Nygaard et al., 2022). If further accentuated,
the mistrust and uncertainty may constrain further development of Arctic
tourism, particularly in the High Arctic and Arctic border regions.

While the current political turmoil has an obvious impact on tourism in the
Arctic, the role of economic development is more difficult to assess. Today,
most places in the Arctic suffer from poor access and small transport volumes
(Hall and Boyd, 2005). Consequently, in order to secure a sufficient income,
tourism businesses there are dependent on a small number of tourists who
spend a relatively high amount of money. This promotes forms of luxury
tourism, which defines the region as an exclusive destination and accessible
only to the economically well-off (Suopajärvi et al., 2022). This resembles
what characterizes tourism to Antarctica, where high costs filter tourist
access as well, which interestingly is not documented in the scientific literature. Exceptions to this can be found in urban places such as Reykjavik and
Rovaniemi. This indicates an urbanization of Arctic experiences, but possibly

also a reimagination of what the Arctic is and could be (Müller et al., 2020). This may be more urgent than anticipated, considering the rapid climatic change and the need to rethink the region for a "post-Arctic" era (Varnajot and Saarinen, 2022) – or for situations such as the one caused by the COVID-19 pandemic. Indeed, the pandemic made visible how we can blur the traditional images of Arctic tourism, such as exoticness and extraordinariness, and approach Arctic tourism from the perspective of proximity (Jóhannesson and Ren, 2024; de la Barre, this volume).

However, even in a situation of increasing prices for touristic mobility, Arctic tourism may indeed benefit from a displaced northern demand for tourism in the southern hemisphere. If travel to remote wilderness and nature-based destinations such as Antarctica, Patagonia, and New Zealand becomes more expensive, Arctic tourism may indeed come to be the intervening opportunity. For being a destination luring tourists from the major demand markets in the global north with exotic adventure, the Arctic is accessible and not too remote when compared to competing destinations in the south (Müller, 2015).

Pathways for Arctic community development

Many chapters in this volume refer to Arctic tourism as a performative practice, exercised by tourists and locals alike (de la Barre, this volume; Granås et al., this volume; Huijbens, this volume; Höckert and Rantala, this volume; Jóhannesson, this volume; Kvidal-Røvik et al., this volume; Ren and Markussen, this volume). They highlight the complex relations between stakeholders, human and non-human, and indigenous and various kinds of newcomers when people's attention targets dimensions beyond the economic aspects of the tourism industry. They also challenge the notion of the Arctic as being merely a tourist destination and a playground for adventure-seeking tourists (Pedersen and Viken, 1996). Instead, the region is highlighted as also being a home that contains and comprises communities, people, animals, etc. This makes it relevant to ask, what are local actors' perceptions, viewpoints, and experiences of living in a place labelled as a last-chance destination (Müller, 2022) – or as immobile and frozen in time (Jóhannesson et al., 2024).

Hence, while attention is often paid to the impact of tourism on employment and business (e.g. Grenier and Müller, 2011), the agendas presented here highlight the role of tourism for residents. In this context, it is also important to see tourism as one among several agents of change. As Tuulentie and Müller (both this volume) point out, tourism is just one industry that requires land

and other resources. Sometimes these industrial interests may be in line with each other while at other times they may collide and compete, not only with each other but also with interests present in the local community (Byström, 2019). Not least traditional indigenous industries are exposed to such pressures, which also influence the already complex process of becoming and being an indigenous entrepreneur (Viken and Müller, 2017; Leu, 2019; Granås and Mathisen, 2022). Hence, tourism development is also about negotiation and planning, balancing different local and non-local interests. Against the backdrop of recent interest in Arctic resources, which is expected to grow considering new climatic preconditions for resource exploitation and trade (Evengård et al., 2015), Tuulentie (this volume) calls for a just transition that recognizes local interests.

However, the future of Arctic tourism is also dependent on the tourists' demands and fashions. Currently, the Arctic is hot, not only because of public political and industrial attention but also because of popular media representations of Arctic communities (Maher and Hardy, this volume). These shape a specific imaginary of Arctic communities and their inhabitants, representing a distinct political economy of the region as a resource frontier (Moscato, 2017). Of course, the content of such representations may change, but already today a path dependency can be noted (Lehtimäki, et al. 2021).

The Arctic in the Anthropocene

An important question that arises from the research agendas presented here is that of whom the Arctic region is for. Tourism, among other sectors, has contributed to making the Arctic a global region, and stakeholders even beyond the Arctic have ideas and opinions about how tourism in the Arctic should be developed (Tuulentie, this volume). Hence, in the Arctic arena, radical positions of conservation on the one hand and industrial development on the other collide and illustrate diverging philosophical and political positions regarding the future of the earth in the Anthropocene era (Huijbens, 2021). While Huijbens (this volume) calls for practices that value place and encounters therein, little so far points in such a direction, considering the environmental and geopolitical turmoil currently shaping the region.

This situation is obviously not unique to the Arctic, though the absence of decision-making power in the region implies a particular fragility and dependence on outside stakeholders within politics and industry. Similar research involving Antarctica has indicated that future scenarios for tourism in polar areas are dependent on a wide array of factors (Liggett et al., 2017). Hence, the future of polar tourism is not predetermined. Instead, it is jointly made by the local and global tourism industry, governments on various geographical scales, tourists, and Arctic residents. Research carries the potential, and should have the ambition, to influence the future pathways of Arctic tourism by providing knowledge and insight to those who make Arctic futures through their decisions and practices. Hence, researchers should acknowledge which kind of future Arctic realities they enact themselves through their research (Jutila et al., 2024; Ren and Markussen, this volume).

What Arctic tourism will look like during the 21st century is still uncertain. Structural factors as well as individual agency, both within and outside the Arctic region, will be decisive for how tourism develops. The research agendas presented here entail attempts to understand and sometimes influence how these factors are negotiated and performed. Obviously, they resemble different theoretical perspectives and emphasize diverse aspects of the tourism system, but this multiplicity and variety are probably necessary in order to meet the complex realities of Arctic tourism and the natural and socioeconomic systems that frame it.

References

Bennett, M. M., and Iaquinto, B. L. (2023). The geopolitics of China's Arctic tourism resources. *Territory, Politics, Governance, 11*(7), 1281–302.

Byström, J. (2019). *Tourism Development in Resource Peripheries: Conflicting and Unifying Spaces in Northern Sweden*. PhD thesis. Umeå University.

Cooper, E. A., Spinei, M., and Varnajot, A. (2020). Countering "arctification": Dawson city's "sourtoe cocktail". *Journal of Tourism Futures, 6*(1), 70–82.

Evengård, B., Larsen, J. N., and Paasche, Ø. (Eds.) (2015). *The New Arctic*. Springer.

Granås, B., and Mathisen, L. (2022). Unfinished indigenous geographies: The endurances and becomings of a Sámi tourism venture. *Polar Record, 58*, e18.

Grenier A. A. and D. K. Müller (Eds.) (2011). *Polar Tourism: A Tool for Regional Development*. Presses de l'Université du Québec.

Hall, C. M., and Boyd, S. (2005). Nature-based tourism in peripheral areas: Introduction. In C. M. Hall and S. Boyd (Eds.), *Nature-based Tourism in Peripheral Areas: Development or Disaster*, 3–17. Channel View.

Huijbens, E. H. (2021). *Developing Earthly Attachments in the Anthropocene*. Routledge.

Huijbens, E. H., and Alessio, D. (2015). Arctic 'concessions' and icebreaker diplomacy? Chinese tourism development in Iceland. *Current Issues in Tourism, 18*(5), 433–49.

Jóhannesson, G. T., Welling, J., Müller, D. K., Lundmark, L., Nilsson, R. O., de la Barre, S., Granås, B., Kvidal-Røvik, T., Rantala, O., Tervo-Kankare, K., and Maher, P. (2022). *Arctic Tourism in Times of Change – Uncertain Futures: From Overtourism to Re-starting Tourism*. Nordic Council of Ministers.

Jóhannesson, G. T. and Ren, C. (2024). Cultivating Proximities: Re-visiting the Familiar. In O. Rantala, V. Kinnunen and E. Höckert (Eds.), *Researching with Proximity. Relational Methodologies for the Anthropocene*, 75–88. Palgrave Macmillan.

Jóhannesson, G. T., Lund, K., Thorsteinsson, B., Jóhannesdóttir, G. R. (2024). Introduction. In B. Thorsteinsson, K. A. Lund, G. T. Jóhannesson and G. R. Jóhannesdóttir (Eds.), *Mobilities on the Margins*, 1–13. Palgrave Macmillan.

Jutila, S., Höckert, E., and Rantala, O. (2024). Becoming fragile. In O. Rantala, V. Kinnunen and E. Höckert (Eds.), *Researching with Proximity. Relational Methodologies for the Anthropocene*, 43–57. Palgrave Macmillan.

Laine, J. (2017). Finnish–Russian border mobility. In D. R. Hall (Ed.), *Tourism and Geopolitics: Issues and Concepts from Central and Eastern Europe*, 178–90. CABI.

Lasserre, F., and Têtu, P. L. (2015). The cruise tourism industry in the Canadian Arctic: Analysis of activities and perceptions of cruise ship operators. *Polar Record, 51*(1), 24–38.

Lehtimäki, M., Rosenholm, A., and Strukov, V. (Eds.) (2021). *Visual Representations of the Arctic: Imagining Shimmering Worlds in Culture, Literature and Politics*. Routledge.

Lemelin, H., Dawson, J., Stewart, E. J., Maher, P., and Lueck, M. (2010). Last-chance tourism: The boom, doom, and gloom of visiting vanishing destinations. *Current Issues in Tourism, 13*(5), 477–93.

Leu, T. C. (2019). Tourism as a livelihood diversification strategy among Sámi indigenous people in northern Sweden. *Acta Borealia, 36*(1), 75–92.

Liggett, D., Frame, B., Gilbert, N., and Morgan, F. (2017). Is it all going south? Four future scenarios for Antarctica. *Polar Record, 53*(5), 459–78.

Lundén, A., Varnajot, A., Kulusjärvi, O., and Partanen, M. (2023). Globalised imaginaries, Arctification and resistance in Arctic tourism – an Arctification perspective on tourism actors' views on seasonality and growth in Ylläs tourism destination. *The Polar Journal, 13*(2), 312–35.

Lundmark, L., Müller, D. K., and Bohn, D. (2020). Arctification and the paradox of overtourism in sparsely populated areas. In L. Lundmark, D. B. Carson, and M. Eimermann (Eds.), *Dipping into the North: Living, Working and Traveling in Sparsely Populated Areas*, 349–71. Palgrave.

Marjavaara, R., Nilsson, R. O., and Müller, D. K. (2022). The Arctification of northern tourism: A longitudinal geographical analysis of firm names in Sweden. *Polar Geography, 45*(2), 119–36.

Moscato, D. (2017). The political economy of arctic reality television: The spatial communication of Ice Road Truckers and Deadliest Catch. *Arctic Yearbook*, 2017, 339–50.

Müller, D. K. (2015). Issues in Arctic tourism. In B. Evengård, J. Nymand Larsen, and Ø. Paasche (Eds.), *The New Arctic*, 147–58. Springer.

Müller, D. K. (2021). Tourism in national Arctic strategies: A perspective on the tourism-geopolitics nexus. In M. Mostafanezhad, M. Córdoba Azcárate, and R. Norum (Eds.), *The Geopolitics of Tourism: Assemblages of Power, Mobility and the State*, 91–111. University of Arizona Press.

Müller, D. K., Carson, D. A., de la Barre, S., Granås, B., Jóhannesson, G. T., Øyen, G., Rantala, O., Saarinen, J., Salmela, T., Tervo-Kankare, K., and Welling, J. (2020). *Arctic Tourism in Times of Change: Dimensions of Urban Tourism*. Nordic Council of Ministers.

Müller, S. (2022). *From Last Chance Tourism to Gone Destinations? Future Narratives of Svalbard as a Post-Arctic Tourism Destination*. Master thesis. University of Lapland.

Nord, D. (2016). *The Arctic Council: Governance within the Far North*. Routledge.

Nygaard, V., Suopajärvi, L., Bjerke, J. W., Elomina, J., Engen, S., Iversen, A., Lidestav, G., Kyllönen, K. M., Leppiaho, T., Moioli, S., Nojonen, M., Rantala, O., Bogadóttir, R., Edvardsdóttir, A. G., Koivurova, T., Lesser, P., Lynge-Pedersen, K., Ólafsdóttir, R., Paulsen, Strugstad, M., Rautio, P., Skum, M., Tuulentie, S., and Tømmervik, H. (2022). *Geopolitical Tensions and Drivers of Different Industries in the European Arctic*. ArcticHubs -project, NORCE. https://projects.luke.fi/arctichubs/wp-content/uploads/sites/47/2022/12/869580_deliverable_3_political-drivers-for-development-of-different-industries-in-the-european-arctic.pdf.

Palter, J. B. (2015). The role of the Gulf Stream in European climate. *Annual Review of Marine Science, 7*, 113–37.

Pashkevich, A., Dawson, J., and Stewart, E. J. (2015). Governance of expedition cruise ship tourism in the Arctic: A comparison of the Canadian and Russian Arctic. *Tourism in Marine Environments, 10*(3–4), 225–40.

Pashkevich, A., and Stjernström, O. (2014). Making Russian Arctic accessible for tourists: Analysis of the institutional barriers. *Polar Geography, 37*(2), 137–56.

Pedersen, K., and Viken, A. (1996). From Sami nomadism to global tourism. In M. F. Price (Ed.), *People and Tourism in Fragile Environments*, 69–88. Wiley.

Previdi, M., Smith, K. L., and Polvani, L. M. (2021). Arctic amplification of climate change: A review of underlying mechanisms. *Environmental Research Letters, 16*(9), 093003.

Suopajärvi, L., Nygaard, V., Edvardsdóttir, A. G., Iversen, A., Kyllönen, K. M., Lesser, P., Lidestav, G., Moioli, S., Nojonen, M., Ólafsdóttir, R., Bergström, D., Bjerke, J. W., Bogadóttir, R., Elomina, J., Engen, S., Karkut, J., Koivurova, T., Leppiaho, T., Lynge-Pedersen, K., Paulsen Strugstad, M., Rantala, O., Rautio, P., Siikavuopio, S., Skum, M., Tuulentie, S., and Tømmervik, H. (2022). *Global Economic Drivers in the Development of Different Industrial Hubs in the European Arctic*. ArcticHubs-project. University of Lapland. https://projects.luke.fi/arctichubs/wp-content/uploads/sites/47/2022/09/d1.2-global-economic-drivers-in-the-development-of-different-ind ustrial-hubs_submission-1.pdf.

Tervo-Kankare, K., Kaján, E., and Saarinen, J. (2020). Costs and benefits of environmental change: Tourism industry's responses in Arctic Finland. In N. Ooi, E. A. Duke, and J. O'Leary (Eds.), *Tourism in Changing Natural Environments*, 10–31. Routledge.

Timoshenko, D. S. (2020). Sustainable tourism development in the Russian Arctic: Challenges and prospects. *IOP Conference Series: Earth and Environmental Science 539*(1), 012097.

Timothy, D. J. (2010). Contested place and the legitimization of sovereignty through tourism in polar regions. In C. M. Hall and J. Saarinen (Eds.), *Tourism and Change in Polar Regions*, 306–18. Routledge.

Varnajot, A. (2020). *Rethinking Arctic Tourism: Tourists' Practices and Perceptions of the Arctic in Rovaniemi*. PhD thesis. University of Oulu.

Varnajot, A., and Saarinen, J. (2021). 'After glaciers?': Towards post-Arctic tourism. *Annals of Tourism Research, 91*, 103205.

Varnajot, A., and Saarinen, J. (2022). Emerging post-Arctic tourism in the age of Anthropocene: Case Finnish Lapland. *Scandinavian Journal of Hospitality and Tourism, 22*(4-5), 357–71.

Viken, A. and Müller, D. K. (Eds.) (2017). *Tourism and Indigeneity in the Arctic*. Channel View.

Index